Preparing Students for Life Beyond College

D1570481

At a time when STEM research and new technologies are dominating the curricula of colleges and universities, this important book refocuses the conversation on holistic education for all students. Organized around the most important and difficult questions that students face, *Preparing Students for Life Beyond College* explores a vision of education that will enable students to talk about universal issues openly and honestly, preparing them for life beyond their formal education. Featuring a variety of traditional and innovative pedagogies, strategies, recommendations, and case studies, this practical resource provides student affairs practitioners and higher education faculty in a variety of disciplines with concrete approaches for developing campuses and classes that encourage critical thinking and reflection. This exciting book prepares colleges and universities to help students create meaning in their lives—no matter the discipline, campus location, or delivery system.

Robert J. Nash is Professor and Official University Scholar in the Humanities, Social Sciences, and Creative Arts in the College of Education and Social Services at the University of Vermont.

Jennifer J. J. Jang 張文馨 is Associate Director of Student Diversity Programs and Adjunct Professor of Mandarin Chinese at Champlain College.

Preparing Students for Life Beyond College

A Meaning-Centered Vision for Holistic Teaching and Learning

Robert J. Nash
Jennifer J. J. Jang 張文馨

Routledge
Taylor & Francis Group

NEW YORK AND LONDON

First published 2015
by Routledge
711 Third Avenue, New York, NY 10017

and by Routledge
2 Park Square, Milton Park, Abingdon, Oxon OX14 4RN

Routledge is an imprint of the Taylor & Francis Group, an informa business

Library of Congress Cataloging in Publication Data
Nash, Robert J.
  Preparing students for life beyond college: a meaning-centered vision for holistic teaching and learning/by Robert J. Nash and Jennifer J. J. Jang.
  pages cm
  Includes bibliographical references and index.
  1. Holistic education. 2. Education, Humanistic. 3. Education, Higher—Philosophy. 4. Education, Higher—Moral and ethical aspects. 5. Education, Higher—Aims and objectives. 6. School-to-work transition. I. Jang, J. J. II. Title.
  LC990.N37 2015
  370.11—dc23
  2014036971

ISBN: 978-1-138-81502-5 (hbk)
ISBN: 978-1-138-81503-2 (pbk)
ISBN: 978-1-315-74703-3 (ebk)

Typeset in Perpetua and Bell Gothic
by Florence Production Ltd, Stoodleigh, Devon

Printed and bound in the United States of America by Publishers Graphics, LLC on sustainably sourced paper.

Contents

CONTENTS

Preface

> The true college will ever have one goal—not to earn meat, but to
> know the end and aim of that life which meat nourishes.
>
> W. E. B. DuBois

We hold dear the main goal of what a "true" education ought to be, according to
W. E. B. DuBois in our opening epigraph. For us, the the aim of a college
education is to prepare students to learn and to live holistically both during and
after their college experiences. What we believe makes our book important, and
unique, is that we explore systematically, and practically, the "end and aim" of an
education that is more about *meaning-making* than it is about how to "earn meat."

We base our meaning-making curriculum on what we call the "Meaning-Quest."
This Quest consists of eight sets of "core meaning-making *Quest*-ions" that all our
students, each in their own ways, bring to our classes each semester. These Quests
will resurface in our students' lives throughout their life cycles. In the chapters
to come, we will spell out the major Quests that will enable our students to realize
their life dreams. We will also ask several college faculty and staff who have gone
through our university-wide meaning-making course to illustrate in a series of
brief, personal, applied reflections how they work with students to overcome these
stumbling blocks. Also, throughout the book, we will include selected pieces of
writing that our students have shared with us about their own particular quest for
meaning.

Our overall objective in this book, as well as in our meaning-making teaching,
is to help students to integrate the self, subject matter, vocational training, moral
development, religio-spiritual inclinations, interpersonal relationships, and service
to others into a holistic learning experience that will prepare them for life beyond
their formal education. We will demonstrate that a college degree must do much
more than just prepare students to earn a living, as important as this goal is; it
must also prepare them to live a satisfying, meaning-filled life. This entails that all
of us on a college campus learn how to nourish students' heads and hearts as well

as their bodies and future bank accounts. Therefore, we need to prepare our students to get beyond the "meat" of daily survival in order to discover the "soul" of education—wisdom, vocation, love, spirituality, morality, and service to others. It is the "soul" of education that will make each of us whole human beings, and there is no quick and easy formula to make this happen. This is a lifetime project that needs to start, at the very latest, during the college years.

Here is what we believe our book will accomplish for administrators, faculty, support staff, and students on college campuses everywhere:

- Develop a powerful rationale for encouraging students to discuss, with specific examples, how meaning-making is both liberating and empowering.
- Allow a representative group of practitioners to actually write about their own, first-hand experiences with the "tasks" and "stepping stones" connected with meaning-making. This will include their opportunities and challenges, their disappointments and satisfactions, and the practical implications for their work.
- Show how meaning-making can "shatter" complacency, deepen and enrich the traditional mono-disciplinary discourse, and help to move students and faculty out of their academic boxes.
- Recommend some practical steps that educators, administrators, and staff can take for infusing meaning-centered teaching-learning strategies into their existing pedagogies.

HOW WE ORGANIZE THE BOOK

We begin each chapter with a relevant set of maxims that will serve as the thematic compass for each chapter. We will then proceed in each chapter to unpack these maxims as our quarterlife students might experience them. In many cases, we will ask our students to interpret them in their own words. Then we will present a series of teaching strategies that we use in all our courses to respond to the challenges of each of our meaning-making questions. We will end each chapter with a personal/professional reflection contributed by a veteran practitioner in the higher education field (the majority of whom have taken our meaning-making capstone seminar). Each practitioner will offer a series of recommendations, calculated to help teachers, students, and support staff to implement each chapter's specific meaning-making idea. And, as a direct response to our practitioners' reflections, we will produce a brief list of salient, content-related, teaching-learning strategies.

What follows is a short explanation that describes what we cover in our book, and how we do so. All of these chapters, and the content within them, have been inspired by our students through the years, by fellow meaning-making mentors in a variety of teaching, administrative, and advising capacities in higher education, and by researchers and scholars throughout the United States and the world.

Part I frames the vision, and sets the theoretical stage, for a holistic meaning-centered education in the academy. Each of the two chapters in Part I explains the multifaceted meaning of meaning-making for quarterlifers as we deal with the topic throughout the book.

Each of the eight chapters in Part II leads off with a few relevant maxims or inspirational quotes that relate to the particular meaning-making Quest. We then list a range of challenging questions and dilemmas that college quarterlifers face in exploring these Quests. In guiding our college quarterlifers on this journey, we provide a few self-discovery activities in each chapter to facilitate their holistic educational development. Each chapter in Part II also incorporates suggestions for staff and faculty in higher education institutions on how to practice meaning-making pedagogy (whatever the subject matter) and help stimulate college quarterlifers in their search for meaning. To provide some background knowledge on each of the eight ventures in meaning-making, we also refer to relevant literature that promotes exploration, enhances discovery, and advocates for a "meaning to live for."

Finally, Part III provides a series of practical pedagogical (and political) strategies necessary to execute meaning-centered teaching and learning. These final two chapters make a case for interdisciplinary education and the type of leadership necessary to create and sustain it, and, also, provide some suggestions for constructing, and teaching, a "meaning-making capstone seminar." It was Thomas Edison who said, "Vision without execution is hallucination." Part III, therefore, connects the meaning-making vision to some of the strategies that will be necessary for the execution of holistic teaching and learning.

Acknowledgments

I wish to acknowledge my heartfelt gratitude to all those quarterlife, meaning-making students who have found their way to my classrooms during my 47-year calling as a professor.

I am greatly indebted to my wonderful, quarterlife, meaning-making co-author and co-teacher, Jennifer J. J. Jang, who came into my life eight years ago and who, I hope, will remain there always—both as an inspiration and as a wise reality-check. Without her, this book would not exist.

I deeply appreciate the work of all our contributors whose personal narratives greatly enriched our book.

And, finally, I want to pay tribute to my always patient, sagacious, and compassionate wife, Madelyn, whose unqualified support has enabled me to publish fifteen books and over 125 articles, chapters, and monographs during the course of my career.

All of these people give my life a meaning that is both transcendent and grounded.

Robert J. Nash

To all who have journeyed alongside me: family, mentors, and friends. My deep gratitude to your listening ears, beautiful minds, and radiant souls; to your unwavering support, continuous encouragement, and endless love. You inspired me to be a better version of myself, and reminded me that I am enough.

To all of our contributors: Thank you for sharing your voices in making this project a reality. Your narratives are powerful, validating, and essential for our audience.

To my co-author, friend, colleague, and Vermont Dad, Robert J. Nash: I cherish our intellectual connection and kindred spirit that transcend generations, languages, cultures, and time. Thank you for awakening and affirming the natural philosopher in me. You have left a permanent imprint on my life.

With gratitude . . .

Jennifer J. J. Jang

Part I
The Vision

The hyphenated term "meaning-centered" in our book title (and in Chapter 1's title) describes what we believe ought to be the goal of a college education for all students, no matter their major or minor courses of study. The term is inspired by Viktor Frankl's comment that human beings need more than the "means to live": they also need a "meaning to live for" (Frankl, 2006). In Part I, we describe our *vision* of a "meaning-focused" education. In these first two chapters, we preview for our readers the rationale, strategies, applications, and goals of a meaning-making education that will evolve throughout our book. Part I explains the overall template—the "vision"—for everything that will follow in the book.

Chapter 1

A Meaning-Centered Vision for Holistic Teaching and Learning

> Ever more people today have the means to live but no meaning to live for.
>
> Viktor Frankl (1959)

> He who has a why to live can bear almost any how.
>
> Friedrich Nietzsche

Viktor Frankl is the well-known survivor of the Second World War Holocaust death camps. He is also the creator of "logotherapy," which describes his psychotherapeutic methodology geared to helping people make meaning. Frankl, after spending three torturous years in concentration camps, and losing most of his family to the gas chambers, went on to write several books on the importance of meaning-making for all lives. His work has influenced us greatly as two educators who work in the academy. Frankl wrote many times in his books that the main lesson he learned during his agonizing experiences in the Nazi death camps was that his "meaning in life was to help others make meaning in theirs." We believe that this is what higher education should be all about. Frankl's lifelong mission has been to help people to create a "why" (a meaning to live for) beyond the frenetic pursuit of the "means" (the job credentials necessary to accrue "stuff") encouraged by so many career-driven curricula in the academy. This is our mission as well in each of the chapters that follow throughout our book.

THE WHYS TO LIVE

Sadly, at a time when Science, Technology, Engineering, Math (STEM) Research, Massive Open Online Courses (MOOCs), and professional-credentialing education are dominating the curricula of colleges and universities, we seem to be straying further and futher from the vision of a holistic education for all students. For us, a "holistic education" is one that prepares students for life beyond college in every one of its complex, interrelated dimensions: the personal, professional, moral, recreational, relational, social, political, religio-spiritual, healthful, and vocational, and others as well. The major theme that underlies every sentence in our book is this one: A holistic college education goes way beyond the usual question "How exactly will a degree prepare our students *to earn a living?*" What we will be examining in this book is an equally significant, but too frequently overlooked, question: "How will a college education prepare our students *to grow as whole human beings* throughout their lives?"

The first question is a more immediate pragmatic, career-centered inquiry, and, of course, the concern is an important one. The second question, however, describes the inescapable, lifelong Quest for meaning-making and personal flourishing facing our students, and this, too, is a crucial educational undertaking. We are reminded here of Nietzsche's insight about the centrality of meaning-making in creating a holistic life: "He who has a 'why' to live can bear almost any 'how'." Our book unpacks the implications of a college education that concentrates as much on the "why" to live as well as on the "how" to make a living.

Nietzsche, perhaps one of the most misunderstood, personally troubled philosophers of the nineteenth century, knew first-hand how necessary a "why" to live can be in sustaining a life amidst the most challenging "hows." He spent his own relatively short lifetime trying to establish a "why" to live. He was plagued for most of his adult years by a deep, suicidal depression. In his own words, "The thought of suicide is a powerful solace; by means of it one gets through many a bad night." Following a major psychotic breakdown, and after spending over a decade in mental asylums, Nietzsche died in 1900 of frontotemporal dementia (not neurosyphilis as is commonly believed). There are some biographers who claim that Nietzsche actually took his own life (although there is considerable controversy regarding this belief), because he had spent his lifetime agonizing over whether or not life was ultimately meaningless.

The World Psychiatric Association (2014), in its latest study of youth suicide, found that 10 percent of all quarterlife deaths during the last three decades were due to suicide. One in five teens seriously consider suicide annually. Over 1700 die by suicide each year. The number of unsuccessful suicide attempts for quarterlifers, as well as persistent suicidal ideations, among this age group was even greater, even though difficult to pin down with any certainty (Crouse, 2014). If nothing else, these statistics confirm for us the singular importance of helping students to create, and sustain, deep, non-ephemeral "whys" to live beyond the short-term "hows" of making and spending money.

THE QUEST FOR MEANING BEYOND TRAINING

Increasingly, higher education has become a mono-disciplinary undertaking with faculty living in specialized silos of teaching, scholarship, and professional training.

We are proposing that the best way to get faculty, student affairs and academic administrators, and students on the same educational page is for all of us to help students create meaning in their lives—no matter the discipline, campus location, or delivery system. For us, focusing a college campus around the universal student pursuit of meaning is far more preferable than what now exists throughout the United States in colleges and universities. Almost everywhere in the American university today, there is an escalation, and increasing separation, of bureaucratic structures: student services, customer-oriented offices, research- and grant-driven science departments, MOOC units, and upper-level administrative wings. Andrew Delbanco (2012) asks the most relevant educational question of all: "Where, in this house of many specialized mansions, is the college? Does it still exist as a place of guided self-discovery for young people in search of themselves?" For Delbanco, the primary purpose of higher education should be to "aid the learner to acquire a new soul . . . and, hence, to be reborn." Along with Viktor Frankl, we say "amen" to this vision.

Unfortunately, there are few opportunities on most college campuses—either inside or outside the conventional classroom, and either online or offline—as curricula become more vocational and scientifically driven for students to develop those strong background beliefs and ideals that will guide their lives when they graduate. Today's college students are asking their own existential questions of meaning. Their questions are timeless and yet reflect the age in which they live. These questions are a fascinating admixture of the abstract and the practical, the universal and the particular. They represent well the tensions that exist for so many college students who seek to find the delicate balance that exists in the difficult space between idealism and realism; between macro- and micro-meaning. Our "meaning-centered" curriculum is based on these "timeless, existential questions." It is no coincidence, in our opinion, that the word "quest" is at the root of the word "question."

As university educators, we witness first-hand every single day the need for our students of all ages, who represent a multiplicity of identities, to have something coherent to believe in, some centering values and goals to strive for. They are on a *quest* to discover a meaning to live for. They, like us, need strong background beliefs and ideals to shore them up during these times when religious and political wars plague entire societies; when the natural environment continues to deteriorate; and when the fluctuations of the global economy result in recession, deflation, and in the inequitable distribution of scarce resources. The quest for meaning has the potential to unite, rather than divide, an entire college community, no matter how different its individual constituents might be.

Here are some very compelling statistics to confirm our point directly above: the American College Health Association (2012) reports that, in a sample of 76,000 students from a variety of diverse backgrounds and identities, 86 percent felt overwhelmed, 82 percent felt emotionally exhausted, 62 percent felt very sad,

5

58 percent felt very lonely, 52 percent felt enormous stress, 51 percent felt overwhelming anxiety, 47 percent felt hopeless and purposeless, and the rest felt dysfunctionally depressed. So, too, a 2013 survey of 30,000 college graduates, undertaken by Gallup and Purdue University, found that while an undergraduate education might have prepared many of them for "great jobs," it did little or nothing to prepare them for "great lives." Only three percent of these graduates felt that their education helped them to achieve "well-being." Well-being, according to Gallup, includes five areas of human flourishing: a deep sense of meaning and purpose, a rich personal and relational life, financial stability, social and community belongingness, and healthy physical activity. These areas of human flourishing are what we mean when we talk about the quest for meaning beyond training. Career credentials are in and of themselves no guarantee that our students will go on in their lives to experience "well-being."

Giving Students Permission to Pause

In our own teaching experience, we have found that students of all socio-economic, national and international, racial and ethnic backgrounds—whether working full-time as somewhat older, blue-collar, first-generation college students or attending college as traditional, middle-class, second-, third-, or even fourth-generation college students—come to our courses on meaning-making with the need to make sense of the unknown, sometimes terrifying, future that awaits them. What these quarterlifers have in common is dealing with questions like the following: After they graduate (if they do at all), how will they pay off the tens of thousands of dollars in loans they have had to borrow to finance their education? How do they hold up under the emotional stress when their friendships, and, in some cases, their family relationships, go awry? What do they do when their work becomes unsatisfying, and they don't want to get up in the morning to put in one more monotonously empty day on the job?

How do they deal with such issues as the widespread sense of disillusionment and panic caused by a results-driven, lockstep education; or those dreaded occasions when they hear that someone they love suffers from the ravages of a metastatic malignancy; or when they face life-altering decisions triggered by failing grades or complete loss of interest in their major (and minor) fields of study; or when they learn that the person who means the most to them in the whole world no longer loves them; or, worst of all, when they no longer love themselves?

Education for making meaning holds the promise of giving a plugged-in undergraduate, and graduate, population permission to stop and pause in the middle of *going through the motions*. Education for making meaning enables students to talk about the deeper existential questions and universal life issues openly and honestly, and face-to-face, with significant others on campus. Meaning-making conversation forces students to take a giant step away from the number-one addiction in the United States—internet addiction (Young, 2010). This includes electronic gaming, smartphones, instant messaging, texting, e-mail, and all the other terminally numbing social media that control students' lives. Most of all, though, an education for meaning-making helps students to understand the folly of living their lives totally obsessed with a goal-driven, get-rich-and-successful, as-quick-as-possible, plan for the future.

We are a pair of college educators (Robert is a professor, and Jennifer is a student-affairs diversity administrator and scholar) who co-teach two elective courses each year on the philosophy of meaning-making for quarterlife students. Robert has written a bestselling book (2010), with Michele Murray, on the topic of meaning-making, and he and Jennifer have presented on the topic of meaning-making in a number of venues to both faculty and student services professionals throughout the United States. Most telling, though, is that back on our respective campuses, record numbers of undergraduate and graduate students from a variety of majors throughout our university voluntarily enroll in these elective courses. Why, you might ask, would students choose to take a course that, at best, is an outlier (and, often considered "soft") in the modern university? The answer is both simple and complex. We hope that the story of "Lorna" in the next section sheds more light on this question.

THE STORY OF "LORNA"

We begin this section with a description of a quarterlife student who studied with Robert several years ago. Even though she is a unique human being, so many of her issues are generalizable among those students who are asking the universal meaning questions that we will be introducing in Chapter 2.

When Lorna was in her late teens and early twenties, she was deeply troubled. She was a first-generation, blue-collar college student, who made the decision to attend college against the wishes of her divorced, high-school dropout mother who needed her to enter the workforce immediately after high school to help her pay the bills for a large family. Lorna was brilliant, creative, and beautiful, with an IQ that put her in the genius category; but, even though she had always been grateful for her "privileges," she was also miserable and unhappy. A survivor of a broken family, adolescent cancer, fraternity-house rape, and a restless soul who experimented wildly with drugs and sex, and someone who to this day battles with a serious eating disorder, Lorna, for years, had led a life bereft of any deep meaning and purpose that can sustain her at all times.

Her search for some kind of sustainable meaning to life led her to many dead-ends. She asked people around her too many questions about the meaning of her life, and she got too few answers to satisfy her. She was always the doubter, the outsider looking in, during these dialogues with her friends, mother, and seven siblings, as well as with people she respected as successful professionals. Lorna eventually went on to earn three degrees, including a doctorate, at an excellent university. Today she is a professional educator of the highest integrity and influence in an elite, post-secondary institution. She fills a room with her charisma and power, even though her physical stature is slight.

But, despite her enormous professional successes, even today, at times, she can also be melancholic and despairing, just as she was when she was an undergraduate. She sometimes succumbs to an anxiety so profound, and to migraine headaches so pounding, and to a personal confusion that is so impenetrable, that all anyone who loves her can do is to hold her, comfort her, and wait for the raging storm of turmoil within her to subside. She often lives her life in a precarious dance with fear, and she dreads the thought of losing her grip and falling into a hole with no bottom.

She yearns for an unmedicated, non-therapeutic certainty that she can build her life on, because everything seems to be so up in the air. At times, she searches for a definitive belief system that will answer her persistent meaning questions and calm her perpetual restlessness. She craves clear-cut resolutions to political and philosophical problems. She is tired of living her life immersed in one personal, existential challenge after another, one bad intimate relationship after another, one psychotherapist after another, one ethical dilemma after another, and never being able to reach a final solution that is permanently satisfying. But, deep down, she is smart enough to know that certainty is an illusion; that her life is a crapshoot; that accidents can happen anytime and anyplace and usually do; and that no truth is guaranteed, especially the truths of those who claim to be in the possession of an infallible religious, political, psychological, or philosophical revelation that will redeem her, and others, forever.

And, so, during these dark nights in Lorna's soul, she continues to seek out people who might help her to restore some meaning to her life. She knows deep down that her heart will probably continue to be restless until the day she passes. Like so many students today, Lorna's life is fragmented. She often experiences good and evil as interchangeable aspects of her daily existence, and much of the time she can't tell one from the other. The freedom to create her own life in her own way is good, to be sure, and she is acutely aware of her educational and career "privilege," but it also carries with it the terror of failure, isolation, and hopelessness.

Others are eager to recommend cure-all antidotes for her terrible angst. Some urge her to go on the low-carbohydrate, South Beach diet, take exercise classes, travel to the South Sea Islands, Greece, or Rome, get into yet another round of intensive psychotherapy, take Zoloft, find Jesus, Allah, Jehova, or Sophia, join an ashram and start meditating, do yoga and mindfulness exercises, give up coffee, chocolate, and sugar, and/or study philosophy. A former college mentor has recommended that she take post-doc courses and become an innovative interdisciplinarian, keep a daily journal, do more publishable writing and national gigging so that she is sure to get tenure, and get involved with community service as a welcome distraction from the unending demands of her university professorship. Some of her closest friends tell her to get married, have children, and "stop taking yourself so seriously." Maybe all, or some, of these will help. Maybe they won't.

The fact remains, though, that Lorna, like thousands of other students who have come through our college courses during the last four decades, suffers from what we call a *crisis of meaning*. Some students experience the crisis as a *clash* of conflicting meanings. Others confront it as a *surfeit* of seductive, albeit risky, meanings. And still others contend with an utter *vacuum* of meanings in their lives. To compensate for the crisis of meaning in the early twenty-first century, we find that too many current quarterlife generation students believe if they can just improve their economic situations and lose a little weight, perhaps secure good grades or a promotion at work, then everything will be okay. Their summa cum laude degrees, toys, travels, stocks and bonds, two cute little kids, cars, and homes will make them happy for the rest of their natural lives. And don't forget the comprehensive health plan.

Lorna is exhibit A of the type of quarterlifer we want a meaning-making education to serve. It was in one of Robert's earlier meaning-making courses that Lorna decided to become a professor. It was the first time in her life as a student that she received the encouragement she needed to explore her most personal meaning questions. She did this without shame and guilt, because others were doing the same. She found affirmation, and liberation, in the seminars. She read widely, she wrote frequently, she asked questions, and she began to "re-create" her life by honestly examining what gave her meaning and what didn't. As she said: "I need a career where I can 'profess' a belief in what's really important to me. And I want to encourage others to do the same." While Lorna is far from being fully meaning-contented and at peace with herself and the world, she no longer experiences her life as a pointless obstacle course.

Lorna's life corroborates the philosopher, developmental psychologist, and physicist Robert J. Havighurst's observation that students in the twenty-first century will need to create, and understand, "complex identities," and a sense of "purpose," in order to be "prepared to cope with uncertainty and to live a life of meaning." The truth is that each and every one of our students, regardless of their unique group and individual differences, have more in common with the Lornas of the higher education world than we might think. In contrast to the disdain of some radical social justice activists, Lorna's quest is not a "luxury" experienced only by the "privileged" among us. Each of our students, like Lorna, are in the midst of their own meaning-making crises—some incidentally, some moderately, some intensely, to be sure—but all are dealing with the challenges of making meaning in their lives. We often wonder why most colleges and universities throughout the United States rarely, if ever, address these crises directly—either in classrooms (except for a few humanities courses) or in special campus sites devoted to such an endeavor (except for a chapel or a counseling center).

We will explore in greater detail the need to create meaning within a framework of eight meaning-making Quests in Chapter 2. This is an in-depth exploration that "Lorna" above, along with most of our quarterlife students, rarely, if ever, get to undertake in their specialized, pre-professional studies throughout their college years. In contrast to this educational void, we will be advocating a type of education that will enable students to talk about these deeper questions and universal life issues openly, honestly, and face-to-face with significant others on campus.

Chapter 2

The Meaning-Quest for Quarterlifers

> The modern world needs people with a complex identity who are
> intellectually autonomous and prepared to cope with uncertainty, who
> are able to tolerate ambiguity and not be driven by fear into a rigid,
> single-solution approach to problems, who are rational and can control
> their behaviour in the light of unforeseen consequences, and who are
> altruistic and enjoy doing for others.
>
> Robert J. Havighurst (1972)

Here, in a nutshell, are the core meaning-making questions that come up again and again among our quarterlifers and post-quarterlifers. (Some of these categories appear in Alexandra Robbins's 2004 work on quarterlifers. The interpretations and questions, as well as additional categories, however, are our own, inspired by all those students we have worked with in our courses, and in our consultancies, throughout the country. *We offer different, non-duplicative renditions of these questions, in addition to dozens of new ones, in each of the following chapters.*)

- *Hopes and Dreams*—What is it that I want to do with my life? How do I find my passion? When do I let go of my dream? How do I find the intersection between my talent and my passion? What is the balance between achievement and fulfillment? What if I don't get what I want by a certain age? How do I start over, if I find I need to? When is the right time to make a commitment? Is it possible to have a fulfilling relationship and a fulfilling job at the same time? What if I make the wrong choice on either side? Am I stuck forever?
- *Values, Morals, Ethics*—Just who is it I'm striving to become as a moral being, and is this possible given all the craziness and contradictions in my life? What is "good moral character" anyway? What does the phrase "moral compass" actually mean, and do I have one? What is it I really believe about right and wrong? What does it mean to live a "good life"? Does being a

good, moral person mean not making compromises? What does it mean to be an ethical professional? How can I find moral communities (outside of the traditional worship places) that bring out the best, and not the worst, in me? Aren't all values, morals, and ethics relative anyway? Doesn't goodness depend on the context? What am I willing to risk in my job by way of moral conviction? I have a sense of the moral being that I would like to become, but is it possible or realistic for me always to act *in*, rather than act *out of*, character at school or in my workplace? What if my personal values are in direct conflict with my workplace's official code of ethics? At what point does my personal code of ethics override the institutional code where I work?

- *Religion and Spirituality*—What is the right religion for me? Why am I so critical of my childhood religion? Why is it that a non-institutional spirituality seems, at times, to be so powerful for me? Will my parents be disappointed if I don't remain loyal to our family's religion? Why does God seem so far away from me on some days, and so close on others? Can any spiritual good come from doubting? Do I need a religious faith to be a moral person? Is there any other way to make a meaning that endures without spirituality? Why is it that so many of my college friends think of religion in such negative terms? Will I be able to make it in the world without experiencing the consolations of organized religion along with its supportive communities? In what religion will I bring up my children, if I have any?

- *Core Relationships*—Why is it so hard to live alone but also so hard to sustain a relationship? Is there really such a person as a "soulmate?" How will I know when I fall in love with "The One?" Am I loveable? How do I avoid feeling "stuck" in my relationships? Why can't I find close, enduring friends who stay the course without drifting away? Is there something about me that causes this? Why is the thought of moving back in with my parents so terrible? Now that I've moved away, how do I make friends? Who will be my true friends, will I ever fit in, and how will I know who I can trust? At the present time, who are the top five people in my inner circle, and how long will they remain in my life?

- *Intersecting Identities*—Who am I in relation to my skin color, social class, sexual orientation, religious background, and gender? How does my international citizenship affect my sense of self in this country? How do these various identities, and others, help to define who I am and who I want to be? Why can't I like who I am, whoever that might be? What does it mean when people accuse me of being "privileged," or "non-privileged"? Why does it sometimes seem that people are so quick to put others in an identity box? Is there any commonality that makes us all human beings underneath our skin color, sexual orientation, neighborhoods, and private parts, or are we irreversibly diverse according to one or another identity?

- *Career, Vocation, and Job*—Am I studying what is right for me? Is college really necessary for my future success? Is it true that I'll be changing careers many times before I retire? If yes, then what's the point of taking all this time to prepare for a particular career? Will I always have to choose between doing what I love or making lots of money? Does my work always have to be so competitive and bottom-line? Is it possible to find a career that is congruent with my personal values? What does "balance" look like when work and stress build up? How will I ever be able to learn all the skills I need to be financially savvy?

- *Civic Engagement*—How can I fulfill what I've been told is my civic responsibility to improve the world locally, nationally, and internationally? If I want to give something back to a world that cries out for my help, how can I get involved both while in school and afterwards? How do I pick my social causes? How can I avoid becoming a self-righteous activist on behalf of a pet cause like so many environmentalists, social justice advocates, civil libertarians, Tea Partyers, and pacifists I know? Is active civic engagement even possible for me given all the demands on my time both now and in the future? How will my volunteer activities help me to build a career for myself and, possibly, go on to graduate school for further professional training? Is social engagement, volunteer work, and advocating for social justice and equality nothing more than a *de rigueur* "penance" for those of us who belong to the "privileged" classes?

- *Self-Care, Wellness, and Balance*—How will I ever learn to take care of myself so that I don't become just another mentally exhausted, workplace fatality going through the motions? How can I avoid burnout, and what some people call "compassion fatigue," both at school and in the career I'm preparing for? How can I practice a little self-compassion when the multiple demands on my life are so intense? Is multi-tasking the healthiest way to live a life? Is it really possible for someone to be psychologically, physically, spiritually, and socially healthy, all at the same time? Or is "self-care compromise" the reality that I will face for the rest of my life? What happens when my commitment to school and work are in direct conflict with other commitments in my life, such as tending to my close relationships, religio-spiritual needs, physical activity, the outdoors, and hobbies?

MEANING-MAKING IS A PROCESS MORE THAN A PRODUCT

We appreciate what the philosopher Alan Watts (2009) once said about music:

I believe that in music, one doesn't make the end of a composition the *point* of the composition. If that was so, then the best conductors would be those who

13

played the fastest! People would go to a concert just to hear one, final crashing chord . . . because that would be the end!

We believe that in higher education today too many students are pushed through a factory-driven education model revving up for the elusive and ultimate career success at the end. But, as Watts said, the end of a symphony is not the primary objective for the conductor. The focus is on the music that is being played all the way through. Like a musical composition, a meaning-making education ought to be an opportunity for all of us to sing, or dance, *while* the music is being played, rather than waiting for the cymbals to crash and for the end to come.

For us, meaning-making is always more of a verb than a noun. Meaning is the process; purpose is the product. We believe in an educational dynamic that is organic, interactive, and, at times, spontaneous. We believe in "eureka!" flashes of insight (crashing cymbals, so to speak), tentative responses rather than final answers to the deepest questions, and much mutual sharing of stories, passions, and values. Too often, today, our students cease being natural wonderers and philosophers after graduating from kindergarten. They then proceed to become numbed and dulled, as they march along the educational treadmill from elementary to graduate school. In contrast, we want a meaning-making education to be an opportunity for all of us in academia to grow in wisdom, especially when times get hard.

We have found that no matter the age, stage, wage, or any other difference, all of our students have a need to make meaning of their lives. Just who, and what, constitute the quarterlife generation? The quarterlife period (roughly between the ages of 18 and 32) is frequently a tumultuous time for most of our students, because it triggers an overwhelming anxiety about the past, present, and future. So many of our quarterlife students are plagued with worry about failure—living up to others' expectations, letting go of the comfortable securities of childhood, coming to terms with the growing tension between freedom and responsibility, and constantly comparing themselves to peers and coming up short. For so many quarterlifers, their existence seems vapid.

LIFELONG CYCLES OF MEANING-MAKING OPPORTUNITIES

Because the majority of our students are quarterlifers, they are all working on what Robert J. Havighurst (1972) calls the "developmental tasks"—those difficult, sometimes arduous challenges that are a precondition for living a full, rich life from birth to death. For Havighurst, these tasks are physical, psychological, and social. We will emphasize throughout our book the qualities that Havighurst believes (cited in our opening epigraph) all quarterlifers will need to cultivate during, and after, their college educations if they are to live full, rich lives of meaning. They will have to build complex identities. They will need to be "intellectually autonomous" and always ready to "cope with uncertainty." Not only must they be prepared for the inevitable ambiguity and uncertainty throughout their lives, but they will need to resist the fear-driven temptation to seek "rigid, single-solution approaches to problems." They must learn to take a thoughtful step back (to pause) in order to deal with all the "unforseen circumstances" that will make an appearance during their lifetime. Finally, they will need to cultivate the virtue of altruism as one way to create meaning—by "doing for others."

We appreciate Havighurst's pioneering, neo-Piagetian research on developmental tasks. He took the work of developmental stage psychologists such as Jane Loevinger, Margaret Mahler, Maria Montessori, Judith Rich Harris, William Perry, James J. Fowler, and Lawrence Kohlberg, and propelled it one large step forward. He spoke less of stages and more of cycles and developmental tasks that all human beings share in common. And, most important, he covered the entire range of a person's life. He thought in terms of overlapping, evolving life cycles, not discrete, completed age stages.

We prefer not to think of the quarterlife (or mid-life or later-life) experience as a *crisis* (as Robbins and Wilner do) but rather as a series of exciting, real-life possibilities for students to make meaning. While it is true that some students do live their quarterlife years in a narrative of panic, stress, and insecurity, others live in very different narratives of meaning. Havighurst has influenced us greatly both in our teaching and in our conceptualization of meaning-making. His work speaks dramatically to us in the following ways, because we consider ourselves to be both pragmatists and philosophers, just as he was.

- First, like Havighurst, we think not in the metaphor of stages but cycles of meaning-making, which include central developmental questions and challenges that recur throughout the life span. Our students (both traditional and non-traditional) have crossed several age groups—from the late teens to the early eighties. What they all have in common is that they are on a "meaning-making quest."

- Second, we do not use the term "tasks," as this word results in meaning-making sounding like difficult or arduous work or labor assigned to someone—something such as a chore or job to be finished at some specified time. We prefer to think of meaning-making as a series of questions that recur throughout a person's life—some of which can be answered, some of which will never be. We have added a number of questions to Havighurst's work (based on Howard Gardner's "multiple intelligences"—Gardner, 2006a), and these include the emotional, intellectual, religio-spiritual, artistic, intrapersonal, interpersonal, philosophical, artistic, and cultural.

- Third, we draw from a number of disciplines in addition to the psychological, and these include philosophy, religious studies, sociology, anthropology, psychology, socio-biology, culture studies, educational theory and practice, leadership theory, and policy studies, among others.
- Fourth, we enlarge, deepen, and enrich the work of early developmental theory researchers by finding a common thematic ground—meaning-making—that serves as the foundation, rationale, and ultimate goal of human development.
- Fifth, we make the claim that no single group on a college campus owns the meaning-making life. Meaning-making mentors represent a variety of disciplines and make their homes in a number of on-campus sites. They are genuine interdisciplinarians and multiply-talented practitioners. These mentors come from all corners of the higher education house, including the academic, the administrative, the counseling centers, career services, student-activities offices, religio-spiritual centers, diversity centers, and human wellness centers, to mention only some. (Some of the material in these previous sections appears in a different format in Nash and Jang, 2013 and 2014.)

WHO WE ARE AS EDUCATORS

We have decided to introduce ourselves as teachers by identifying five brief guiding principles that we follow in teaching about meaning. Our goal is to talk briefly below about these principles without resorting to the use of show-off pedagogical jargon—the kind of specialized vocabulary used by a variety of educational specialists. We have found that our students become less and less responsive to public (or private) expressions of meaning-making in a classroom setting whenever we resort to using "technical tenure terms" to describe ideas that are actually far more profound, and useful, when they are simply stated. This is why we respect maxims. Intellectual complexity is a paradox. One of our basic beliefs about academic language is that the more convoluted and thick it becomes, the less powerful are the ideas it purports to describe. In fact, the ideas themselves tend to disappear from view whenever highly specialized language takes center stage. The thick argot becomes its own end.

But, having said this, we are also aware of an irony: We have found that our students love knowing the etymologies of words as much as they enjoy making personal sense of the maxims that we often share with them. Most quarterlife students know very little, if any, Latin or Greek; and so Robert, a lover of both these classical languages, is more than willing to share his etymological interests with them. Most know little or nothing about the origins and evolution of word meanings. Most are excited to learn that words are living things and constantly changing. Most are empowered when they learn that since the Paleolithic period, tens of thousands of years ago, human beings have been in the process of making up all the words, every single one of them; and we continue to do so. And, as we do, we are constantly changing the meanings of these words which, in their own mysterious way, then turn around and change us. Therefore, we are able to create meaning with our words, and these words, in turn, have the potential to touch our, and others', hearts, minds, and souls. In the principles that follow (and throughout our book), we make it a point to share with our readers our own love of words and the roots from which they change and grow.

Anyway, here is who we are:

- *We are philosophers*. We love ideas. We play with them. We try to get our students to have "fun" with ideas. At times we talk *while*, and not necessarily *after*, we think. We encourage our students to do the same. We make meaning with our students in conversation with them, and we do this with each other as well. We are always on the alert to dig deeply into thoughts and feelings, sometimes slowly, sometimes quickly. We follow a simple principle introduced by Socrates: all of knowledge begins in wonder. First there are the questions, and then there are the answers. We have found that young children are the most natural wonderers, because they start, and continue, their quest for wisdom with the never-ending, sometimes irritating, question—"why?" We are committed to getting our quarterlife students to go back to their early years and fall in love once again with the questions. Sadly, many of them have said that they stopped wondering in school when they left kindergarten, or at least the earlier grades. After that, schooling became a site for answers, not questions; certainty not uncertainty; data not dreams.

- *We are teacher-midwives*. We strive mainly to encourage our students to give birth to themselves. To educate (L. *educere*) is "to lead out of." We believe with Socrates that our students possess more natural wisdom and understanding than most of us, or them, realize. Thus, we spend a lot of time trying to "draw out" our students, before we fall prey to the temptation of "pouring into them" the authoritative data, facts, knowledge, and technical skill sets that we possess and believe that they should too.

  As teacher-midwives, we "evoke" (L. *call from or call forth)*—we call forth to our students and ask them to join us in the meaning-making process by sharing their insights. We rarely, if ever, try to "provoke" them—to "call out" students—to deliberately goad, prick, irritate, or anger them. Neither do we spend all our time trying to "invoke" the experts in the sense of always giving these authorities the final word, indeed the ultimate blessing, on what constitutes "The Truth" about meaning-making. Finally, we make it a point at all times never to "revoke" the contributions of students, especially in public. We will never withdraw our support from them.

17

Neither will we arrogantly "repeal, rescind, or annul" their meaning-making contributions.

Obviously, as readers will readily observe throughout our book, we value the insights of scholars and thinkers. We quote authorities on meaning-making frequently and respectfully. We always encourage our students to understand, and unpack, these insights with generosity and hopefulness. But we try never to leave the impression that the ideas of authoritative others are infallible—no matter the majesty of their reputations—or that their writings carry the inerrancy of papal encyclicals.

■ *We are pedagogical constructivists.* Please understand, however, that we are not anti-objectivists. The pursuit of a lowercase truth that might reside outside of us is a worthy endeavor in academia, particularly in the sciences, and one that we respect greatly. Our constructivism, in contrast, is method-ological. We want to help our student meaning-makers to understand that they, and they alone, are responsibile for authoring (constructing and construing) their lives. If this means that some students wish to choose objectivism as their dominant way of understanding the world, then so be it. We support this perspective with enthusiasm. This is what the existentialists mean when they write about the virtue of authenticity (L. *authentes,* self-making, genuine)—the inescapable realization that each of us must accept the truth that, when all is said and done, we alone are the autonomous authors of our meaning-narratives. We confer meaning on the world at least as much as the world confers meaning on us.

■ *We are pedagogical pluralists.* There are many pedagogical possibilities for teaching about successful meaning-making. So, too, there are innumerable ways for students to make meaning. In this sense, an emphasis on difference and diversity in meaning-making can be educationally rewarding. We are always learning from one another's worldviews, no matter how different or how similar; or how outrageous or how orthodox. We are all co-learners in the classroom, and elsewhere across the campus, because nobody owns the final word on meaning-making. We are respectful of our students, and each other, in the root sense of the term "respect" (L. *respicere*)—showing a willingness to "look back on" our own meaning-assumptions in the light of what others have shared about theirs.

■ *We are pedagogical storytellers.* Socio-biologists, philosophers, anthro-pologists, psychotherapists, and sociologists have confirmed that storytelling has been one of the most useful survival tools that human beings have created throughout history. Our stories draw us together. They empower us. Unfortunately, if they are too rigid, they can also tear us apart. They can wall us off from others' stories. To narrate is to survive, but only if we are willing to listen without making *a priori*, pontifical judgments about the rightness or wrongness of stories. Nelson Mandela has said that "as we let our light shine, we unconsciously give others permission to do the same." What better way to encourage authentic self-expression than to draw out the stories that give our students' lives meaning—thus, "letting their light shine." We would even go one step further: What better way for us as educators to build empathy and rapport in a classroom setting, or elsewhere, than for us to tell *our own* stories—with humility, honesty, and courage? Storytelling is both a craft and an art. Sharing our meaning-making stories orally is the craft; writing about stories is the art. In this way, we merge both craft and art throughout the meaning-making venture.

WHO WE ARE AS WRITERS

First of all, we think of ourselves as public intellectuals. Public intellectuals aim to convey their insights in a language that is non-elitist, non-technical, and non-authoritarian. We hope that our book will help faculty, administrators, and student affairs specialists to deal with many of the meaning-making questions that confront students each and every day of their lives. We craft our book in a way that is down-to-earth, clear, and accessible to non-scholars, as well as to scholars, who represent a variety of professions and disciplines. Thus, our book is impassioned, but most of all, we want it to be engaging, inspiring, direct, conceptually informed, research-based, and practical. This is a book about the meaning of meaning-making for students and the need for faculty and administrators to create a meaning-making curriculum on college campuses.

While we have the greatest amount of respect for the scholarly disciplines (both of us have been trained in the disciplines—Robert in philosophy, anthropology, English, and religious studies, and Jennifer in international studies, leadership and policy studies, and intercultural education), we deliver our ideas without having to filter them through the sometimes impenetrable jargon of the scholarly disciplines. We write as public intellectuals and as down-to-earth practitioner-scholars. At times, we write in a personal narrative style. We also include in this book short, written meaning-making insights from our undergraduate and graduate students whenever appropriate. And at the end of each chapter we feature a summative, practice-based reflection by individual practitioners/faculty/scholars who see themselves as meaning-making mentors in the different types of university work that they do. All of these experts, with a few exceptions, have taken meaning-making courses with us at some time during their careers.

OUR WRITING STYLE AND OUR THEMES

Throughout our book, we use a style of writing that Robert created called Scholarly Personal Narrative (SPN) (Nash, 2004; Nash and Bradley, 2011; Nash and Viray, 2013 and 2014). This is also a writing methodology that we teach our students in all our meaning-making courses. SPN strives for an ideal mix of particularity and generalizability, concreteness and abstractness, practice and theory. SPN writing has four major components: it starts with the identification of key *themes*; then it connects these themes to the writer's *personal stories* in order to exemplify and explicate the points being made; then it draws on relevant, pre-existing *research and scholarship* in order to ground and enrich the personal narrative; and, finally, it ends up with *generalizable ideas and applications* that we hope might connect with our readers in some way.

In this book, we identify specific meaning-making themes. Then we use our personal experience in our classrooms, and throughout the campus, region, and nation, to narrativize and exemplify these themes; then we reference the relevant scholarship to further develop an understanding of meaning-making theory and pedagogy; and, finally, we identify as clearly as we can the practical take-aways for our readers who might be interested in becoming meaning-making mentors both inside and outside the college setting.

It is important for the reader to understand that SPN does not present the author as some omniscient, third person authority. The author's voice is personal, clear, fallible, and honest. It is also humble and open-ended. SPN writing shows some passion. It is not a detached, "objective" examination of a topic. Instead, we want our book to be a thoughtful, first-person attempt to make a point, and to teach a lesson, by drawing on our own professional-personal experiences whenever appropriate in order to provide a real-life context for meaning-making teaching and learning.

The Meaning-Quests

In Part II, we probe in depth eight sets of meaning-making questions. We present each of these questions as quarterlife "Meaning-Quests." In separate chapters, we explore the following topics that emerge as primary concerns for students of all ages and stages throughout the life cycle: Hopes and Dreams; Morality and Ethics; Religion and Spirituality; Core Relationships; Overlapping Identities; Careers and Vocations; the Call of Service; and Self-Care and Balance. Each chapter's content contains germane theoretical explanations, scholarly analysis, student responses, and, at the end of each chapter, actual practitioner reflections. Each chapter also features our own personal perspectives on the core meaning-making issues we raise. We intend for all the chapters in Part II to be both inspiring and practical; to be intellectually defensible and professionally motivating.

Chapter 3

How Do I Realize My Hopes and Dreams?

The potential of the average person is like a huge ocean unsailed, a new continent unexplored, a world of possibilities waiting to be released and channeled toward some great good.

Brian Tracy

At the center of your being you have the answer; you know who you are and you know what you want.

Lao Tzu

A vision is not just a picture of what could be; it's an appeal to our better selves, a call to become something more.

Rosabeth Kantor

Go confidently in the direction of your dreams! Live the life you've imagined.

Henry David Thoreau

We have found that the quarterlife cycle of our students' lives is one of perplexity and complexity. Students struggle to find themselves, and most cannot remember who they were before the world told them who they needed to be. They are often distracted by what the current economy tells them they need to like, follow, and purchase. They have lost focus, and they mindlessly conform to media-portrayed images of aesthetic beauty and the latest clothing fashion trends.

Although potentially tumultuous, we agree with Paulo Coelho's maxim: "People are capable, at any time in their lives, of doing what they dream of." It is never too late to actualize our dreams. In order to do what Coelho suggests, people need to know first how to dream, and then to understand the content of their dreams. Thus, our question on hopes and dreams is two-fold: 1. Do our students have dreams, and, if so, do they know what they are? 2. If yes, then what stops them from doing what they love, enjoy, and dream of? This two-fold question is not a matter of what our quarterlife students *should* do, or are *supposed to* do, but what they genuinely *want* to do with their lives. Jennifer often reminds us of something that Marie Forleo says when it comes to hopes and dreams, "you've got to name them in order to claim them."

FREQUENT QUARTERLIFE QUESTIONS ABOUT HOPES AND DREAMS

> Every person dies, but not every person really lives.
>
> William Wallace

What follows are some of the most common deep-meaning questions regarding their hopes and dreams that we hear each and every day, in one form or another, from our students. As our students go through the quarterlife cycle, they become more aware of their own finitude. Time passes all too quickly as their undergraduate years begin to fade, and sooner or later they must face an uncertain future. At some point, each of our students grasp the harsh truth of Wallace's maxim: Yes, their death is inevitable, and who knows when—but what will they need to do in the interim to "really live"? The questions below capture some of their larger existential concerns. And Val's letter that follows puts each of these questions into a wrenchingly dramatic, personal perspective:

- What is it that deep down *I* want to do with my life, not what *others* want me to do with my life?
- What do I need to do in order to be successful in life, and can I be successful on my own terms?
- What does "passion" mean anyway, and why is it important to live a life of passion?
- Can I combine all my passions, or do I have to choose just one?
- Is it realistic to follow my dreams when it seems that I'm plagued more by my nightmares than my hopes?
- Why are my mentors always the first ones to question whether my dream is a practical or realistic one?
- What is my long-term vision for my life, and why should I even have one?
- Isn't it better to live one day at a time, and let the chips fall where they may?
- What do I enjoy doing the most in my free time, and will I ever feel this way about all the things I have to do throughout my life?
- What am I doing in my life now that I want to continue doing? What aspects of my present life do I wish I could take a pass on . . . forever?

- Is there something at the end of all of this? Do I know what it is? Is it worth what I am doing now to get there?
- Is there really something "more" than what I see and get every single, boring day?
- What kind of life do I want to look back on?

A Sad Letter from Val

What follows is a fictional letter that captures the downside of "hopes and dreams" concerns that we hear from so many students today, both in our classrooms and nationally in our consultancies. We have tried to incorporate in this single letter how "lost" so many of our quarterlifers feel when they "lose track of their dreams," or, worse, when they find that they have no "hopes or dreams" at all to guide them. We do not mean for "Val's" letter to be an isolated, grand example of a "lost" generation of quarterlifers. Sadly, her letter is far more representative (even typical) of the quarterlife generation than we might expect, and we are seeing more and more students like her in both our undergraduate and graduate programs.

Dear Jennifer and Robert,

When I first read those quotes you shared with us by Lao Tzu and Rosabeth Kantor, they really hit me like a bomb. Lao Tzu wants me to check out the "center of my being," because it is there that I will have the answers regarding my hopes and dreams. And Rosabeth Kantor urges me to be clear about my life's "vision," because it will reveal my better self. What the f——!

Here's what I believe at this difficult time in my life. I am lost. Somewhere on this twenty-three-year journey that has taken me through basketball games, ballet recitals, flute lessons, theatre productions, student government elections, honors receptions, sorority functions, cancer fundraisers, volunteer trainings, and more jobs than I care to count, I forgot to define myself. I lost track of my dreams. Though I have found myself in Venezuela, Spain, Mexico, Canada, and all across the United States, I have forgotten to discover myself. In my years of babysitting, tutoring, spending time with friends, reminiscing with my grandparents, caring for my parents, and loving my significant others, I have neglected to nurture myself.

So here I stand today, a "hot mess" if you will, lacking the will power, the strength, the hopefulness, the courage to say "no," or to put myself first. How, might you ask, can I do all of the things I have done, go all of the places I have gone, know all of the people I have known, and still question who I am? How have I ended up in this stark space where all my hopes and dreams have disappeared?

25

The answer you and Lao Tzu may say can be found if I look inside myself, but when I turn inside to look, I see a swirling mass of vague memories surrounded by a churning spiral of questions. Who am I? Where do I go from here? What do I enjoy? What happens if I quit? How do I take control of my life? Why am I so scared? What am I afraid of?

I wish that I could write this statement as a bold conclusion to a challenge I have overcome. I wish I could share with you the peace and tranquility that I discovered on my journey of resolution. My journey has not ended though. Instead, I blaze forward much like a blind rat in a maze, unaware of where I am going and bound to return to places I have been, because I cannot always tell the differences between my past, present, and future.

I believe in a lot of things, but I just don't know if I can believe in them for myself. I believe that it is okay not to be perfect, but I just can't lower my own standards. I believe it is possible to live a meaningful and happy life, but I just don't know what happiness means to me. I believe it is possible to set and achieve goals, but I just don't know what mine are. I believe I can find my way, but I just can't find the map.

Let's be honest. I know I am far from perfect, and yet I'm still trying. Actually, I don't even know what or who I am trying to be perfect for. I have also spent so much time trying to make other people happy, I have neglected to define what makes me happy. And now, as I begin to realize that life is short, I desperately want to take control of my life, to find what is meaningful for me . . . but I can't right now, because I am lost . . . and I don't know where I am going. I have no idea what my hopes and dreams are. Worse, I'm not sure I really want to know for fear of never being able to realize them. I'm really sorry that this letter is such a downer, but, I hope you can tell I don't want to continue living such a hopeless and dreamless life. Please help me.

Val

OUR UNDERSTANDING OF HOPES AND DREAMS

We will return to Val's letter at strategic points throughout the rest of this chapter. But, at this time, we want to talk about the meaning of hopes and dreams as we present them to our students each semester. *Hope* is a theological virtue in the Catholic Church. In this context, hope is all about the expectation of a life after death. Hope inspires human beings, because it promises everlasting happiness in an afterlife in the beatific presence of the God who created them. Theological hope keeps us from despair and discouragement, because we know that, at the end of our human lives, something greater, purer, and more joyful awaits us. While we respect this Roman Catholic catechetical notion of hope, it is not what forms our understanding of the term.

Rather, for us, *hope* is more closely allinged with C. R. Snyder's (2003) humanistic research on hope. Snyder believes that the ideal of hopefulness is what gets all of us through the hard times. Hope is actually a gritty, courageous way of thinking. Hope is a cognitive process that prepares us for disappointment and failure, but it is also more likely to pave the way for success and happiness. Hope is more than the simple expectation that things will get better if only we are patient enough to see them through. Instead, hope is the practical preparation we need in order to be successful in the world. Hope is a learned behavior. For Snyder, hope is knowing (and trusting) deep down that each of us can set realistic goals for ourselves, learning how to follow through and realizing these goals, and, most important, believing that we have the determination and the talent to accomplish what we need and want. Hope is pragmatic.

Dreams have long been the exclusive province of psychoanalysis, since Sigmund Freud introduced this therapeutic approach to analyzing the unconscious wellsprings of human behavior. For Freud, dreams are directly related to pathology. Everything we do is motivated by our unconscious, primal impulses. In order to live in a civilized society, we need to understand what motivates us unconsciously and then proceed to repress our worst instincts. One way for us to understand our baser impulses is through carefully examining our dreams. Dreams are our unconscious, unguarded way of taking an uncensored look at our most primal desires and motivations. Thus, for Freud, dream analysis in psychotherapy is the key to unlocking the repressed secrets of the ID. While we respect those students of ours who have benefitted from this psychoanalytic take on their dream states, this is not our approach to the relationship of dreams and meaning-making.

For us, the Old English root of dream (*dreme*—a fond hope or aspiration that serves as a motivational device to achieve our full potential) makes the most sense in dealing with quarterlife meaning-making. Both short- and long-term goals are intimately tied to our fondest dreams. While our dreams may not always be rational, they are almost always full of passion and excitement. They infuse, and motivate, our quest for meaning with creativity, imagination, and daring. Dreams can be both personal, interpersonal, and transpersonal. They can be small or big, practical or impractical, safe or risky.

We take our lead on dreams from Norman E. Rosenthal, MD (2013), who, in his decades of dream research, has found that our dreams are what give birth to our goals. The first step is to recognize, and establish, our goals based on our dreams, and then to cultivate the determination to act on them. Rosenthal has three simple rules for activating dreams and transforming them into achievable goals: 1. Recognize and respect all of our unique and authentic dreams (those greater and lesser ideals that motivate us); 2. Take our dreams seriously, especially when others might be ridiculing or minimizing them; 3. Hold on to our dreams firmly, with determination, and let them grow into fruition.

27

Rosenthal has found in his research at the National Institute of Mental Health that those who do not let go of their dreams, who wait, persist, and are willing to try new things, and who are able to make changes to their initial goals when necessary, are the most likely to succeed in realizing their fondest hopes and aspirations. These people are also the happiest in their workplaces, in their relationships, and on their campuses. At the very least, according to Rosenthal, holding onto our dreams helps us to develop new strengths and skills and gives us the motivation to realize our fullest human potential. Without our dreams, we are less than we could become.

The Omnipresent Fear of Failure

Rosenthal's research leaves many of our students feeling liberated and empowered, because they finally seem to receive the permission and freedom to do what they feel they really yearn to do. For those of our students who have never been encouraged to dream, however, this can be a real-life nightmare, haunting them during their quarterlife years and way beyond. This is the state of mind that Val is now dealing with. The questions are painful for her to face: What do I *do* with my life? What am I *supposed* to do with it? What can I *actually* do with it? What *should* I do with it?

We have faith that all our students, including Val, at some level, have an ability to use their imaginations to tap into their inner geniuses and intuitions. And so, whenever the time is ripe, we ask them these questions: Do you know how to dream? Would you be willing to write a short reflection on a recurring, edifying dream in your life? Can you sketch a symbolic picture, or many pictures, of your future? Can you write a poem about it? When is the last time that you had a soul-satisfying dream about the years to come in your life? We ask our students questions like these, because we understand how constrained their hopes for the future can be. In a heavily-formatted society, quarterlifers often find that their future paths are proscribed through direct and indirect acts of pressure by people they respect and who "want only the best" for them.

On the other hand, those students who know what they desire, and are certain of what they love—who have discovered their passions, and uncovered their strengths, and who have realized their calling—are optimistic and excited about their futures. Sadly, quarterlifers like Val let their songs of hopes and dreams hibernate quietly within them. But some refuse to remain in hibernation; suddenly these hopes and dreams burst to the surface. These are the wonderful moments the public sees on those "Got Talent" shows when a no-name performer who has never received any singing lessons goes on stage and "blows away" the judges and audience. These performers are willing to gather the courage, and to take the chance, to share their hopes and dreams with the world. What is it that stops most of us, including Val, from pursuing and doing what we desire, love, and enjoy?

We believe, along with our epigraphists, that it is mainly fear and doubt that steal away our self-confidence and sense of agency.

Fear is that invisible, but immensely powerful, force that commands the human psyche and shapes behavior. So many of our students live their lives in fear. We ask them to heed the words of an inventor, Charles F. Kettering, with over 140 patents, and honorary doctorates from nearly 30 universities. He said: "Believe and act as if it were impossible to fail." And so, we ask our students these two questions: What would you try to do if you knew that you could *not* fail? And then we ask them this question: What would you try to do even if you knew you *would* fail? It is in their response to the second question where they are most likely to find what they are truly passionate about. Unfortunately, too many quarterlifers never let themselves get to the second question.

We need not let fear stop us from taking risks. All of our epigraphists encourage us to stop waiting for that *perfect* time to take a risk, and for that fortuitous opportunity to knock on our door. In fact, we are ready when we want to be ready. So we need to take a chance and learn as we go. We learn from both success and failure, benefit and risk. Regardless of the outcome, we will emerge from the adventure transformed. George Washington Carver, a chemist who discovered over 325 uses for the peanut, said: "Ninety-nine percent of all failures come from people who have a habit of making excuses."

The crippling effect of perfectionism is another factor at play with fear. Both perfectionism and fear are near-fatal kissing cousins. Many of our students know what they desire and want to go after, but their sense of perfectionism takes over and cripples them with the fear of being less than perfect. That is a lot of self-imposed pressure to live up to, and so most of our students never start. As Jack Canfield said, "We miss 100 percent of the shots we never take. Instead of spending this whole time aiming at a target, we need to fire away and adjust our aim as we go." Quarterlife students spend much of their time aiming at the target, attempting to get the perfect scenario and circumstance, and, tragically, they miss 100 percent of the shots they never take.

For us, Anne Lamott (1994) comes the closest to exposing the fallacy of perfectionism, particularly for *authors* who have a tendency to stall when writing, or, worse, who never finish what they start. Her words ring so true for us as we deal with those perfectionist students who are working on theses, dissertations, and other types of compulsory writing projects. These students seem to be more concerned with winning the equivalent of a Pulitzer Prize or a MacArthur Genius Award than they are in just starting, sustaining, and finishing a "good-enough," not necessarily a "best-enough," manuscript. Here is what Lamott says:

> Perfectionism is the voice of the oppressor, the enemy of the people. It will keep you cramped and insane your whole life . . . perfectionism is based on the obsessive belief that if you run carefully enough, hitting each stepping-stone

29

> just right, you won't have to die. The truth is that you will die anyway . . . so have a little fun [while you're hopping from stone to stone].

Perfectionism, unfortunately, leads to doubt. Doubt steals away our self-confidence and self-determination to realize our hopes and dreams in life. Doubt is sometimes the silent, but also the loudest, most destructive, voice inside our heads. This is the voice that says, "I can't." "I'm not ready." "I'm not good enough." When we doubt, we become hesitant. Instead of coming from a place of abundance, we act out of scarcity and fear. We send ourselves messages of "what if?" and "not enough!" Self-doubt eats us up inside, and keeps our natural boldness, power, and magic from expressing themselves. Instead, we become hollow and fragile. In contrast, Goethe (1820) once said: "Whatever you can do, or dream you can do, begin it. Boldness has genius, power, and magic in it. Begin it now. Now!" The important question for our quarterlife students is this one: How is it possible for you to regain all your natural powers even, and especially, during those moments when you feel most hollow and fragile? We believe our strength is regained through exploring the intersection of our passion and talent, where most of our hopes and dreams reside.

STRATEGIC TIPS FOR HELPING STUDENTS FIND THE INTERSECTION BETWEEN PASSION AND TALENT AND THEIR SELF-WORTH

We believe that each of our students has a deep, inner hunger for something more. As meaning-making mentors, we play an important role in helping them realize what that "something more" is. As educators, we know that because our students are uniquely composited as individuals, there is no one prescribed answer to what success means to our students collectively. We understand that, no matter what the degree of their uniqueness might be, all our students must come to terms with meeting Maslow's hierarchy of basic needs. However, there is no one industry, one career, one religio-spiritual set of beliefs, one guaranteed timeline, one lifestyle, one significant other, or one magical combination of all of these that will offer each one of them the magic formula for living happy, fulfilled, and satisfying lives.

So many of our students are non-plussed when they learn that the "magic formula" for being happy and successful is actually a fraud. As Ellen Goodman (2007) humorously puts it in defining "normal":

> Normal is getting dressed in clothes that you buy for work, and driving through traffic in a car that you are still paying for, in order to get to the job you need to pay for the clothes and the car, and the house you leave vacant all day so you can afford to live in it, and all of this is supposed to make us happy but actually leaves us feeling emptier than ever.

Magic formulas for realizing hopes and dreams are most often profit-driven myths perpetuated by the marketplace. Some of our students grow angry, or, worse, despairing, when they find that the promises of the marketplace are really lies, based on selling a consumer's dream that quickly turns into a nightmare. Ironically, based on the United Nations' National Happiness Index (2013), the United States is not among the happiest countries in the world, even though it consumes a huge portion of the world's resources. According to this Index, the United States ranks seventeenth, and it continues to drop in the world rankings. These rankings include five categories: "healthy life expectancy, having someone to count on, perceived freedom to make choices, freedom from corruption, and prevalence of generosity."

Below are a series of tips for helping students to find the intersection between passion and talent. We believe that passion and talent are the necessary preconditions for realizing our hopes and dreams. In the following paragraphs, we make a few distinctions that might provide conceptual clarity between the ideas of *passion and talent*. Then we will share a series of questions that we use with our students to help them identify, and think more deeply about, their hopes and dreams, and their passions and talents. We conclude with an array of resources that we have used in order to help our students to go further in their self-exploration.

Passion

We need to encourage students to be clear about their passions and their talents, and how to find the intersection that connects them. *Passion* is a word we often hear in career services offices, but it is not a concept that we discuss openly and at length in the high school or college classroom. Few of our students have ever taken the time to identify, and explore, their passions. Sometimes when we ask our students to free-define the word "passion" their initial responses always connote something irrational, or suffering, or even anger. After we discuss the term for a while, our students realize that passion can also convey excitement, enthusiasm, inspiration, love, and affection for an activity. Often a passion for something can be the cause, or it can be the effect, of one's natural talents. In fact, most people who display special talents, and who express strong commitments, are also passionately invested in them. Unfortunately, "find your passion" has become a cliché, but like most clichés there is an element of truth in it. And, so, we make it a point to engage our students in a conversation about the upside of passion and how the realization of their hopes and dreams is dependent on how passionate they are about achieving these.

Some simple passion-questions that we ask our students to help them zero in on their hopes and dreams are these:

- What are a couple of activities you engage in frequently that evoke strong, positive emotions from you?
- What are you most enthusiastic about (what do you most look forward to) when you get up in the morning to start your long day?
- Who and what do you love the most in the whole world, and why?
- What hope and/or dream—either personal or professional—has stayed with you the longest in your life up to now?
- Do you know anyone who is obviously passionate about the work they do? If so, how do they express this passion?
- How hard are you willing to work in order to translate your passions into the practical realization of your hopes and dreams?
- What do you do when you find that you are losing some of your lifelong passion for special activities in your life?

Talent

Obviously, realizing our hopes and dreams takes more than passion. Passion is the great motivator. But *talent* is the ability to translate our passion into practice. All of our students have a native ability, a natural aptitude, for excelling in a specific pursuit. Identifying this native ability ought to be one of the primary goals of meaning-making education. For us, education needs to be all about cultivating those natural abilities that will infuse our students' personal and professional lives with enduring meaning. All of us know students who drift from one major to another, from one school to another, from one job to another. Sometimes this drift is important for students in order to find their authentic calling in life. Unfortunately, however, too much student-drift is the result of a meaning-making vacuum in the classroom, in the counselor's office, in the residence hall, and in a number of other on-campus sites. How often, we sometimes ask our students, has anyone who works at our university asked you such talent-questions as the following:

- What is it you think you do really well—both in and out of the classroom?
- What comes faster and smoother to you when you have to learn something new?
- If someone were to apply the adjective "natural" to you—what special skills, talents, qualities, or dispositions would the adjective describe?
- What is it that you are able to learn in less time, and to master, than other things?
- Which of your activities draws the most compliments from others?
- Do you think there are some things that you do phenomenally well?
- What natural abilities would you like to spend more time developing?
- How has your formal schooling helped you to cultivate the special talents that you possess? If not at all, why not, do you suppose?

Extrinsic Self-worth vs Intrinsic Self-worth

During a conversation with a colleague recently, Jennifer learned about how to distinguish a *Doing* culture from a *Being* culture, where people earn their lovability and self-worth as a result of what they *do* rather than who they *are*. In a subsequent conversation, Jennifer and Robert were able to identify *extrinsic* self-worth cultures as different from *intrinsic* self-worth cultures. It is important for us to make this distinction, because it helps us to deal with all students, particularly those from diverse backgrounds, whose sense of lovability and self-worth are derived primarily from what they are able to achieve, to provide, and to become. How proud do they make their families because of their accomplishments?

Some of these students are international from collectivist cultural back-grounds—e.g., Greece, Brazil, China, Taiwan, Japan, Korea, Vietnam, etc.—and they are eager to please, never really sure of themselves, always seeking approval, and lacking self-confidence, even though they have been highly successful achievers in so many ways. They want to be helpful, sensitive, and considerate, and many are drawn to the call of service. They were socialized in their cultures to believe that their worth and meaning derived from being the best student, the best child, the best sibling, the best professional, and the best learner. Hence, they strive to please mainly by *doing*, rather than simply by *being*.

All of the above is important to the focus of this chapter, because when it comes to passion and talent, different types of students, including international students, may fulfill their hopes and dreams in different ways. They may express their passions in unique ways, or, as all too frequently happens, completely repress them. The upshot of this dynamic is that students from an extrinsic self-worth background find themselves creating hopes and dreams for their futures that are more compatible with what others want as opposed to what and who they want to become. In this ironic sense, therefore, students from extrinsic self-worth backgrounds "be" by "doing." And students from intrinsic self-worth backgrounds "do" by "being." Finally, when it comes to meaning-making, some students make meaning extrinsically, some intrinsically, and some seek a balance.

STRATEGIC TIPS FOR HELPING STUDENTS TO IDENTIFY HOPES AND DREAMS

We don't need to have all the answers to all our students' questions all the time. When asked a question as big as *what do I do with my life?* one realistic response might be this one—*at this point in your life, what would you* like *to do with your life?* You can return the question to the questioner. Draw the student out by asking *what* and *why* often. If they say running makes them happy, ask why? Dig deeper. What is there about running that makes them happy? Some students are eager to do this external processing with a professor, administrator, or staff member at a university. All we have to do is to be the genuinely attentive listener that all students

33

crave in their lives! Here are a few "Hopes and Dreams Prompts" that we have used to get our students to write and to share openly with classmates:

- Describe your ideal day.
- If you could do anything for a living, what would that be?
- If money were not an issue, what would you do with your present time as well as the rest of your life?
- If you knew you could not fail, what would you choose to do?
- What would be worth doing, even if you knew you would fail?
- What and who do you aspire to become knowing it may not always be realizable?
- What do you want to experience in your life over the next five or ten years?
- How do you propose to make this happen?

As educators, we need to help our students be clear about what their hopes and dreams might be. There are times when all a student needs is for educators to bring up this topic, either personally or collectively, and simply ask: "What is it is that you truly want for your life?" Many students will then go off and reflect on their own. On the other hand, sometimes when students say, "I don't *know* what I want," it is because they are afraid to *own* what they want. They are afraid that once they get clear on what it is they desire so deeply that it hurts, they will come up short, fail, look stupid, or not be loved. Hence, they hesitate to go after, or worse they completely abandon, their dreams.

We believe strongly that each of us, at some time in our lives, knows what we want to be and how we want to pursue this. However, the pressures from outside are strong for us to conform and to move away from satisfying our deepest desires. The key for us as educators and administrators is to continually encourage our students to be steadfast, and go after what they really crave. As the 1913 Nobel Laureate for Literature, Rabindranath Tagore, said, "You can't cross a sea by merely staring into the water." Actualizing our hopes and dreams means exercising our passions and putting our talents to work in the world.

A Personal Reflection from a Practitioner on Realizing Hopes and Dreams

Michele C. Murray, Vice-President for Student Development
Seattle University

"Grounded in Why"

At the end of his weekly Billboard Top 40 Countdown, iconic DJ Casey Kasem (also the voice of "Shaggy" from the *Scooby Doo, Where Are You!* cartoon series) signed off with his trademark line, "Keep your feet on the ground and keep reaching for the stars!" As a kid, I never gave this encouraging statement much thought—it was simply the signal that the week's number one song had been played and the countdown was over. But now, years later, I find Kasem's signature line to be full of wisdom, even if it is a little syrupy.

There is a sage truth in the paradoxical advice to be both grounded in a certain reality and hopeful and courageous enough to reach for, and realize, even the most powerful dreams. Staying grounded means knowing who I am at the core of my being—my values and beliefs, the source(s) of my joys and passions—and having a realistic understanding of who I am in relation to others. The more grounded I am, the more secure I am in who I am, and the less I try to be someone I am not. Being grounded is not being stuck. Having my proverbial "feet on the ground" is my position of greatest strength. If I am grounded, I am not constrained by other people's conceptions of who I am or what my life should be, and that allows me to be free . . . free to dream and free to reach for the stars I know are out there.

Having the freedom to reach for the stars is one thing. Knowing which star (or stars) is the one I should reach for is something else entirely. Of the millions and billions of possibilities out there, which is the right one for me? Which star, or constellation of stars, is most connected to who I am at the core of my being? In a way, these are variations of the classic question: What should I do with my life?

I am no stranger to these questions and have asked them of myself over and over again as I make meaning of my life. In one way or another, these are also the perennial questions I hear from students. Whether fretting over which graduate program to pursue or which career path to follow, students I encounter spend a lot of time questioning their choices, trying to distinguish between them, and attempting to determine which is the best choice for them. Truth be told, I did the same when I was in college. I wish I knew then what I know now, and so I try to spread the lesson experience has taught me about figuring out what to do with my life: You are asking all the right questions but in the wrong order.

Why Comes Before *What*

The questions I asked as a college student, and those I hear students asking today, are about the stuff of hopes and dreams. They want to know definitively what they should do with their lives as if naming the goal will solidify their identity. It is easy to understand why this is so. In just about every small-talk, cocktail party conversation people talk about what they do as if it defines who they are and confers some sort of value upon them. The pressure students feel to name what they do is understandable, indeed. So it comes as a shock to them when finally being able to name what they want to do leaves them feeling empty.

There is a reason that Kasem first recommended his listeners to keep their feet on the ground before he encouraged them to reach for the stars. It is the same reason that

35

Simon Sinek's TED Talk, "How Great Leaders Inspire Action" has been viewed almost 18 million times. You can't reach your dreams without first being grounded in who you are; you can't get to the "what" without first understanding the "why." In Sinek's view, our "why" is our purpose and our beliefs. The why is our grounding, our inspiration, and motivation. The "what" is the manifestation of our purpose and beliefs. The what has no shape, depth, or meaning without the why. Or put another way, if we want to realize our dreams and know which stars to reach for, we need to be sure we are grounded in our own sense of purpose, our own why. As Sinek points out, people fail to reach their objectives when they focus too much on the *what* without having a meaningful *why* to drive it. It is the *why* that really matters.

What Comes Before *Why*

Regrettably, simply recommending that someone go find a meaningful why is woefully inadequate. Without a map to the why, it is all too easy to end up with a collection of meaningless whats, and this I know from personal experience. In my younger years, like my students today, I had countless career fantasies. One year I wanted to be a child psychologist and then a forensic psychologist. The following year I flirted with optometry and then music or television news and then public relations. (Never during any of that time did I ever imagine a career in education.) I was intrigued by the way those possibilities sounded and by what I imagined my life could be. My process of identifying what I should do with my life was like buying a suit because it looks good on a mannequin only to find that the fit, size, and color were all wrong for me. I was grasping at any star because I was not grounded enough in myself to find my own.

The stories Parker Palmer (2000) recounts in *Let Your Life Speak* mirror some of my own experiences. I was, as Palmer suggested, trying to tell my life what I wanted to do with it rather than listening for what my life wanted to do with me. So focused on the what of my career choice was I, that the why had escaped my notice. But similarly to Palmer, the clues to my deepest longings and desires—my whys—were hidden in the plain sight of my life.

Throughout high school and college, I was attracted to activities that involved other people, and I was often chosen to lead groups. I enjoyed problem-solving and being creative. I was at my best when I had time to think and reflect, and I felt the most sense of reward when I was helping other people live into their best selves. All of these clues to the particular constellation of stars that are right for me were hidden in my activity, but I missed them. I mistook the activity—the what—for the why. Rather than conferring identity upon me, my activities were a shorthand for what I truly loved and brought a sense of joy to my life. When I understood that the activities were an expression of love and joy, I found my why. For the first time in my life I began to feel grounded and could see more clearly which stars were mine for the reaching.

Love Is *Why*

When students come to me similarly confused about what they want to do with their lives and turned around by all the choices before them, I like to share one of my favorite, inspirational poems, "Falling in Love." In the words of the unstoppable Tina Turner, they often ask, "What's love got to do with it?" And in the words of Fr. Pedro Arrupe, S.J., the Jesuit leader to whom the poem is attributed, I often respond: "Everything!" Arrupe writes: "What you are in love with will affect everything and it will decide everything." I explain: This is not a simple erotic love. This is the love that enkindles the internal fire and says, "This is who I am!" Arrupe's concept of falling in love speaks to a spiritual longing for congruence and alignment—the kind of love that brings order and meaning, depth and understanding.

Arrupe knew that the inspiration for the *what* comes from the *why*. His words are echoed in favorite quotes from famous luminaries such as Maya Angelou and Steve Jobs, who say that the secret to success is to do what you love. To anyone searching for *why*, the advice is the same: Fall in love. There you will find your *raison d'être*, your purpose, and your pathway to success. The answer to the question, "What should I do with my life?" begins with another question: "What do you love?" Answer this question first because your reaching the stars depends on you being grounded in your *why*.

REALIZING HOPES AND DREAMS: A SUMMARY OF SALIENT RECOMMENDATIONS FROM MICHELE MURRAY

As the highest-ranking student affairs professional on her campus, Michele's work with students is always consistent with helping them to identify, and realize, their fondest hopes and dreams. She makes it a point to reinforce their hopes. She listens intently, and non-judgmentally, to their personal and professional goals. She is sensitive to both their reasonable, and not-so-reasonable, fears about the future. She is able to get them to express, and own, their passions. But she is also tuned in to their sense of failure, and so she helps them to acknowledge their talents and to "fall in love" with the prospect of actually being able to live out their hopes and dreams.

Here, in a nutshell, are a few of her recommendations, in her own words:

1. Remind students that they need to be grounded and secure in who they are before they can reach for the stars. Ask them what grounds them the most at this time in their lives. Get them to articulate their dreams and their possibilities. Encourage them to re-examine their current courses of studies, and to be as honest as they can about whether the current career path they are pursuing is motived as much by them as by others.

2. Get students to explore their "whys" in every course they take and in every activity they get involved with on and off campus. Many people (of all ages) fail to reach their objectives when they focus too much on a particular *what* without having a meaningful *why* to drive it.

3. Ask students to re-examine and re-evaluate their "whats", because without a plan (even if it is continually evolving and changing), the "whys" have no ultimate compass to guide them. Both the "whys" and the "whats" are intextricably related in the pursuit of our fondest hopes and dreams.

4. Encourage students to identify the "whys" and "whats" that they truly love. Get them to ask: "What activities in my life provide me with the greatest sense of joy and love?" The macro-question—"What should I do with my life?"—always begins with another question: "What do you love?"

Chapter 4

Who Am I Striving to Become as a Moral Person . . . and Why?

[What have I learned from my lifelong depression and my suicide attempt?] I need to live the moral life. I choose to live responsibly and consciously. I choose to live fully. I choose not to drop into the abyss of despair and depression . . . I choose to take risks and to put myself out there, on the line, over the line, to help others.

Kelly A. Daley

In the touch-and-go of modern-day life, in a world grappling with chaos and the uncertainty of an unknown and unpredictable future, in a fragile society struggling with conflicts between technical know-how and long-established values and beliefs . . . [one question] lies at the heart of the human endeavor: "How best may I live, endure, and achieve, in the presence of, and in conjunction with, my fellow human beings?"

Karen Ho

For me, morality is couched entirely in terms of other human beings. Human beings are the source of each other's joy and suffering. Human beings create and destroy bonds with each other, and all we can do is try to build bridges that connect one another.

Allison Handler

The epigraphs that open this chapter are taken from a series of Ethics Prize Essays sponsored by the Elie Wiesel Foundation for Humanity. The volume, *An Ethical Compass: Coming of Age in the 21st Century* (2010), includes 30 essays written by undergraduate college students during the last two decades. What all these essays have in common is, in the words of Elie Wiesel, "that they showcase young people who are sensitive to the sufferings and defects that confront a society yearning for guidance and eager to hear ethical voices." Wiesel, and a panel of independent investigators, read thousands of essays submitted by quarterlife college students who were asked to reflect in personal ways on their moral beliefs. The result is a volume that personifies Wiesel's profound conviction that all young people must "think higher and feel deeper" in their college experience if the world is to deal successfully with all the "salient humanitarian challenges of our time."

WHY IS CREATING A "MORAL COMPASS" IMPORTANT FOR COLLEGE STUDENTS?

The term "moral compass" is fast becoming an ethical cliché in the United States. Today, advocates of a particular religion, political ideology, or even a philosophy of life will judge the validity of a person's "moral compass" according to whether or not it is consistent with the teachings of a preferred ethical system of what constitutes right and wrong behavior. For example, the political and social conservative William Bennett has written a book titled *The Moral Compass: Stories for a Life's Journey* (2008). Bennett's prescriptive take on the best "moral compass" for young people is based on Christian family values, masculine virtues, community responsibility, and a firm belief in God. And, from another perspective, President Barack Obama, a liberal, social activist Democrat, has said that the "true moral compass" is one that supports "democratic freedoms against those who would intimidate, torture, and murder people for exercising the most basic first-amendment freedoms" (2004).

We, however, are using the term "moral compass" in a more all-encompassing, less partisan manner. For us, having a moral compass means knowing how to act "in character." It means knowing what gives our lives moral meaning and then acting accordingly. It means being consistent: knowing who we are, where we came from, and who we would like to become. It means being acutely aware of the ethical story about our lives that we would like to write in the best of all possible worlds. It means being conscious of how our background moral stories influence our foreground moral actions, both for good and for bad. It also means being aware of the impact of our past and present communities that have been so central in defining each of as moral beings.

Finally, possessing a moral compass means being true to those dispositions, qualities, motives, and intentions that define us to ourselves as authentic moral meaning-makers. The Harvard psychologist Robert Coles (1989) offers this familiar, yet still enticing, definition of character: "Character is how you behave when no one is looking." He says this, because, in our opinion, he understands that moral character is the embodiment of our entire lives lived in a variety of small communities (such as families and churches), shaped by pivotal moral and ethical teachings in a number of secular and sacred institutions, and touched by influential others who come into our worlds at various points, and, even when they are gone, stay with us in lingering moral memories throughout our lifespans.

According to Coles, these ideals, communities, events, traditions, and people are "always looking" at us whenever we make our moral choices. They provide what sociologists call the basic "habitus" (those taken-for-granted assumptions that make our particular experience of the world seem like good, common sense) for shaping our continuing moral narratives.

If Coles's definition of moral character is accurate, and we think it is, then to act "out of character" is to betray everything that is precious to us. It is to compromise, to turn away from our ideal moral selves, to abandon those defining communities, stories, and qualities of character that nourish and sustain us. In contrast, having a consistent moral compass to fall back on points us in the right direction during those dreaded times when we feel our lives are devoid of a sense of meaning; when we have lost sight of our "true moral north." Every single student we have ever met must face the prospect of veering off the moral path during times of great challenge in their lives, and when they do, they will need to get back on track.

Our semester-long course ("Ethics of Helping Relationships") on ethics, morals, and meaning-making—an elective for undergraduate and graduate students in our professional school—is currently one of the most popular courses in our college. (Robert created this course four decades ago; it was the first course of its kind nationally in a college of education and social services.) Today, the course always closes out at pre-registration, and waiting lists are lengthy. We are not surprised that students show up on the first day of class sensing that a course like ours is important for them to take, but not always sure why they should register for what their friends and families might label as an "impractical" course. After all, they wonder, what will be the payoff for them if they decide to "stay the course" and spend an entire semester reading, writing, and talking about morality and ethics? Will future employers really care whether they have, in the words of Elie Wiesel quoted above, learned how to "think higher and feel deeper" about the salient ethical challenges of the twenty-first century?

During the first class, we usually share pertinent moral statements like the epigraphs that open this chapter, and we ask our students to try to make sense of them by reflecting on them in frank and personal ways. For example, in response to Kelly Daley's self-disclosure about her lifelong depression and suicide attempt, a few students just don't understand how these terrible experiences would lead her to "want to live the moral life." What is the direct connection, they ask? Shouldn't she be in therapy or on anti-depressant medication? Many others, however, understand right away that only by choosing to live responsibly and consciously can Kelly "choose to live fully." Because some of our students live in their own "abyss of despair and depression," and a few of them have even tried, or seriously contemplated, ending their own lives, they know that helping others can be a life-enriching way to help themselves. With Kelly Daley, they understand that life takes on a larger and deeper meaning, when they decide to expand their

41

moral spheres of vision; when they choose to put themselves out there, "on the line, over the line, to help others."

Still other students want desperately to achieve a groundedness in their lives. They need something solid to fall back on at a time when everything is up in the air. They resonate with Karen Ho's sentiments above concerning the never-ending hustle and bustle of the everyday world. How, they ask, can they deal in a healthy and holistic way with the terrifying uncertainty of an unknown future that awaits them? How will they be able to live true to their best selves when there seems to be so much pressure to fit in, to acquire technical skills, and to be a money-making, career success in the world beyond the college campus? With Karen Ho, they seek to create values and beliefs that will stand the tests they will face for the rest of their lifetimes. They want to build an extensive and responsive community of significant others throughout their local and national regions that will bind them together rather than tear them apart.

When we are successful in encouraging our students on the first day of class to think honestly and openly about what might give their lives an enduring moral meaning, they understand that living a compassionate life in conjunction with others is what will ultimately save themselves . . . along with the human species. They realize, as does Allison Handler above, that even while they are competing with their peers and colleagues in the school place and work place for scarce benefits and noteworthy achievements, in the end, what really matters is "to build bridges that connect people to one another." After all, if an obsessive quest for success, drug and alcohol addiction, sexual profligacy, and cut-throat, show-off competition are the ultimate outcomes of the so-called "good life," then, at some point in history, each of us will end up destroying ourselves along with one another.

ASKING THE KEY MORAL MEANING-MAKING QUESTIONS

In this section, we offer a series of moral meaning-making questions that we ask our students to consider during the first few classes of the semester. We purposely try to keep these questions open-ended, non-judgmental, and *evocative*, even though many of them might be difficult for some students. We strive to draw out, not close down, our students, particularly when the subject matter is sensitive in nature and even controversial. Students have told us that rarely, if ever, have they been given an opportunity in a high school or college classroom, or in any campus setting for that matter, to explore some of these questions. Neither, by the way, have faculty, staff, and administrators taken the time at our university to talk about some of these issues with one another in a series of cross-campus, meaning-making consortia. We believe that it is time for all of us to have these types of conversations.

1. What gives your life meaning? What makes life worth living for you?
2. Have you read any books (fiction or non-fiction) in the last several years you can honestly say have changed the way you think about (or live) your life? Which ones? How so?
3. What beliefs, morals, or ideals are most important in guiding your life at this time? Which ones would you pass on to your children? Or to your friends if they asked?
4. Do you believe your life should have a purpose? If yes, what is *your* purpose? If not, why not?
5. Can you give some specific examples of how your important beliefs, morals, or ideals have found actual expression in your personal and/or professional life? If you can't, why not?
6. Whenever you must make an important personal/professional decision, what pivotal moral beliefs or ideals do you sometimes fall back on?
7. Do you think there is a "plan" for human lives? Is there one for your life? If yes, where does the "plan" come from?
8. When your personal/professional life appears most discouraging, hopeless, or defeating, what holds you up or renews your hope?
9. Why do you suppose some persons and groups suffer more than others? Why do some persons and groups experience more success and happiness? Why is it that some persons and groups act more ethically or unethically than others?
10. Will human life in general go on indefinitely, do you think, or will it ultimately end? If you don't care for the question, why not?
11. Some people believe that without religion morality breaks down. Do you agree or disagree? Why?
12. What do you think of this statement? "Ethically, we're all *egoists*, because, if we're completely honest with ourselves, we must admit we act out of enlightened (or unenlightened) self-interest in everything we do."
13. Or this statement? "Egoism is ultimately a selfish philosophy. Without a commitment to *altruism*, people's actions would be unimaginably self-centered, cut-throat, and hopeless."
14. What do you think of this statement? "There are *no moral absolutes*, because morality is totally relative to a particular culture, group, belief system, or personal preference. We're all inescapably different."
15. Or this statement? "There are indeed *moral absolutes*, because regardless of cultural or personal differences, people do, in fact, agree on a number of core moral principles. In some ways, we're all very much alike."
16. If we, your instructors, were to ask you the following questions, how would you answer us? "Why should we treat you fairly, when it might be to our advantage to treat you unfairly?" "Why should we tell you the truth, when it might be to our advantage to tell you a lie?" "Why should we keep a

43

promise we made to you, when it might be to our advantage to break the promise?"

17. Why should anyone bother about being moral at all? Why should you try to act ethically in an organization that seems inherently unethical? Why not just do what feels good, or what you can get away with, or what suits your fancy at the moment, or what gets you promoted? Under what conditions would you ever be able to impose a moral judgment on anyone, or to hold anyone morally accountable in the work you do?

Some Student Responses to the Key Moral Meaning-Making Questions

Before the semester is over, and in thinking about all these questions in depth, students will have had the opportunity to examine what makes them tick morally and ethically. Here are some representative student responses in their end-of-course, narrative self-evaluations regarding what they learned about themselves as moral beings throughout the semester. (All the responses are anonymous, and each of the entries has, to some extent, been narrativized, and/or composited and modified, in order to protect the privacy of the writers.)

If I don't know what I stand for morally, then who the hell am I? If I can't act ethically to the best of my ability in all my living and work spaces, then what am I? How is it possible for me to find any meaning in my life, particularly during these undergraduate years of self-indulgence and confusion, if I'm all over the place with my beliefs and actions? My main take-away from our course this semester is the importance, indeed, the necessity, of identifying what is really important to me as an evolving moral person. In class we talked about the moral insights of Maya Angelou, and this is the quotation of hers that I found most pertinent to my own moral journey: "Courage is the most important of all the virtues, because without courage you can't practice any other virtue consistently . . . your moral character will be erratic." Well, please know that, because of this course, I am learning what I want my moral character to be . . . I want courage to be the cornerstone of how I interact with the world. I want to achieve moral consistency, intentionality, and a passionate sense of mission and purpose in everything I do both on and off campus.

"What holds me up when everything is falling down around me?" This question really got me thinking this semester—my first year of graduate school. I graduated from an elite Ivy League college last year whose new President went public recently with his embarrassment and shame over the runaway abuse on our campus of alcohol, drugs, academic cheating, and, especially, sexual violence toward women. One of our texts this semester, Julian Baggini's *What's*

It All About? Philosophy and the Meaning of Life (2004), helped me to understand the out-of-control pursuit of hedonism for its own sake on my undergraduate campus. Too many of us lived our empty, "falling-down" lives with a "carpe diem" mentality. "Seize the day; eat, drink, and be merry for tomorrow is just too scary to think about; and, in the end, brute pleasure is all there is, whatever the cost to ourselves and others." Well, after living four self-destructive years of hedonic angst on my campus, and after studying Baggini this semester, I now interpret "carpe diem" very differently. "Seize the day" does not mean drowning myself in aimless, escapist pleasure, because there is no tomorrow worth living for. In contrast, for me, it means that time is short, and this is the only life I have. I shouldn't squander it. I can leave my mark on the world only by living up to my highest values. In the relatively short time I have left to live, I want my life to be a virtuous example (to all those who will come after me) of integrity, authenticity, and commitment to helping other quarterlifers whenever they feel the urge to succumb to a mindless, adolescent hedonism. Yes, this is what I took away from our course this semester, and I'm damned grateful for the opportunity to redirect my life.

I realize that I make most of my moral decisions emotionally and intuitively. I guess my moral compass is more affective than cognitive. I just go ahead and do what I feel, not necessarily what I think, is the right thing. I grew up in a family where feelings and intuitions were highly respected. I remember my now-deceased grandmother who actually raised me saying: "Go with your emotional gut when you face very difficult decisions. Gut responses can be trusted more than head responses. You can't fool your heart, but you can play all kinds of crazy games with your head." Now, don't get me wrong. I use both my head and my heart to make important moral decisions in my life, but my heart is still my most trusted resource. I think it was Pascal who said that "the heart has reasons the head knows nothing about."

I don't know whether my life, or life in general, has any underlying purpose. I'm not religious or spiritual. What I do know, though, is that I am the only one who can make meaning of my life. I, alone, need to decide when I am acting ethically and when I'm not. I, alone, need to take full responsibility for my judgments and actions in all areas of my life. My life is basically meaningless if all I do is play the "blame game." I used to do this all the time, you know, until I realized that my out-of-control drinking habit was nobody's choice but my own. However, where I differ from the A.A. "gospel" is that there is no "higher power" in my life that determines my choice to be drunk or sober. I am my own "highest moral power," and I thank everyone in this course for helping me to see this.

45

I learned this semester that I do need "moral absolutes" to guide me. There's got to be a moral compass for me that doesn't keep wavering all the time. There's got to be some fixed moral meaning that does not allow me to deviate from the "right path" whenever I think this is the easiest thing for me to do. If there isn't an undeviating path, then everything is up in the air all the time. Everything is just "shit luck," as a friend of mine always says. I just don't get the relativists. I don't do well when I float about untethered to anything solid. I need to come back to earth, especially during those times when I am uncertain about everything. I can only do the "good" if I know what the "good" is, right?

There's got to be some commitment to justice and equality in the world I live in, or else we'll all be self-serving monsters to one another. If I don't expect you to treat me fairly, and vice versa, then how can we ever trust one another? One crucial learning I took away from our course this term is that "moral karma" is my basic ideal. Whatever I do to you will come back to me eventually. If I treat you fairly, then sooner or later I will be treated fairly. And if I exploit you, then sooner or later I will be exploited. One tangible result from learning about myself as a moral meaning-maker this semester has been for me to become an active member of my off-campus Peace and Justice Center. In fact, I was just elected an official member of the Board of Governors.

I loved reading Jeremy Stangroom's book, *Would You Eat Your Cat?* (2010), this semester. We had such great conversations during this unit of ethical decision-making. Just about every single one of the "key ethical conundrums" in the book spoke to me in some way. I became acutely aware that, no matter how sure I might have felt about doing what's right in my life before taking this course, I could have gone in so many different ethical directions in these case studies. Would I eat my cat if I were starving? Maybe yes, maybe no. Would I have assassinated Hitler if I had the chance? Maybe yes, maybe no. Is it ever right to have sex when I am drunk? Maybe yes, maybe no. Is suicide always wrong? Maybe yes, maybe no. Is torture sometimes justified? Maybe yes, maybe no. Am I personally responsible for the environmental degradation all around me? Maybe yes, maybe no. In case you're wondering, it's the "maybe" in each of these dramatic choices that pose the greatest challenge for me. I realize that I am a situationalist as a moral meaning-maker. My moral motto seems to be— "It all depends on the situation." Does this mean that I am just one of those "subjective relativists" that the author of our book criticizes? Or am I actually a "sensible realist"? Maybe yes, maybe no, to each position. I've got to think about all of this stuff more. Thank you for getting me started.

My favorite reading in the course was the Dalai Lama's *Beyond Religion: Ethics for a Whole World* (2011). After our intense, very personal discussions in class,

I became aware that my reason for being is based on my compassion both for myself and for others. As the Dalai Lama says, "it is only through a compassionate concern for other human beings that all our ethical values and moral principles arise, especially justice." I also learned from the Dalai Lama, but more importantly from my classmates, that harboring "afflictive emotions" such as anger, resentment, jealously, meanness, possessiveness, and hatred will only destroy me in the end. Thanks to this course, I intend to become a lifelong meaning-maker who will try to cultivate what the Dalai Lama calls "key inner values." These include patience, forbearance, forgiveness, non-attachment, generosity, self-discipline, contentment and joy, and justice. These "key inner values" will keep me on the meaning-making track for the rest of my life. Thank you so much for this transformative insight.

What our students are saying in the above writing excerpts demonstrates for us a truth that emerges from every course we teach on moral meaning-making. Whoever they are, and wherever they come from, all students know at some level that they ignore at their own peril those moral beliefs that sit below the surface feeling like dead weights. Their moral ideals, even if hidden or denied, are really living things. And these living things can give their everyday lives purpose, meaning, and direction—not to mention a little peace of mind. Our students understand that without knowing what it is they believe deep down about right and wrong, good and bad, love and hate, wisdom and ignorance, compassion and indifference, etc., they will be doomed to live their futures bereft of serious convictions about anything truly worthwhile (see Nash, 1997).

STRATEGIC TIPS FOR GENERATING SUCCESSFUL CONVERSATIONS ABOUT MORAL MEANING-MAKING

What follows are a series of well-intentioned tips for teaching about moral meaning-making. For us, whether we are teaching, offering workshops, advising, consulting, or training, the conversational quality of the relationships that we build with our particular audiences is pivotal for our success . . . or failure. Moral meaning-making is more about process than product. Ultimately, it is up to each and every individual and group on a college campus to create what postmodern theorists call an "undominated conversation" about faith, work, civic life, and ethics and morality. The challenge for us as teachers and administrators is to encourage all of our constituencies to articulate their most cherished moral beliefs to the rest of us in languages and stories that speak effectively to those of us who might come from contrasting philosophical, political, and religious places.

There may or may not be a common moral language to achieve this objective, but we believe it is still worth trying to find one. We have found that we can sometimes get students and colleagues to open their minds and hearts to each other whenever we try to exemplify the following virtues in our interactions with others: capaciousness, resiliency, narrative ingenuity, empathy, rapport, non-manipulation, self-critique, negotiation, openness to otherness, patience, and an inexhaustible sense of irony and humor. Here are our tips (for further information on teaching about ethics and morality, see Nash, 2002):

1. To quote Edward Tivnan (1996): "We are all bundles of opinions and beliefs, of theories and prejudices about how we and our world are or ought to be." This is to say that what we all have in common as we go about the project of teaching for and about moral meaning is the fact that our views are at one and the same time true and false, whole and partial, strong and weak, each in their own ways. Thus, we need to listen to others as we would be listened to; we need to question and challenge others as we would be questioned and challenged; we need to pontificate to others only under the condition that we want others to pontificate to us.

2. Mark R. Schwehn (2005) proposes that four virtues—humility, faith, self-denial, and charity—are necessary for respecting, rather than changing, the meanings of others. *Humility* presumes that we attribute at least a modicum of wisdom and insight to others. *Faith* means trusting that what we hear from others is worthwhile in some way. *Self-denial* suggests that, at some point, we need to consider the possibility of abandoning at least a few of the meanings we cherish in the name of intellectual integrity and moral honesty. *Charity* is all about attributing the best motive, and being willing to respond to serious differences of moral opinion with generosity.

3. We must always work a little harder to detect even a tiny bit of truth in what at first might sound to us like the biggest bunch of nonsense. What constitutes "truth" and "nonsense" depends, of course, on *our* perspective, just as it does on *theirs*. This is not to suggest that moral truth is an illusion, or that every view of moral truth is equally true or equally false. It is simply to say that defective intellects, moral characters, or religious convictions often have little or nothing to do with why people actually reject, or accept, one or another version of moral truth. Usually rejection or acceptance have more to do with personal interpretation, socialization, and unique perspective than with a willful recalcitrance, ignorance, or sinfulness on the part of the gainsayer.

4. Nobody, and this includes students, faculty, and administrators, ever makes moral judgments outside of particular narratives of meaning. Thus, the implication is that all moral narratives, no matter how desirable, are infinitely contestable, because they are infinitely interpretable, as is every single story that has ever existed from the beginning of human time. Stanley Fish (1982), the literary theorist, has said that narrative interpetation and perspective "go all the way down." Thus, one person's zero-level, non-

negotiable moral premises are what another person might very well think of as begging all the really fundamental moral questions. Whose moral "down" down there is truly determinate?—Fish is asking. Thus, the challenge for moral-meaning educators is not to surrender to the lure of skepticism or cynicism. Rather, it is to approach *all* narratives about moral meaning with curiosity, modesty, caution, critical judgment, and, when appropriate, with a sense of humor. It is to encourage all the moral narrators in the campus conversation to tell their stories with conviction. Moreover, it requires that all the rest of us listen, ask questions, challenge these stories when necessary, and, most important, learn from them whenever they are resonant for our own situations.

A Personal Reflection from a Practitioner on Becoming a Moral Person

Lara Scott, Center for Student Ethics and Standards
Assistant Director of Academic Integrity and Conflict
Resolution Programs, The University of Vermont

"This Isn't Who I Am: Reflections on Moral Character in the World of Academic Integrity"

It is such a privilege to work with young people during critical transition periods filled with difficult questions and a lot of emotion. In the best of times, it's an honor to be witness to self-reflection, new awareness, accountability, and perspective building. In the worst of times, it is painful, and sometimes disappointing, to observe an inability or unwillingness to recognize self-responsibility and impact. In my work as Coordinator of Academic Integrity, these critical transition points are the moments that follow an alleged violation of university policy. It is in these moments that I find there is great potential for moral and ethical development.

Students show up in my office in any number of ways: apologetic, defensive, ashamed, angry, disappointed, sad, fearful, inquisitive, etc. While students may show up differently, the common thread is the opportunity to reflect on their own morals and ethics. I believe inherent in Academic Integrity are opportunities to consider beliefs, values, morals, and ethics. I also believe it is essential for educators to focus on learning and development of the whole student. So, I choose to provide space and time for students to think about their own ethics and morals as they relate to their academic integrity conduct situations.

I work to offer students opportunities to be reflective and to make meaning from conduct situations. I do this by listening intently with respect and compassion; asking reflective and challenging questions; and being honest, direct, and clear about impact

49

and expectations. As in all relationships, both parties make contributions to their interactions. My contribution and responsibility is to offer opportunities for learning, their contribution is to decide to engage with those opportunities, or not.

Listening Intently

The way I view listening altered drastically four years ago when I read evaluations from a class I teach. That semester, multiple students wrote, "What I was thinking and what I had to say mattered." Reading this instantly shifted how I think about student voice, the importance of making space for it, and letting students know they've been heard. Thinking specifically about my role as an administrator, I've also become more mindful of the positional power I hold and how it can impact students. Being cognizant of this power dynamic, I listen intently to show students their voice and their experiences are valued.

In challenging conversations, of which Academic Integrity conduct conversations often are, genuinely listening can alter an interaction tremendously. My experience is that once students feel heard and understood, they are much more willing to answer questions, able to see the perspective of the referring instructor, and open to hearing messages about University expectations and policy. The dialogue quickly shifts from one about accusations and facts to one about what's going on for the student, what led to the conduct situation, and what they've learned. What this tells me is that students are willing to engage because they've been heard, and they believe someone, an administrator, cares about what they have to say; they matter.

In individual meetings, I can tell when students feel heard because they begin to open up. It is at this point when I often hear something like, "This is not who I am, Lara." This is always an interesting moment because this, seemingly little, comment opens the door to a discussion about ethical development. My experience has been that most college students I interact with care a lot about their moral character. They allude to it by making statements like the one above, and they show genuine disappointment in themselves when they feel they've acted out of character. Robert and Jennifer talk about Moral Compass as "knowing what gives our lives moral meaning and then acting accordingly." When students meet with me it becomes clear that what they espouse and the actions they chose are out of alignment. In these moments of dissonance, through conversation and willingness to respond to difficult ethical questions, many of my students start working to realign what they know to be true about themselves *or* to redefine what has become a new truth.

Many students I meet with are trying to determine if the values they were taught are ones they want to choose to personify, believe, and live by moving forward. For some, an academic integrity hearing forces them to think about their ethical selves when otherwise they may not choose to. My focus on listening to truly hear, and responding with compassion and respect, I believe, encourages students to engage in this ethical conversation openly.

Asking Reflective and Challenging Questions

What have you learned from this situation? Why is trust one of your top three values? Who, besides you, does this case impact? Do you think your choices in this situation reflect how you know yourself, your character?

These questions are some of the most common questions I ask students in individual conduct meetings and class-based workshops I facilitate. In part, I ask questions because I am an inquisitive learner. More importantly, questioning is a central piece of my philosophy where I believe learning can be more meaningful when students arrive at it with support and guidance, but without being told "the answer." As such, I spend much of my time in conduct conversations asking questions and challenging students to develop at least initial thoughts and responses with me.

In our workshops, specifically, students tell me they never thought about how they define morals and ethics before, and that the most impactful activities were the values sort and the ethical dilemmas. They tell me they find it helpful to hear others' perspectives and they enjoy figuring out what they'd do in ethical dilemmas and why. They also respond to *why*, *what if*, and *how does this connect* questions infused throughout to help students clarify their individual values and consider whether previously taught/held beliefs continue to fit their current lives. Students' engagement with this tells me that they are, as Robert has called it, "evolving ethical/moral progressors, not born transgressors." When offered genuine opportunities to reflect on their decisions, consider what they value, and determine how they want to be seen, students are very often willing and able to take on the role of ethical progressor.

Being Direct, Clear, and Honest about Impact and Expectations

Infused with genuinely hearing what students have to say and using questions as a mode to explore big ideas and assist in ethical development, there is also the cut-and-dry judicial-affairs policy of which students need to be informed. At its basic level, my work is about expectations and appropriately holding students accountable. There are many philosophies about how best to do this, and regardless of the chosen methods, I have a responsibility to be clear about the university's expectations. I have found that being direct, clear, and honest when it comes to talking about policy and expectations is effective and important for students. I have also found that including impact in conduct conversations integrates values and, consequently, ethics into the discussion.

About two years ago, I scheduled a meeting with a student to talk about a sanction. The student used derogatory language in a written reflection to me, which resulted in an incomplete sanction. More importantly, there was a large, negative, impact on those who read his words. As I often do, I chose to ask open-ended, non-judgmental questions so I could better understand this student's choice of language. I also chose to be direct, clear, and honest about the impact his choice of words had on me, personally and professionally.

51

It quickly became clear that my willingness to be honest about the impact on me, and direct about what my concerns were, pulled him in. Immediately, this student responded to me looking to better understand my perspective. He was not defensive; he did not shut down. Rather, he asked questions and worked to clarify his intent. Our conversation rapidly shifted to ethics and morals. We talked in depth about values held by different cultures, what he believes is right, how he wants to be seen by his peers, and what the university expects of students. As he left, he shook my hand and thanked me for taking time to talk with him about my concerns. In the end, I didn't necessarily agree with all he said. But what I realized was that in my work, being honest and direct about impact and expectations is yet another way to open the door to students beginning to reflect on, and develop, their ethical and moral selves.

Conclusion

In my work with college students, I've come to realize that Academic Integrity policy work is a wonderful venue in which to engage students about moral character. There is great opportunity in the conversations I have, and the sanctions I assign, to ask students to reflect on their moral philosophy of life. I have found over time that students are more willing and able to engage in this thinking when I use compassion and respect to listen and respond, ask questions that challenge students to think deeply, and provide honest and direct feedback.

The interactions I have with students going through the academic integrity conduct process are often interesting and powerful. However, because I typically meet with a student only once, I'm also reminded that I don't always know if there will be an impact from the relationships I develop and conversations I have, or, how or when it will occur. What I do know is that when I offer students an opportunity to think about who they are and how they want to be in this world, they typically take that opportunity.

As a result of multiple follow-up e-mails and many "thank yous" in evaluations, I am reminded that I do make a memorable impact. And, sometimes that result is more than I intended at the time. This realization is one example of what keeps me engaging with students in the ways that I do. A colleague once told me that social justice education is so powerful for her because once she learns something new she can't *un*learn it. I take this to mean that once we learn something new we are always, at minimum, aware. I find this to be true for personal ethics as well. Once students reflect and have awareness about their own moral being, they remain aware, and that awareness continues to show itself as future situations and decision-making points arise. Developing one's ethical/moral being is important and on-going work. It's an honor to be part of the journey, even if I never know the end result.

STRIVING TO BECOME A MORAL PERSON: A SUMMARY
OF SALIENT RECOMMENDATIONS FROM LARA SCOTT

Lara's professional reflection confirms the importance of helping students who have been accused of academic dishonesty to create a "moral compass." They need to know what, and how, it is to "act in character." Lara's questions to those students who come before her for judicial review are meant to help them determine what they value by way of moral principles and whether their actions are consistent with these values. They often need a "refresher course" on their development as moral meaning-makers, and Lara's conversations with them serve exactly this purpose. She has been highly successful in helping students to line up their own sense of personal integrity with the principles of academic integrity that are her job to profess and protect. Here are some generalizable strategies that Lara uses in order to help students locate themselves morally and ethically:

1. She listens intently to students' personal, moral meaning-making stories in order to be able to draw out implications for the standards of academic integrity that they may have violated.
2. She asks challenging questions meant to evoke moral responses. She sometimes poses ethical dilemmas to students in order to encourage them to think deeply and broadly about ethics and morality.
3. She is always clear and honest with students vis a vis official judicial affairs policies. While she does not compromise these policies, Lara is always open to questions and concerns that some students might have about academic integrity policies and procedures.
4. She keeps front and center at all times the key *raison d'être* of her work as a judicial affairs professional—to help her students develop a keen, consistent awareness of who they are as ethical/moral beings and to exemplify in action what they profess to believe morally.

Chapter 5

Can I Be Both Religious and Spiritual at the Same Time?

My [therapeutic] approach assumes that life has arisen from random events; that we are finite creatures; and that, however much we desire it, we can count on nothing besides ourselves to protect us, to evaluate our behavior, to offer a meaningful life schema. We have no predestined fate, and each of us must decide how to live as fully, happily, and meaningfully as possible.

Irvin D. Yalom

Faith is first among the cardinal virtues because everything proceeds from it including and especially love. Faith is the leap into the unknown—the entering into an action or a person knowing only that you will emerge changed, with no preconceptions of what that change will be. Its antonym is fear.

Fenton Johnson

Something breaks suddenly into our lives and upsets their normal pattern, and we have to begin to adjust ourselves to a new kind of existence. The experience may come through nature or poetry, or through art and music; or it may come through the adventure of flying or mountaineering, or of war; or it may come simply through falling in love, or through some apparent accident, an illness, the death of a friend, a sudden loss of fortune. Anything which breaks through the routine of daily life may be the bearer of this message to the soul.

Bede Griffiths

I am religious, because the ultimate questions human beings ask—What is the meaning of existence? Why are there pain and death? Why, in the end, is life worth living? What does reality consist of and what is its object?—are the definitive essence of my humanity.

Huston Smith

I believe because it fills my life with depth, and mystery, and beauty
. . . I believe in God because it makes my life more interesting, less
rational, and, finally, more worthwhile. I believe in God because my
heart—not my head—tells me it is true.

Kent Gilges

Because of an unprecedented student demand in his professional school, Robert created a religion, spirituality, and education elective four decades ago. It was the first such course ever offered outside of an arts and sciences college in the United States (Nash, 2015). There was no precedent for it anywhere, even in sectarian religious colleges and universities. The study of religion in this country has long been relegated to the liberal arts and humanities and to divinity schools. The main reason for offering such a course in a College of Education and Social Services was that undergraduate and graduate students were asking more and more about the function of religion and spirituality in their lives, as well as in the lives of their future clients, students, and social service constituencies. They were asking what we call the "deep metaphysical questions." And these were the questions that nagged away at them, despite all their efforts to avoid, or deny, their relevance.

QUARTERLIFE METAPHYSICAL MUSINGS

For us, the word "metaphysical" means more than simply its root etymology—"going outside the physical world." Rather, the metaphysical quest of our quarterlife students is similar to something Gregory of Nyssa, the fourth-century theologian, called *epektasis* (Gr.)—a "straining toward deep meaning." For us, this is a straining toward a luminous darkness, toward an unsatiated desire for something more, something of inexpressible depth, something not "once and for all" but "once and for always a mystery." Or in the words of Bede Griffiths in the epigraph above, metaphysical suggests "anything which breaks through the routine of daily life [and could be] the bearer of a message to the soul."

All the epigraphs at the beginning of this chapter signal the types of questions and concerns that began to come up for our quarterlife students four-plus decades ago in Robert's courses, and continue to do so right up to the present. In fact, whatever the generation of students, and whatever the stage of development, the questions are unrelenting and unchanging. They emerge for all of us as much for personal—as well as for practical—reasons. The questions continue to surface at various times throughout our lives—during times of stress and relaxation, sorrow and joy, and agony and ecstasy. Sometimes they seem to appear out of nowhere. These deeper questions are unavoidable. They represent the metaphysical component of our existence . . . without which we would have only the physical-scientific explanation as the ultimate rationale for each and every event in our lives.

And while the physical rationale might satisfy some, and we fully acknowledge that it has served its empirical/scientific purposes well, still it doesn't satisfy all, nor should it.

In the spirit of Irvin Yalom, the existential psychiatrist, in the epigraph at the opening of this chapter, many students wonder about the extent of their finitude. Is there anything beyond their everyday existence that they can look to for answers during those times that confound all of us, that rock our lives with tragedy, that will help us to live our lives with meaning, even though life could very well be meaningless? Is the meaning of life all up to us and no force outside of us? If so, if everything is random, where do we go to put together the chance-fragments of our lives?

Not all of our students are willing to buy into Yalom's take on existential meaning. Here is a typical response:

> If I don't believe that everything, or at least something, happens for a reason, then what's the sense of living? There is so much shit in my life, that without at least a glimmer of hope that there is something larger and more enduring, then my life seems pretty pointless. If everything is just shit luck—sometimes good, sometimes bad, but most of the time just aimless—then I am not only hopeless; I am powerless as well. Nope, I need something more. I'm closer to Fenton Johnson's take on life than Yalom's.

However, our students are sometimes skeptical when they read Fenton Johnson. Is he right when he says that each and every one of us must make the "leap into the unknown" at some point in our lives? Is this what faith is all about—trusting that there might be answers to the most unanswerable questions, if only we are willing to take the risk to venture into the unknown? Is faith truly the "cardinal virtue" without which there can be no love? And is the opposite of faith really "fear," or is it actually a rational skepticism?

Here is a typical response we sometimes get from our more cynical students regarding Fenton's "leap into the unknown":

> It seems to me that a leap of faith can be a leap of cowardice. I'm a realist. I know that I'm the one who needs to get a job, make money, plan for my future, raise a family, and be successful. This is what my college education is all about, and why I'm willing to run up huge loans to finance it. Leaping into faith, while it sounds nice, can also be a leap away from responsibility and from everything else that only I am responsible for, including my close friendships and intimate relationships. My job in life is to make the "unknown" something that will soon be "known." Isn't this what planning for the future is all about? How, please tell me, is this an act of cowardice?

57

And, yet, whenever we read the works of Huston Smith and Kent Gilges in class, many quarterlife students connect immediately with their insights. Their responses are similar to this one:

> My life is so damned screwed up sometimes that I just have to stop and ask Smith's question—"why in the end is my life worth living?" Why is any life worth living? Life is so fragile, so unpredictable, so demanding, that I need to know who, what, and why I am. I'd love to be religious, like Smith, and maybe someday I will be. He doesn't seem weird to me at all, like he does to some of my friends.

Another type of response that we get from some students to the deep metaphysical questions is more in the spirit of Gilges:

> I want desperately to believe in a God—not necessarily in the God of my parents or church pastor—but in a God of "depth, mystery, and beauty." I'm a business major, and everything has answers; everything can be reduced to profit margins; everything is a matter of costs and benefits; everything can be measured and calculated. I'm tired of this kind of "head-truth" because it enslaves me; it leads to wealth addiction. I want to find spiritual peace in the God of my heart, not in the material satisfactions generated by my head. Does this make me an irrational escapist? Does this heart-need of mine preclude success in the everyday world? My girlfriend calls me a "Godophile," and then she smirks. Why?

ASKING THE CORE RELIGIO-SPIRITUAL MEANING-MAKING QUESTIONS

Whether Christian, Muslim, Jewish, Buddhist, or Hindu in religious belief, or whether theist, agnostic, atheist, or "apatheist" (Robert's neologism—"who cares?") in non-belief, students come to our course each semester with all shapes and sizes of spirituality. While it might be fashionable for quarterlifers to declare that they are "agnostic" or "atheistic" when it comes to "religion," but "open-minded" when it comes to "spirituality," deep down every single one of our students has thought, at times, about the core, spiritual meaning-making questions.

For example, Robert had a two-hour conversation recently with two 20-year-old students after the first class of the semester. They had asked to speak with him privately. One of them led off the conversation with this comment:

> Robert, you ask questions about metaphysics that students our age just don't ask because they don't mean anything to us. Most of our generation never attends a church, synagogue, or temple. Most of us deal with our personal issues

by talking with close friends either in person or on Facebook. What counts the most to us during times of personal "storm and stress"—to use your phrase—is to deal with our setbacks quickly, in our own way, and then get on with it. A song lyric that really speaks to our generation says it all—"When I grow up, when I grow up, when I grow up, I won't have to think so much . . . I'm so glad I'm living in the USA with my BMW and my MBA."

What started off with a student's skeptical comment calculated to educate a late-life professor on the realities of the current, quarterlife generation eventually turned into a probing, back-and-forth conversation about the deeper meanings of life. As we do in our classes, Robert asked these two students the following types of questions in a non-judgmental, very personal way. And he shared some of his own responses to them vulnerably, openly, and honestly. We have found in our teaching that particular types of probing, spiritual questions transcend all age, gender, racial, ethnic, and socioeconomic groups. Whatever the questioners' particular identity differences, what remains universal is the salient spiritual need that students have to ponder the imponderable. They need time in and out of the classroom to wonder, to speculate, to ask the truly difficult questions, the questions that end up exasperating most of us, because they threaten our deep-down, secure and certain places. Examples of these types of spiritual questions are:

- In the larger scheme of things, if there is one, why does what I do really matter?
- Why do I experience those sudden, uninvited moments when I regret the vanishing of a past I have barely lived and can only faintly recall; a present that continues to slip away from me until it, too, becomes a rueful reminder of possibilities forever lost; and a future that looms as being more ominous than hopeful?
- Is there something more to life, to *my* life, that gives it purpose and rationale? Since the beginning of human time, approximately 100 billion people have been born, lived, and died. To what end, if any? Is the ultimate purpose of my existence to make at most an 80- or 90-year appearance on a tiny speck in the cosmos and then to pass on and out of an existence that is essentially ephemeral and always indifferent?
- Why is it so difficult for me to believe in the existence of something greater than the here-and-now, yet, despite the difficulty, why do I continue to long for, and to seek, a larger meaning, an illumination, that I can hold onto throughout all the vagaries of my life?
- Why do I cling to the elusive hope that transcendence is real, that inner wisdom is ultimately attainable, that it is possible to live a life with genuine dignity and integrity, that somewhere, somehow, I can find a sustaining meaning in it all?

59

Some of our students, like the two who sat with Robert for a couple of hours, answer these questions in a variety of ways. Some respond by constructing narratives of spiritual meaning that are quite private and personal. Others are much more public about their spirituality, sometimes locating themselves within the frameworks of conventional religious traditions. Some students are grounded in doctrinal certainty; others are nagged by incessant doubt. The spirituality of our students manifests itself in many forms. We have found in working with our quarterlife students, however, that most of them need some sense of organic unity with others and with nature; and at least an occasional glimpse into what is real and enduring at the core of it all; and an opportunity to discern the peace and harmony that exists beneath and beyond the world's strife and imbalance; and a starting point for explaining those aspects of life that seem either enigmatic or ultimately unknowable.

In our teaching, we frequently generate class conversations by asking the following types of religio-spiritual questions:

1. Do you make a distinction between religion and spirituality? If yes, what is the difference for you? What is your own religious background? Do you still practice?
2. What larger belief about the meaning of your life gets you up in the morning and off to work, and off to face your responsibilities, day after day, especially when you don't want to? What gives you the personal strength to carry on?
3. Is there a master plan to your life? Or is it all about blind chance?
4. Why is suffering so pervasive in the world? Why tsunamis? Why New Orleans flooding? Why political, religious, and nationalistic wars? Why earthquakes?
5. Why do some people call themselves "spiritual" rather than "religious"?
6. Do you think your actions make any real difference to anyone or anything in the larger scheme of things? If yes, why? If no, why not?
7. When's the last time you had a conversation about religion or spirituality with a family member, a friend, a teacher, a counselor (choose one)? How would you describe the conversation? If you haven't, why do you suppose you haven't?
8. What would you say to this bestselling author, Christopher Hitchens, who made these comments: "Religion poisons everything." "God is not great." "Religion kills."
9. How long do you think you would be able to talk intelligently about the particulars of their faiths with students who might represent such backgrounds as Islam, Christianity, Buddhism, Hinduism, atheism, Judaism, Confucianism, or Taoism? Which one of these would you like to know more about?

10. Have you ever had any courses in high school that covered some of the world's religions? Why or why not did this happen, do you suppose?
11. How would you describe the general religious or spiritual leanings of the people in your nuclear and/or extended family?
12. Would you be comfortable talking about religion and/or spirituality with someone you just met? Why or why not?
13. What do you think of the research in positive psychology that says the happiest people in the world are the most religious . . . by far?
14. What is it that turns you off the most about organized religion? What turns you on the most?
15. Can we be good, moral people without religion?

We can say, without exception, that the thousands of students who have passed in and out of the elective course each semester on religion and spirituality that Robert developed decades ago always manage to find at least a few questions in the above list that capture their attention and focus the discussion . . . often for hours at a time. The question that forms the title of this chapter—"Can I be both religious and spiritual at the same time . . . or how about neither?"—is the one that never fails to ignite, and to inspire, a quarterlife discussion about the meaning of what we call "metaphysical meaning."

A RATIONALE FOR CREATING A SPIRITUALITY OF TEACHING AND LEARNING

In the last few years, we have been trying to create a pedagogy we call a *spirituality of teaching and learning*. In all the classroom work that we do, we are motivated by Tennyson's aphorism—"there is more faith in honest doubt than in half the creeds of the world"; by the unwavering conviction that a genuine spiritual faith must somehow find a way to wrestle with the demons of honest doubt. The objective is not to overcome the doubt, because this is neither possible nor desirable, but to fully incorporate it into any final declaration of spiritual belief and call to action. For us, honest doubt is a spiritual student's intuitive sense that no ecclesiastical leader, or dogma, or doctrine, or sacred book, or teaching, or ritual can ever capture the fullness of life's ultimate mysteries. It is the humble understanding that, when everything is said and done, one's frail and wavering spiritual faith is all that is left to fill the interval between saying too much and saying too little about what is essentially incommunicable.

Spirituality, as we conceive, and approach, the topic in our teaching and writing, is not necessarily God-bestowed, an incarnation, or even coming to a vivid awareness of some supernatural presence. Nevertheless, we are fully aware, and respectful of, all of these phenomena, because for many of our students, they inhabit a central place in their spirituality, and well they should. Neither does post-millennial sprituality seem to have much in common with New Age occultism. Instead, for us, a spirituality of teaching and learning simply calls for the student, and the teacher, to undertake, in trust, an inward journey together whose ultimate destination is to fashion a deeper, personal response to the mystery of existence.

A spirituality of teaching and learning, regardless of the subject matter, puts the central emphasis on the student's (and the teacher's) continuing quest for a richly textured interior life. It recognizes the pivotal communal nature of this activity whenever it is undertaken in an educational setting. It encourages, at all times, the development of a richer, more complete spirituality on the part of individuals, one that reaches for a meaning far beyond the mere academic mastery of a number of scholarly disciplines and the cultivation of a number of professional skill-sets.

A spirituality of teaching and learning, among other things, attempts to elicit candid, first-person accounts of the larger meaning of students' lived experience, whenever these meanings are appropriate to the subject matter at hand. And it attempts always to exemplify such qualities as truthfulness, courage, and integrity. We consider these to be the cardinal spiritual virtues not only of teaching and learning, but of living a virtuous life as well. We predicate our call to create a spirituality of teaching and learning on the well-tested assumption that, given an ethos of mutual support and caring in the classroom, our students will not hesitate to talk with one another about how their deepest beliefs, ideals, hopes, fears, doubts, and, yes, spirituality (or lack of it), influence their daily lives.

Our students are eager to do this, we believe, because they live during a time when it seems that more and more people are talking about topics that seem less and less important. So much talk in America today is wasted in vapid chitchat (e.g., e-mail and online chat rooms, Facebook, texting, and tweeting), in angry name-calling (radio and television talk shows), in academic one-upsmanship and intellectual nitpicking (many college seminars), in so-called "reality" television, and in an endless cycle of media-generated, self-serving political "spin." Sadly, the kind of spiritual talk we are encouraging in the college classroom, as well as in other campus venues, rarely occurs anywhere else in America—not in the family, not on the therapist's couch or even in the priest's confessional; and certainly not in the professor's, or student affairs professional's, office, or in the dean's, provost's or college president's suites.

In our own classroom teaching, spiritual talk will sometimes take our students on a trip through the great monotheistic religions of the world. At other times, it will take an Eastern direction. And often it will settle for non-theistic forms of spiritual commitment as found in nature, loving relationships, philosophy, literature, art, and music. We are convinced that absent the opportunity to travel this inward journey—without the challenge of creating a personal spirituality of meaning—the outward life of the student, sooner or later, threatens to become desiccated and burned out.

We believe strongly that the deepest places where one's spirituality comes from is rooted in love, compassion, service to others, forgiveness, understanding, social activism, patience, making deeper, emotional contact with one another, and learning how to live peacefully and harmoniously in pluralistic communities of difference. If we are willing to focus on the relevance of our students' spiritual quests in discussions both inside and outside the classroom, then perhaps we can begin to open a deep-learning dialogue with them before it is too late. On a college campus, there are so many faith-based, or faith-absent, identities, whether openly disclosed or not, that characterize members of all groups on a campus. We believe that it is in the best interest of our universities and colleges to make room, not only for the more conventional, and approved, multicultural conversations among a diverse student body, but also for the open expression of spiritual and religious beliefs. This, for us, is a genuine, multi-identitied approach to discussions of social justice, pluralism, and diversity.

As faculty and staff, we have a golden opportunity to nurture students further in their life journey to find internal and external happiness. Many studies undertaken by positive psychologists reflect the increase in suicide, drug and alcohol abuse, as well as a myriad of other self-harming behaviors and disorders, on college campuses (see, for example, Layard, 2005; Lyubomirsky, 2007). These studies show that short-term pharmaceutical and talk therapy solutions do little to reduce the high rate of unhappiness omnipresent on all college campuses, whether secular or sectarian. What does work, according to this research, are strong, core beliefs in something larger than the self.

STRATEGIC TIPS FOR TEACHING AND LEARNING ABOUT SPIRITUALITY ON COLLEGE CAMPUSES

What we offer here in our closing section are some tools that we have employed in our pedagogy in order to create, and foster, a spirituality of teaching and learning in our classrooms and in other college venues. We will address our readers directly by presenting a series of general recommendations that we hope all faculty and staff will consider:

1. Take a pedagogical risk, and undertake a closer, sub-textual examination of the subject matter you are teaching. What exactly are your goals for selecting and teaching the subject matter, and what message are you trying to send to your students that may not be implicit in the subject matter itself? How can you reconfigure your subject matter to get beyond the mere presentation and testing of information, and the cultivation of specific career skill-sets? How can you re-present your subject matter so that students can deepen, enlarge, and expand their multi-layered search for truth?

63

2. If you can, form a circle of conversation with yourself and your students. Talk *with* your students, not *at* them, as often as possible. Everyone in the spirituality learning circle needs to be equally seen and heard. As a teacher, you cannot arbitrarily separate yourself from your conversation circle's process and content. In fact, at times you must be at the forefront of self-disclosure in order to gain your students' trust. You need to learn how to *disclose* rather than *impose* and *depose*. You must be open to mistakes and misunderstandings, both for yourself and for your students. There are no definitive, right or wrong answers in the process of teaching and learning about spirituality. There are only questions. No conversation ever ends; it only stops for a while, to be continued at another time. No religio-spiritual narrative is ever finally and fully formed; instead, it keeps on developing throughout a person's lifetime.

3. Begin to create a safe space for your students to ask the deeper questions and to make the soulful connections between the subject matter, career preparation, and their personal pursuit of meaning and purpose. Allow for facilitated moral conversation (Nash et al., 2008) by building trust—by assuring the confidentiality of names and stories in students' spiritual disclosures that may be directly linked to someone known, and by fostering genuine honesty and respect for varied opinions. A pedagogy of spirituality cannot take the form of a debate. You need to be an advocate (*advocare, L.* someone who *calls to* others not someone who *calls out* others) for each and every student regardless of their religio-spiritual orthodoxies or unorthodoxies.

4. You will need to *exemplify* a pedagogy of openness and flexibility in your practice all the while you are attempting to *explicate* your subject matter. Draw out your students' belief stories in reference to spirituality. Find out what gives their lives meaning. Be generous in your willingness to help them see the connections between the subject matter you are teaching and their pursuit of spiritual meaning. If you begin to get stuck, evoke ideas and suggestions from students regarding what more they would like to happen in classroom conversations, and how and why studying this subject might bring more meaning into their lives. If given the opportunity, students can be incredibly insightful about what they need from their teachers.

For example, if a student is studying, or majoring in, business, education, psychology, astronomy, or chemistry, ask what draws them into these courses of study? Do they have a personal story—such as having lived through a relative's risky venture into creating a small business, or tutored children in a local school or day-care center, or witnessed first-hand a death or serious illness in the family, or dealt with a mental disability in the life of someone they love, or marveled at observing a shooting star as a child, or been captivated by the way the body works. Too often we give our students important technical subject matter and vocabulary, relevant facts and data, and significant statistical knowledge, without asking them to think more deeply about how the information in a particular course will touch their lives long after they have finished taking the tests, earning their diplomas, and entering long-awaited careers and professions.

5. Experiment with helping students to reflect on the deeper meanings, and origins, of the subject matter you are teaching them. This can happen most naturally in the humanities, of course, because so many of these disciplines are grounded in a variety of reflective responses to the perennial enigmas of the human condition. It is more difficult, but not impossible, to do deep meaning-analysis, if you are a scientist, for example, teaching such *natural sciences* as evolutionary biology or cellular biology within the framework of a so-called *objective* scientific method.

As a scientist, give yourself permission to do some pedagogical experimentation. Step outside the objectivist worldview at least occasionally. Encourage students to reflect on the sheer wonder, and pleasure, of knowing the human body—how it works, its homeostatic flow, the creation and recreation of cellular elements from old to new, what the possible genesis, and ultimate goals, of such elements might be, and what philosophical or religio-spiritual connections these might have to the more data-based content of the disciplines that students are studying. In some profound sense, as Einstein himself pointed out, every scientific discipline, no matter how objective and rational, contains confounding mysteries that can be approached only by imagining and creating meta-scientific hypotheses to explain them. For example, get students to formulate their own imaginative, leap-of-faith hypotheses of origins and destinies that might transcend the conventional, methodological mandates and assumptions of each of the scientific disciplines.

In another cognate area—the *social sciences*—encourage students to explore how a wide range of social scientists differ in their understanding of a topic such as human consciousness. Help them to reflect on why there seems to be a universal human need to enlarge consciousness by looking for something larger than the self, in order to explain the unknown. Take time to help them delve deeply into the ontological and metaphysical questions that have remained unanswerable throughout human history. Why, despite our sophisticated social science research methodologies, epistemologies, and our advanced technological prowess, do our metaphysical questions persist? Why do they continue to *haunt*, at times even *taunt*, us? To what extent do our various tribes of social influence condition us to affirm, or deny, the religio-spiritual basis of our existence.

Similar issues can be raised in teaching the *arts* by exploring, not only how artists depict their worlds through multiple mediums and styles, but also by examining what serves as the spark of inspiration in their own narratives of meaning—whether these be religio-spiritual, philosophical, literary, or even political. What are those unprovable, non-empirical background assumptions that inevitably influence their artistic expressions?

The subject matter of the *humanities* comes closest to getting at the deeper existential questions. We believe that one way to save the humanities in our career-driven higher education curricula is to convert humanistic study into a journey of spiritual meaning-making for our students. In the end, there is nothing more practical for helping our students to live a good, happy, and fulfilled life. In fact, we are convinced that all subject matter, no matter how diverse its methodologies, content, and goals, is a potential resource for making spiritual meaning in the teaching-learning venture.

A Personal Reflection from a Practitioner on Being Spiritual, Religious, and Life-Loving

Robert Lair, Professor of Religious Studies
St. Michael's College, Colchester, Vermont

The Need for Real-World Soul-Searching in the College Classroom

Jordan handed me his last paper assignment for my first-year seminar called "The Examined Life" *exactly 67 days before he fatally hanged himself in his dorm room closet.* The morning that I heard the news, I rushed to my office and spread out the five papers that he wrote for me during the semester and read them word by word, with more depth and probing than I've ever read a set of student papers in my life. It was as if time had stopped. My usual distractions had stopped. I didn't hold a pen or pencil. I didn't hear my phone ringing. I didn't notice that it had started to snow or that the winter birds were congregating again outside my window in the holly trees. It occurred to me that I had never read a student paper with as much attention to "humanness."

As I read, I felt like I was strapping lead weights onto my ankles and wading out into the ocean of his words, the weights dragging me deeper and deeper in my search for some kind of clue, something that I should have seen, some kind of hidden meaning, some kind of coded cry for help. But no matter how far I went into the depths, I couldn't find him. He hadn't let me in. His "examination of his life" was objective, arm's length, just another set of papers for "school," which he made clear he had always hated. School, he said, had nothing to do with his real life.

For seventeen years, I have asked my students to share their life stories in my philosophy and religion seminars, insisting that they try to find the interface between themselves and the "academic" work they do for class. The starting point for reading Nietzsche, I tell them, is that late-night experience when they're reading *Zarathustra* and their minds start to run their soft hands over the bumps and bruises of their everyday lives. That is when they fall in love with philosophy, or find that religion can be relevant. I ask my students to write about the deepest parts of themselves. I challenge them to find the places where their lives intersect with the experiences of Viktor Frankl and Blaise Pascal, with Thich Nhat Hanh and Paul Tillich.

I get drug stories when they read Huxley—long rambling essays about LSD trips and the "doors of perception" swinging open. Two of my students were heroin addicts last semester. One of them came up to me at graduation with his mother, father, and two younger brothers, and I've never seen a more beautiful group of people in my life, the picture perfect family from Connecticut. The father took my hand and thanked me, with a slight twitch around his beautiful mouth, for everything that I did for his son. I scrutinized all of their faces. It was immediately clear to me that they knew that Craig had shared with me that he was a heroin addict, and that he told me he was "slipping" from time to time, and that he told me about finding his best friend dead on his living-room couch from an overdose. They were so grateful that Craig had a confidante, but all I really did was ask him to share with me what he really believed. All I really asked him to do was to write about Tolstoy's *The Death of Ivan Ilych* with a little bit of honesty. How could he not write about his friend dying on his living-room couch? He told me that it haunted him, that death haunted him, the prospect of his own death, as well as the prospect of the deaths of his friends around him.

A couple of years ago a student stood up in class and read a paper about running away from home when she was thirteen. I imagined her buying a quart of milk with her own picture on the side of the carton. She talked about eluding the police for three years, about her drug addiction, about her flophouse snowboarding-drug-dealing-den of iniquity, about how it felt to have no identity, to be invisible to the world, about the ecstasy of snowboarding, young and free and completely stoned out of her mind. When you are talking about ecstatic states in a religion class, about happiness, about what the novelist Walker Percy called "Angelism," or the desire to see with the eyes of God, this woman's experience matters! The crushing existential disappointment that came when she woke up in the morning looking for her next fix mattered too. The power of the narrative threads in her life drove her academic hunger, and what came cascading out when she was given the permission to use her life experience in her scholarship was nothing short of astonishing.

A Christian woman from Benin once asked me if she could write her "Credo" (I Believe) paper about anything she wanted. She was thrilled to be given the opportunity to talk about something that she experienced when she was six. She watched a man beat a woman to death in the market, because the woman wouldn't let him steal a T-shirt from her. She told about how the village men caught the thief and killer and decided to kill him in turn: "So then they tied his legs together, and tied his hands together, then they tied him against the pole, and put a car tire around his neck, poured kerosene all over him and lighted him on fire. We all watched him scream for help and let him die."

67

She spoke about how the incident broke her young heart, and she wondered every day why nobody helped the woman who was killed or, for that matter, the thief who tried to steal from her. How could the world stand by and let these people be killed for no reason? She became obsessed by the need for compassion, forgiveness, and justice in the world, and she says the story is the heart of her personal mythology, and the driving force behind her academic aspirations.

I wonder how many times Jordan, my student who committed suicide, was tempted to write about his existential crises, to open up, to let go. I had a woman once write a paper about being up on a chair with a bathrobe tie around her neck ready to kill herself. She wrote about it in her "Credo" because she figured that she got off the chair for a reason; she said "yes" to life for a reason, and she knew that these reasons must be related to the things she held most sacred in her life. Specifically, her boyfriend was looking forward to her watching a Boston Bruins hockey game with him that night. She also didn't want to impose her dead body on her roommates.

Viktor Frankl tells us in *Man's Search For Meaning* that the ones who survived the death camps were the ones who had something to live for; they had some kind of task, or idea, or experience, or person to keep them going. My student never told her boyfriend about the chair and the bathrobe tie. She just snuggled up in the crook of his arm and watched the Bruins game with him, and perhaps for the first time in her life she knew, quite consciously, what she was living for.

The fate of doing philosophy and religion in my twenty-first century classes hinges on my students' capacity to link Kierkegaard and Chogyam Trungpa and Thomas Merton and Lao Tzu to the simple act of telling stories about things they really care about in their lives. The stories don't have to be dramatic or sensational. A woman once pulled her sweater off her shoulder, before she read her paper in class, to show us a tattoo. For 15 minutes, we all stared at her tattoo as she read her paper about Paul Tillich's definition of a symbol, and about Joseph Campbell's *Power of Myth*; and she told us how again and again she thought about this symbol on the back of her shoulder, a rose compass, that she swore saved her life countless times when she was "lost"; how she'd close her eyes and envision the compass there and wait for quiet direction, for wisdom, for patience, and for love.

I am broken-hearted about losing Jordan. I think of him every time I enter a classroom. Real, open, and honest philosophy is about saving our own lives, about identifying the things that get us off of our "existential chairs." We hold back at our own peril. If we stop telling the stories that are most foundational to our lives, we risk ripping out the very heart of the philosophical enterprise itself, and, therefore, we risk non-existence, nonbeing. In a world of skyrocketing suicide rates on college campuses, the need for this type of real-world soul-searching has never been more important. It's really about a simple movement of the human soul, a simple invitation that we need to always be willing to make to each other, in and out of the classroom: you tell me your story, and I'll tell you mine.

UNDERSTANDING THE NEED FOR "REAL-WORLD SOUL-SEARCHING": A SUMMARY OF SALIENT RELIGIO-SPIRITUAL RECOMMENDATIONS FROM ROBERT LAIR

Robert Lair has been a religious studies professor for many years. Robert Nash, one of the co-authors of this book, has been a frequent guest speaker in many of those classes. Professor Lair is truly an educator who teaches what he believes in such a way that he manages to touch the "human souls" of each and every one of his students. This is one of the many reasons why Jordan's suicide was so wrenching for him. He had made a "soulful" connection with Jordan, just as he had with a troubled Craig, and with the young woman who contemplated hanging herself with a "bathrobe tie."

Long after his courses end and students graduate, Professor Lair maintains contact with them. He continues to be a life-supporting, meaning-making mentor, and a source of inspiration, as their religio-spiritual stories continue to evolve throughout their quarterlife, midlife, and later years. As we have discussed throughout this chapter, Professor Lair always encourages his students to build a satisfying metaphysical philosophy of life. He does not preach at them. He does not prescribe or proscribe. He practices patience, kindness, and compassion. He draws them out without censoring or critiquing.

However, he is not afraid to ask the deep, challenging religio-spiritual questions—both inside and outside of class—that we feature earlier in this chapter. He knows that sustaining a rich, evolving relationship with students both during and after they leave his classroom requires that he be authentic; that he needs always to be there with honesty (and clarity) in order to help them make sense of the inevitable joy and tumult that will characterize their lives until both he and they pass. For Professor Lair, teaching is his vocation, and what "calls" to him the loudest is the profound need that all his students have to be heard from the depths of their souls.

Here are some pedagogical tips for getting students to do some "real-world soul searching" that Robert Lair always tries to use to his, and their, best advantage:

1. Encourage students to get beyond the objective, distancing, third-person treatment of course content. Instead, ask them to start with the subjective, connective, first-person meaning of the content for their own lives and for those they love.

2. Remember, every student's religio-spiritual story of seeking meaning matters. No story is to be censored, dismissed, or ridiculed. Inherent in each story exists a larger meaning that could help others. Stories that explain personal "credos," no matter how idiosyncratic, are to be taken seriously. It is in these stories that human beings have a golden, once-in-

69

a-lifetime, college opportunity to author an honest, religio-spiritual meta-narrative to guide their lives.

3. We need to teach in such a way that we encourage, and enable, students to get off their "existential chairs." Facilitating "real-world soul-searching" in the classroom is a pedagogy whose time has come. Disciplines such as philosophy, religious studies, art, history, psychology, political science, etc., take on a new vitality whenever students can be helped to explore their unavoidable "existential crises" through the humanistic insights of these disciplines.

Chapter 6

How Can I Construct Durable, Loving, and Reciprocal Core Relationships?

> Personal relationships are the fertile soil from which all advancement, all success, all achievement in real life grows.
>
> Ben Stein

> One who stays near vermillion gets stained red, and one who stays near ink gets stained black.
>
> Ancient Chinese Proverb

> There is more hunger for love and appreciation in this world than for bread.
>
> Mother Teresa

> We cultivate love when we allow our most vulnerable and powerful selves to be deeply seen and known, and when we honor the spiritual connection that grows from that offering with trust, respect, kindness, and affection. Love is not something we give or get; it is something that we nurture and grow, a connection that can only be cultivated between two people when it exists within each one of them—we can only love others as much as we love ourselves.
>
> Brene Brown

Even if our students are exchanging thoughts, ideas, perspectives, feelings, and values almost exclusively via the social media rather than in person; and even if they think they hold the world in the palms of their hands with a smartphone; and even if they think they are in full control of their social lives and are way beyond needing to be touched personally at the core of their beings by anyone, they are still being ineluctably shaped by these connections. How so? Because, as the Ancient Chinese Proverb in this chapter's opening epigraphs states: "One who stays near vermillion gets stained red, and one who stays near ink gets stained black."

No matter who the persons are in our circle of near or far contacts, and no matter what the means we use to communicate with them, their influence—their "stain"—will leave its indelible mark on every single one of us . . . and ours on them.

The vast majority of quarterlifers in this fast-paced age of globalization are more connected to one another via electronics than ever been before . . . but, ironically, it is these same students who feel the most disconnected. They, like Jennifer, feel as if they live "neither here nor there"; they, too, find themselves existing always in the "in-between." Where exactly is the "home" in the ether of the internet world? This connection-disconnection anomaly contributes to an overwhelming sense of confusion and isolation. We all know relationships are important. Like Ben Stein's quote in the epigraph that opens this chapter, our lives are heavily interdependent and affected by the relationships we have. Our digital network may have gotten wider, but both our core (and peripheral) relationships have not necessarily deepened.

In a recent seminar conversation, one of our students made this revealing comment about the growing number of superficial relationships among quarterlifers:

> Why do you suppose that "hooking up" is so popular nowadays? "Hooking up" means you can get together with someone physically without having to make a deep, heart-to-heart connection with that person. "Hooking up" is a lot like texting—it's quick, easy, momentarily gratifying, with no strings attached afterwards. It's in and out, and see you later. Well, I, for one, am sick of hooking up. I want close people in my life who are more than one-hour hook-ups. I'm looking for honest, long-term connections, not just with a potential lover but also with close friends.

This quarterlifer confirms the truth of Mother Teresa's maxim in our chapter's opening epigraph: "There is more hunger for love and appreciation in this world than for bread." Our student who is suffering from "hook-up fatigue" might also add:

> Although it may not seem so, there is more deep-down hunger for sustained love, loyalty, and appreciation in my quarterlife-world than for the usual quickie relationship that starts with a text and ends with sex. We just don't know how to create such authentic relationships

ASKING THE CORE RELATIONSHIP MEANING-MAKING QUESTIONS

How ironic for us as meaning-making educators that the personal and social-interaction issues, which are so much on students' minds, rarely, if ever, get covered in any systematic educational way throughout their undergraduate (or graduate) years. Faculty and administrators these days too easily relegate examination of real-life questions about real-life problems to the counselor's office, the pastoral life center, and, perhaps, to a handful of highly specialized staff members employed in student services. In contrast, as meaning-making educators, we believe strongly that the types of questions about core relationships we list below can be inserted into any type of academic curriculum without losing the so-called "rigor" of the discipline. What is the use of highly specialized disciplinary knowledge if, in addition to having its own intrinsic, "critical thinking" value, it cannot be applied to the solution of real-world, *personal* issues and problems?

Why can't we take some time in our coursework to examine each and every one of the meaning-questions in this book through the lenses of the disciplines we teach, such as psychology, philosophy, the sciences, education, business, history, medicine, political science, religious studies, etc.? At the very least, a meaning-making approach to all the academic subject matter and scholarly methodologies that we feature in our higher-education curricula could offer a refreshingly new take on a term that has long since become a cliché in the academy—*relevance*. In Robert's half-century of teaching, he is reminded time and time again by his former students when they come back to visit him that what they remember most about their college education is what they were able to take away that enriched and clarified the internal need to make meaning of their lives. It was this type of learning that effectively prepared them to appreciate, and apply, their more technical, specialized learnings to the external world.

Robert and Jennifer are philosophers, and they are convinced that their discipline continues to illuminate each and every meaning-making issue that students confront during their college years. Lou Marinoff, a professor of philosophy at City College of New York, and creator of "philosophical therapy," believes that it is philosophy, more than anything else, including medication, that can help students deal with the emotional turmoil of the "big questions" (2003). For him, "philosophy can change your life." In fact, the title of his international bestseller, now being sold in 75 countries, is *Plato, Not Prozac!* (2000). And Jonathan Haidt (2006), a professor of psychology and philosophy at the University of Virginia, has written an interdisciplinary bestseller—extolled by psychologists, philosophers, biologists, and medical professionals—titled *The Happiness Hypothesis: Finding Modern Truth in Ancient Wisdom.*

For the first time in human history, many quarterlifers will now spend more than a quarter of their lifetimes in school, wait longer to get married, and be considerably older than their parents were when they have children. And a growing percentage of quarterlifers will never marry or have children at all. All of this also means that our students will be spending more time alone and, as a result, longing even more for closeness, intimacy, and companionship. What follows are the kinds of vulnerable relationship questions we frequently hear from

73

quarterlifers after we take time getting to know them on a deeper level and they become more trusting. These types of personal questions come up time and time again in our meaning-making university seminars, national presentations and follow-up small group meetings, and local consultancies both on and off campus:

- Am I actually loveable, and, if I am, what makes me so?
- Am I really capable of sustaining a close, loving relationship with a partner?
- Why is it so hard to live alone but also equally hard to venture out and take the risk of being closely involved with others?
- How do I avoid making bad choices regarding friends and lovers in my life because I am so lonely?
- How do I deal with all the pressure to conform to the self-destructive practices of some of the groups I yearn to be a part of?
- Are my partner and I really meant to be?
- Is it a myth that there is really "The Right One" for each of us?
- Is it wishful thinking from another time in history that a durable, long-term relationship is still possible between and among human beings?
- How do I avoid settling for less than I really deserve in my relationships?
- Why can't I find close, enduring friends who stay the course without drifting away?
- Is genuine reciprocity in a relationship a realistic expectation, or will I always have to make compromises regarding how much to give and to get in my closest affiliations?
- Why is it that I live in an annoying paradox—wanting at times to separate myself totally from my family of origin so I can be my own person or seeking desperately to cling to them because I need unconditional, secure relationships in my life?
- Why do I sometimes make such bad choices when it comes to inviting lovers into my life?
- Why am I so terrified about the possibility of having to move back in with my family when I graduate?
- Now that I've moved away from family and childhood friends, how do I make new friends without appearing too needy?

A PRACTICAL TIP FOR HELPING STUDENTS TO IDENTIFY PEOPLE IN THEIR CORE RELATIONSHIPS

We sometimes ask our students to apply Jim Rohn's (2012) concept of the "five-person average" in order to assess the depth, and impact on themselves, of their core relationships. Rohn, a world-renowned business philosopher and leadership expert, believes that each of us is "the average of the five people we spend the most time with." This core group consists of individuals whom we almost instantly click with, have the right chemistry, are able to be vulnerable with, and who value reciprocity. They are the people who we let in to see our deeper side, and who we hold near and dear to our hearts. This is the core group of individuals who meet our needs for connection, who share our "tribal" validation, who are the source of our inspiration, who we even want to become like when we grow up, and with whom we feel serene and secure whenever we are in their presence.

Our students appreciate an opportunity to examine their "core group average," because it gives them a chance to look at their closest relationships more systematically. They take the assignment very seriously, because if each of us is the average of our top-five core group, then we can see just how selective (or unselective) we've been in creating core relationships. After all, it is this top-five combination that essentially raises our net worth in terms of who we are and who we want to become. What some of our students discover is that, either consciously or unconsciously, we tend to fill our top-five slots only when we find individuals who fit our criteria. Some of our students are content with leaving a vacancy in their core group because they would rather go without than to lower their standards.

Upon being asked why she had so many vacancies in her core group, one of our students quoted Robert Wyland (2010), a world-renowned marine artist, who said, "There are two types of people—anchors and motors. You want to lose the anchors and get with the motors because the motors are going somewhere and they're having more fun. The anchors will just drag you down." Our student went on to assert that she was "tired of surrounding myself with dead-weight anchors. And, worse, I find myself being a dead weight in other people's lives. In contrast, I want to be a motor who is going somewhere, and I want motors in my life."

A Student's Personal Letter on Several Core Relationship Issues

In our meaning-making courses, students are dealing with a variety of core relationship challenges. Often the most difficult relationships are the very personal ones, the ones that go beneath and above the workplace, the schoolspace, and the playspace. It is no coincidence that the root of the word "core" is "heart" in several of the Romance languages, including Latin. Adult love relationships have adaptational value from an evolutionary perspective (e.g., attachments bond us to one another for reciprocal protection, socialization, and physical survival). But companionate love relationships enrich our psychological states, provide sexual excitement and satisfaction, and fuel our passions for the joy of being with another person totally committed to us. Love, etymologically, fulfills our "heart's" desire. A true love relationship completes us and makes us whole.

The letter below was written by a quarterlife graduate student, Dana Christiansen (name used with permission), who was examining the concept of

75

love for the first time in an academic setting. Almost ready to graduate, this letter writer was grateful for the opportunity to explore, and clarify, several core relationships in her life that were bound to have an effect on her choices for life after graduation. The assignment we gave to our class was this one: Write us a candid, personal letter about some of the struggles, and successes, you are having with core relationships in your life right here and right now. What have you learned from these experiences that will help you to get ready for your future? What might others learn about love and life from reading your letter?

Dear Robert and Jennifer,

As my twenty-first birthday quickly approaches, I recognize that my close relationships are what I most often reflect on when I allow myself the time and humility to explore what gives my life meaning. I find myself thinking of the two people for whom I have the most respect, my sister and my boyfriend. I also find myself reflecting on some difficult relationships that I've had. Finding meaning through difficult situations is an inevitable challenge that everyone must confront at one point or another. The two relationships that I continue to struggle with are the ones with my mother and my friend.

Though I love my mother very much, the relationship that we have is far from perfect. My mother is bipolar, and our intensely emotional relationship has left me wounded. After leaving my house for college, I realized that if I were to live the adult life that I wished to live, I would have to distance myself from her, physically and emotionally. Jennifer Dohrn, one of our course authors, states, "I have begun a process of learning the extent of my own limitations. This is wonderfully healthy. You can give to others in a very full way and still have integrity about your own self." I find myself on a similar journey. Dohrn admits that it is "a process," and I can attest to that as well. Though my mother and I are in a better place, we will always struggle to communicate and speak each other's language, but in recognizing my own limitations with her I have learned a lot about myself. I will always love and care for my mother, but Dohrn helps me realize that it is not my responsibility to fix her.

I was taken with a quotation that we read from Aristotle's *Nicomachean Ethics*: "a 'perfect friendship' is one in which two people not only see one another as 'another self,' as reflections of one another, but who consider one another equally virtuous. Because of this, a good person cannot be friends with a bad person." My friend is not a bad person. I don't even know if I believe anyone is a "bad" person. I have been friends with this person for over five years. Though she has many positive qualities, I have never felt particularly comfortable in our friendship.

I have never allowed myself to be truly vulnerable with her, which is out of the ordinary in my relationships. She and I are polar opposites on many spectrums, politically, philosophically, etc. Her brash disposition and polarizing views often make me uncomfortable. I frequently find myself questioning our friendship, and pondering if I should distance myself and how. It is something I've struggled with for many years, and I have yet to come to a conclusion. I have learned some of the most significant and useful life lessons thus far in reflecting upon my most difficult relationships. For this reason, I continue to work on them, in the hope of finding a balance that I am comfortable with that will enrich the meaning of these less-than-perfect relationships and my life as a whole.

My sister, nine years my elder, has been more like a mother than a sister to me. I can turn to her for anything. When our mother wasn't doing well during my high school years, I would often call my sister in tears, searching for a shoulder to cry on, someone who would just listen. She would always provide me with the patience and understanding that I so desperately needed. She did not treat me as an overly emotional teenager, or minimize my feelings of confusion and dread; she would just listen. She will not give advice unless I ask her for it. Her restraint and poise amaze me, and are qualities that I aspire to attain. She carries herself with the type of self-respect that demands the same in return. The close relationship that we have, cemented by our shared woundedness, vulnerability, and respect affords me the comfort and confidence to aspire to be a better me.

For three years, my boyfriend has been the philosopher of my soul, and I anticipate this will be the case for as long as we are together. He, like my sister, exudes and receives respect. He makes a conscious effort to treat others with kindness and patience, and asks for the same in return. He has given me the strength to be my flawed, authentic self, and as a result our love has blossomed. Soren Kierkegaard states that "the most insightful knowledge springs from, and is the fruit of, an intense and impassioned emotional outpouring." This foundation of respect, of recognizing each other's individual strengths, weaknesses, and needs, has led to a truly meaningful relationship between me and my boyfriend. As one of our course authors notes, "you can't show respect for someone else unless you are prepared to make yourself vulnerable. You can't give respect unless you have the courage to say what you need from the other person."

In reflecting on the important relationships that continue to make my life meaningful, the underlying theme is my ability to question. Will I be brave enough to question the relationships that cause me distress? Am I showing enough respect to the people who I love the most? Am I being the friend, girlfriend, daughter, and sister that I aspire to be? This kind of questioning requires that I "think of alternatives, using my imagination, and then commit to changing those aspects of myself that keep me from being the person I aspire to be."

In educating myself through school, through relationships, and through day-to-day tasks, I hope to unearth questions and aspects of myself that I have yet to face. By reflecting on my failures and my accomplishments in all my various relationships, I hope to continue to aspire to be a fuller, more self-actualized version of myself in everything I do—including my work, my schooling, my family life, my friendships, and all my social groups. As David Wilkins points out, "you need to know your own demons, your own inner working, your own brokenness. Yet, you have to use that very brokenness to create an invitation for connection with people." The work of making meaning in my life will undoubtedly be a lifelong journey, but if I do my best, respect those around me, and never stop questioning, I think making meaning will start to feel less like work and more like life—my life. And, for me, it all starts with healing and sealing my core relationships.

Sincerely,
Dana Christiansen

STRATEGIC TIPS FOR IDENTIFYING, AND EXAMINING, DIFFERENT TYPES OF LOVE—AS INSPIRED BY OUR LETTER WRITER

It is important for our quarterlife students to understand that while there exists a universal physical and psychological need on the part of humans to love and be loved, there are different kinds of love to consider. We offer below four types of love that come up time and time again in our meaning-making experiences with students. We believe that our letter writer, Dana, in the previous section, speaks both directly and indirectly to each of these types, and she has inspired us to think more diversely about love. We will also briefly recommend a few strategies for strengthening core, loving relationships at the end of this chapter that have worked for many of our students.

Familial Love

This is often the very first experience with love for most of our students who have been raised in traditional domestic relationships vis a vis their families of origin. Our strong attachments to close and near, blood relatives are biologically a result of our genetic ties. But there are also strong psychological/social functions that genetically-related family members provide for one another. The Ancient Greeks had a word for the love felt by parents for their offspring—*storge* love. When all is going well, *storge* love provides warmth; physical and emotional security; unconditional acceptance, support, and sustenance; shared values, ideals, and goals; enjoyment and leisure; standards for acceptable social behavior; as well as other types of social training, *etc*. *Storge* love is a higher form of human love, and it is unconditional, always forgiving, and even, at times, sacrificial. (*Storge* love is closely related to the Greek concept of *agape* love, the love that some traditional religious believers think their deity has for them. Agape love is supernatural and otherworldly, and it is primarily about unconditionality, forgiveness, and universality.)

But, alas, familial love does not go well all the time. For some students, like our letter writer above, *storge* familial love has its major ups and downs. For some, it is too idealistic, and, for others, just downright unattainable. And for others, still, it is too authoritarian and demanding. In some cases, family love is simply nonexistent. Our letter writer's relationship with her mother is dysfunctional, perhaps irreparable; while her relationship with her sister is much more in keeping with the trusting, mutually supportive, warmly affectionate love conveyed by *storge*.

At times, however, for our students, familial love is a synonym for nothing more than obligatory love. The love one has for a parent is obligatory for some students like our letter writer who seems to be staying the course with her bipolar mother because she feels a familial duty to support her. Obligatory familial love, in our experience, is more widespread in collectivist cultures than in individualistic ones. But, as in our letter writer's case, there are glaring exceptions to this practice in individualistic cultures. Many of our students hang in there with difficult members of their families because they feel the enormous pressure in some American subcultures of paying dues to one's family.

It might be helpful for our letter writer, Dana, to ask herself if her love for her mother is obligatory, something she displays out of a sense of duty, or, perhaps, out of guilt. Is she motivated by a need to pay back her divorced mother for raising her and making so many personal sacrifices? Does our letter writer mean "caring deep down" for her mother when she says "I love my mother." Or does she mean something less or more or, really, nothing at all? How, exactly, does the love our letter writer has for her sister differ from the love she has for her mother? Should one love a family member only when there is reciprocity and mutuality in the relationship? Is it immoral for someone to walk away from a family member when the relationship is injurious, even lethal, in its impact on everyone involved? How long must a family member stay the course to make things right? When does the duty to self override the duty to others? At what point does establishing a close, lasting relationship with one's family become a matter of personal choice rather than a societally imposed duty?

Friendship Love

One of our students refers to friends as the "family we choose." Robert often says this to his students: "Describe the best qualities of your closest, most trusted friends, and I'll tell you who you, yourself, are striving to become as a person."

Our true friends are us, and we are our true friends—with wonderfully unique differences, of course. Friendship love has much in common with authentic familial love in the sense that it can be caring, tender, and, even, Platonic in nature. Where friendship love (the Greeks referred to this type of love as *philia*) differs from other forms of love, however, is that it is always voluntary, freely chosen and given, and deeply committed to the welfare of others.

And while friendship love has its own challenges and risks (it can sometimes degenerate into mutually destructive groups of co-dependents such as "drinking buddies," "gossip circles," "self-serving, exclusivist cliques," or "mutual admiration societies"), it is, nevertheless, one of the most admirable types of love. This was true not only for the Greeks and Romans, but, also, for a number of religio-spiritual communities both past and present.

It is *philia* love that Aristotle was referring to when he said that "Without friends, no one would choose to live, though one had all the other goods." Friendship love is invariably enjoyable, honest, edifying, and mutually growthful. It is not superficial. It is not exploitative. Everyone benefits. There are new learnings to be grasped every single day from *philia* friends, just as there is a constant overflow of new pleasures and inspirations. Friends laugh together, play together, think together, grow together, and, at times, suffer together. They are always there for one another, even when they might want to be elsewhere.

Friends commend, but they also challenge. Friends accept, but they are also willing to advise and evaluate. Friends support, but not unqualifiedly. In order for friendships to stand the test of time (actually, few friendships in college last beyond graduation, because life changes so drastically when students leave the area, or fall in and out of love, or assume very different lives in different places), students need to be assiduous in keeping *philia* relationships alive. As one of our students remarked a few months after graduation: "I'm suffering from *philia* withdrawal because all of my supports have disappeared. I'm in serious mourning."

Dana, our letter writer, is fortunate to have found a *philia* friend in her older sister, who appears to be the direct antithesis of her non-*philia* friend. She is convinced that her sister will remain true to her through all the ups and downs in her life. Her sister has always been her one constant, somebody whom she could rely upon regardless of the circumstances. Her sister has been, at various times, her "mother," her counselor, her non-judgmental peer, her role-model, her mutual sufferer in "woundedness," and her source of comfort when she most needed it. And, she, in turn, has offered all of these gifts to her older sister.

All has not been lost in her non-*philia* relationship with her friend, though. Dana acknowledges that, even though her five-year non-*philia* friendship has been profoundly troubled, and that she may have to end it sooner rather than later, she has still taken away lasting life lessons that have been "most significant" and "useful." She understands, now, the importance of finding harmony and balance in close relationships, of never having to sacrifice independence for dependence, of always feeling safe enough to seek personal authenticity and vulnerability, and of continuing to seek the shared commonalities necessary for close "virtue" friendships.

Romantic Love

The Greeks often referred to romantic love as *eros*. This is a physical love ruled by the erotic passions. This type of love connotes allure, chemistry, pleasure, physical ecstasy, and bodily attractiveness. While *eros* is certainly an important aspect of any type of loving relationship between people who are physically, and even emotionally, attracted to one another, it is not enough to capture the fullness of romantic love. So many of our college students have never had a romantic relationship with anyone in a way that isn't exclusively erotic. How often have we heard students of all genders and sexual orientations say, in one way or another, "I felt used"? Or, "the sex got old fast, and then there wasn't much left to talk about." Or, "when I didn't, or wouldn't, 'put out', I never saw the other person again." Or, "it was never about 'love,' it was about 'want,' as in I 'want' your body, but forget about all the heart and mind stuff."

The medieval philosophers, such as Thomas Aquinas, differentiated "concupiscent" or "covetous" love from a "benevolent," "soulful" love. For us, the term "romantic love" signifies a relationship that is both erotic *and* also mutually caring and respectful; physical *and* also deeply emotional in the sense that it represents a connection of soulful intimacy. Genuine romantic love unites rather than divides. Romantic love is a mixture of body and soul, heart and mind, passion and reason, excitement and calm, excess and moderation, desire and fulfillment, and, yes, also weakness and strength, sadness and happiness.

Romantic love for us, in the most authentic, holistic sense, gives and receives, and gives and receives . . . over and over again, because in Brene Brown's epigraph, love is something we nurture and grow, not only with others but within ourselves. Our letter writer, Dana, is involved in a true romantic relationship. She has found someone she genuinely cherishes, someone who makes her better than she is, someone who is both a lover and a soulmate, someone she describes as "the philosopher of my soul." He excites her, and he respects her. He supports her feelings and her intellectual musings. He encourages her to question. He supports her never-ending meaning quest, because he, too, is on the quarterlife quest to make meaning.

While all of this might sound overly idealistic to some; and while we are well aware of romantic love's excesses and deficiencies when pushed to obsessive extremes; and while we know that all kinds of love can be used as weapons to exploit and harm others, we also know from years of first-hand experience with love-seeking quarterlife students that there is considerable truth in this maxim of Sophocles: "One word frees us of all the weight and pain of life, and that word is 'love'." Finally, we also agree with an anonymous maxim that has been in circulation for centuries: "The mystery of love is greater than the mystery of death." Or as one of our more scientifically-inclined students once said in class: "I know why someday I will have to die, but I have no rational idea why someday I will have to love."

Self-love

Contemporary positive psychology (newly termed by its creator, Martin E. P. Seligman, as "flourishing" psychology) makes the claim that the best way to create reciprocal, enduring core relationships is to cultivate, and radiate, a strong self-love. Self-love, for the "flourishing" experts, is not meant to be a simple cliché along the lines of "be your own best friend," or "love yourself first, and everything else will follow." While there is always at least a semblance of truth in clichés like these, our notion of self-love digs a bit more deeply.

Neither is our use of self-love meant to be a back-door justification for excessive narcissism, selfishness, or navel-gazing. We have found in our work with quarterlifers that when our students become excessively self-centered, it is precisely because they *lack* an authentic self-love, and so they overcompensate. The irony here is that the more narcissistic the person, the more likely it is that an authentic self-love will be elusive. We prefer to use the term "soulful self-love" in order to describe its depth, its imagination, its sense of transcendence, and its openness to learning from others in order to learn more about the self. Our concept of "soulful self-love" meets all the criteria mentioned in the Brene Brown epigraph at the beginning of this chapter. Particularly relevant is her comment that "we can only love others as much as we love ourselves."

Our letter writer, Dana, is learning how to love herself in the most healthy and functional way. She knows that she can give to others without giving herself away. She can still maintain her own "integrity." She willingly accepts the love given to her by others and uses this as an opportunity for her to return the love. No matter how difficult the relationship, she has the growing confidence that she is capable of emerging from interpersonal conflict better and clearer about who and what she is because of it. She is confident in her ability to be vulnerable without being weak, and she is discerning enough to know when she should stay in a functional relationship and when she should leave a dysfunctional one. She trusts her best judgments because she knows her own "demons," and she has learned from her own "brokenness." She is full of self-respect because she respects others, and she is open to the very real possibility that everyone she knows—no matter how weak or strong—has something important to teach her. Her *raison d'être* at this time is to create an enduring meaning by "healing and sealing my core relationships."

A Personal Reflection from a Practitioner on How to Construct Loving Core Relationships

Mollie M. Monahan-Kreishman, Ph.D.
Independent Speaker and Consultant for Colleges and Universities on
Issues of Women, Gender, Relationships, and Sexual Violence on Campus
Gig Harbor, Washington

Finding Meaning in Mending: Brokenness, Restoration, and the Connections We Find in Between

She sits across from me on a well-worn, woven chair. She shares painful and powerful moments in her transition from an outward gender appearance that does not fit who she really is, to finding ways to be *honestly real* both inside and out. Core people in her life—parents, friends—have responded to her coming-into-her-own in monstrous, caustic ways. Their words and actions have taken her to a breaking point. And now, as she finds new relationships that support and affirm her, I watch her grace and dignity prevail, and she finds ways to fill the cracks with gold.

She is a past student of mine—one of many whom I have had the privilege of sitting with over the years. From student activities and residence life, to the women's center and all of my roles between, I am drawn to campus life for the possibility of making a difference in human life. And outside the space of students' brokenness, I find ways to work on my own, because I cannot be there for them without tending to the fragmentations of my own life as well.

Connections and Disconnections

At a time when brokenness, often emerging from abuse, seems to prevail, how do we, as human beings, find our ways into deep, meaningful, connected relationships? If relationships are at the core of both harming and healing, how do we navigate away from the former and toward the latter? How do we, as student affairs professionals, educators, and administrators, model healthy relationships for and with our students, and how can we remain open to learning from the students themselves? What is it to have meaning-*full* relationships—relationships that are full of meaning, full of support, and full of love?

In thinking through these questions, I turned to a group of people who never cease to inspire and teach me: my students. I reached out to individuals who have bestowed insight upon me and said to me in different ways over the years: my relationship with you is meaningful. I wanted to know what it was about our relationships, from their perspectives, that was so meaningful.

- "You touched a very vulnerable part of my heart."
- "I felt a bond between us."

83

- "We shared [an] experience."
- "I felt safe with you."
- "When I went through a bad depression, you were there."
- "You weren't preachy, but you were never afraid to set me straight."
- "When I was going back to school to finish my degree, you asked me how you could support me."
- "I continue to work on being the woman you always told me I could be."

And yet, in the shadow of such affirmation, I admit that I have not always felt that I made that grade. Indeed, there are times in which I've been so depleted that giving felt impossible.

This is my truth: there are times in my life that I have been my best—able to live, model, and share in the magic that happens when relationships are deep and meaningful. These moments stay with me. They include the quiet, loving glance of my partner, solitary walks in the woods, hugging my five-year-old daughter, watching her explore the garden, hearing her laugh, making her laugh. There are also times when I have not been my best, and in those times, relationships have been harmed or lost entirely. Those moments stay with me, too. They include the self-doubt I experienced as a doctoral student, the realization of a friend's betrayal, and the suffocating, all-encompassing nature of my own journey toward healing after rape. Life is about lessons learned, and the most important lessons are about being human, and *being in* humanity. It is an exploration of self and others, and the connections that both hold us and break us apart.

Meaning from Mending

So what can we learn from honest, sometimes painful, reflections on life and the people in it? How does living a life of reflection become part of being in healthy relationships? I am blessed with a small handful of people in my life who do this, and do it well. They include a few student affairs mentors from my time as an undergraduate student, a faculty member from my masters program, and three very special friends. They live a life in essential connectedness with others. From their actions, I can see emerging what may be some essential ways in which they are called toward this end. What follows is a summary of these strategies for making meaning in building and sustaining core loving relationships.

A SUMMARY OF RECOMMENDATIONS FOR BUILDING AND SUSTAINING LOVING RELATIONSHIPS—WRITTEN BY MOLLIE M. MONAHAN-KREISHMAN

It is critical to acknowledge here that in reality, life ebbs and flows. It is not entirely constructed of lows and highs, but rather exists in the messiness in between.

In these times, we can certainly still be in relationship with others—healthy, lasting ones, at that. We need good relationships to celebrate wholeness in the best of times, to help hold the pieces together in the worst of times, and to simply be together during the times in between. And then—and this is the best part of all—the people who are able to stay with us, to help us hold those pieces together in fullness and emptiness, are, in turn, holding the material of durable, lasting relationships.

It is about taking time to see, care for, and let people know that they matter to us. It is about recognizing toxicity and stepping away, removing it from our lives, and moving into spaces that heal and fill our souls. It is about seeing the brokenness, mending it purposefully, and committing to the deep and meaningful relationships that give us our very reasons to be. It is between the brokenness and the restoration, and the mending and the meaning making, from which the strongest, most powerful connections and relationships are made.

Oriah Mountain Dreamer (2003) writes, "the call is always there, whispering in the soft places of our bodies and hearts, in the longing that reminds us what we ached for at the deepest level" (p. 4). For those who can hear it, it is a persistent, quiet voice, which guides us toward and into an essential connection that we can *be* and *model* and *share*. Five callings I explore here are: seek and see the brokenness, work toward authenticity, refill with love and joy, share the collected wealth, and create space for practicing the art of caring deeply.

1. Those whom I see living in an essential connectedness seem engaged in the labor of seeking and seeing their own broken pieces. Being hurt and feeling pain are essential parts of the human experience, so does it not follow that making *visible* such *invisible* experiences will lead to the most essential and genuine relationships? If the pieces of a broken life are clearly seen for what they are, they have the capacity to restore and expand the magnificence of life when they are shared. Life is a balance, and when individuals and relationships are challenged to breaking points, they have the capacity to become stronger and more beautiful as they mend.

2. They do the hard work that moves them toward what Corey Anton calls, "selfhood within authentic existence" (2001). From the vantage point of one's own life, finding one's own authenticity can come at great sacrifice. It is through such sacrifice, however, that one may gain by way of sharing the beauty of these discoveries with others. These discoveries are made in their own time, if they are made at all, and cannot be forced. The people in my life who have been challenged the most, and who have discovered their own authenticity in this way, find ways to hope in community with others. They have an abundance of appreciation for what life can be, and what life has to give.

85

3. They are purposeful about being with people who and experiences that fill them with love and joy. Like the most precious moments with my partner and daughter, staring wide-eyed at abundant bright stars above the sandhills of North Carolina, every human being has the capacity to be filled with wonder. When life becomes too busy to pause and take in the greatness of the world, it is time to slow down and reconnect with self and others. One must have energy first in order to give energy to others. One must know oneself in order to know from whence the joy and love may come.

4. From places of happiness and fulfillment, they share from our collected wealth of love and loss and the fullness of humanity. It is a sharing of souls—identity intertwined with self and others, leading to an empathy for the human condition. Whether it is by way of time spent listening, planning, or celebrating, they demonstrate that the people around them are seen, heard, and valued. When we feel filled with joy and love, it is effortless to give. And by being-with, powerful and lasting relationships can be made.

5. They are purposeful about modeling and creating space, or home, from which students may practice the art of caring deeply. It is from this inner home-space that they invite students (and staff, for that matter) to write self-reflections and share with one another, or to engage in more and less structured reflections. I've experienced this as a student and as a faculty/staff facilitator. I've watched some of my colleagues do it with great skill. When space for safe reflection is created from a place of authenticity and transparency, exceptional moments and connections can be made.

Chapter 7

How Do All My Overlapping Identities Help Me to Define Who I Am?

A person is not just one thing [only and solely a member of a racial, ethnic, religious, or political group] but many things: a parent, a friend, a teacher, a chess player, a Frenchman, a socialist, a granddaughter, all at once, a multiple and complex entity whom the politics of singular identity reduces to an empty symbol and stuffs into a pigeonhole.

A. C. Grayling (2010)

Culture hides much more than it reveals, and strangely what it hides, it hides most effectively from its own participants.

Edward Hall

Fear is not real. The only place that fear can exist is in our thoughts of the future. It is a product of our imagination, causing us to fear things that do not at present, and may not ever, exist. That is near insanity. Do not misunderstand me. Danger is very real, but fear is a choice.

Will Smith

We intend to use the word *identity* throughout this chapter as a term that connotes the multiplicity of ways that our students strive to define themselves and how they want others to define them. Thus, we are not interested in either promoting, or critiquing, identity politics. We want to go beyond the etymological meaning of *identity* (L. *identitas*), which means *group sameness* or *exact likeness*—i.e., *identical*. In contrast, we believe in the proposition that each human being has multiple, overlapping identities, and all of these make us genuinely unique, even when we share common belief systems and heritages.

We prefer the word *overlapping* to *intersecting*, because, etymologically, the former term denotes identities that coincide with, and extend alongside, a number of other dominant and subordinate identities, sometimes forming a richer, more complex, total identity; while the latter term denotes two, sharply divided identities that, even though they might cross over one another, may not result in any significant change to the dominant identity. On a larger scale, we believe that, in spite of our implicit and explicit, dominant and subordinate, differences, all of us as human beings share a common need to make meaning of our lives. What form this takes is complex, unique, and compelling for each of us.

No single one of our multiple identities sums us up; it is rare that we ever reach a point in our lives when all of the various facets of our personalities overlap with one another in a perfect, definitive unity. Sometimes we are this, sometimes we are that, and, sometimes we are actually none of these but something entirely different. What others *see* will never be all that others *get*. This is what makes us the complex, sometimes mysterious, human beings that we are. We agree with the philosopher, David Hume, that each of us is a "bundle of perceptions," and these perceptions of ourselves, and others as well, change at any given point in time through each and every experience that we have.

For us, an identity is a complex social-psychological-cultural frame of reference that we create, and are created by, in response to the following personal questions we ask throughout our lives: Who am I? What am I? Where am I? How am I? and Why am I? Walt Whitman had it right: "each of us contains multitudes."

WHAT ARE THE RECURRING QUARTERLIFE IDENTITY QUESTIONS?

Identity development is one of the core concerns of our quarterlifers in their pursuit of meaning-making. Our students know that when they can establish and act out their own identities, then, and only then, will they know what they have in common with, and how they might differ from, other people in their lives. A strong sense of self-identity is the precondition for making social connections with others—no matter how different each of us might be. According to the sociologist, Ken Browne (2010), "How you see yourself will influence the friends you have, who you will marry or live with, and the communities and groups to which you relate and belong." If people did not have an identity, they would lack the means of identifying with or relating to their peer group, to their neighbors, to the communities in which they live or to the people they come across in their everyday lives.

We hear several versions of the following questions from our students whenever we initiate a unit on why identity development is an integral component of making meaning:

Who am I?

This is one of the most difficult questions for students who are either transitioning into, going through, or transitioning out of the quarterlife process. This is the question that Erik Erikson (1994) believed was the major developmental element of ego identity. In fact, this question recurs throughout the lifetime of a human being. It never gets answered once and for all. No matter what the age of our students—quarterlife, mid-life, or later life—the core identity question is always "Who am I?" Or in Erikson's terms: What are the "beliefs, ideals, and principles" that have shaped me into the "who I am" today? Here are some other forms that this meta-meaning question of ego identity takes: Who am I in relation to my ethnic and racial heritage, my social class, my sexual orientation, my religious background, and my gender? Am I less, more, or a complex combination of all these multicultural/diversity/socio-economic identities? Is who I am more a product of my various "privileges" (or lack of them) than I think?

Another take on the "who am I?" question that we often hear is more philosophical: Is there a "me" or a "self" that is constant, immutable, and basic, even when all my various identities are in flux? Is the "I" that I am today related in any way to the "I" that I was as a pre-teen, or a teen, or a 20-something? In what ways am I unique, unlike no other human being, or are we all alike more than unalike? In what ways am I like other human beings? Is the "who am I?" inextricably linked with others, so that the more accurate question is "who are we?" Can I be an autonomous person if I become too dependent on others? What exactly does it mean for me to be "interdependent"? Another form that this question takes for many students is this: "Who am I in terms of my family of origin, the family that I will marry into, or the single person that I might choose to be for the rest of my life? To what extent do our primary relationships shape us to be who we are?"

Sometimes we hear a variation of this type of "who am I?" question: Is the "who" I am today the same "who" that I *want to become* tomorrow? In what ways have I consciously changed the "who" I am at the present time from the "who" I was yesterday? Is this even possible? How free am I actually to become the "who" that I might prefer to be at any given time in my life cycle?

What am I?

This identity question is the one that is often uppermost for quarterlife students who are trying to develop competence in a variety of areas. Arthur W. Chickering (1993) lists this as one of his top "vectors." The "what am I competent in?" question is a nagging one for college students at both the undergraduate and graduate levels. Chickering identifies a number of competencies that quarterlifers are working on: skills that are intellectual, physical and manual, and interpersonal. Students are also trying to create reasoning and critical-thinking skills, as well as artistic and

89

athletic competencies. And one of the most sought after, and often the most difficult, competencies for quarterlifers in their quest for identity is to be able to communicate and interact effectively with others in a variety of settings.

The "what am I?" is closely linked to the "who am I?" question. Some students want to identify with a career "what" as early as possible in order to avoid the pain of always being in search of the "right job" that will acccurately define them to themselves, family, and friends. Some declare career majors early, some later, and some change major areas of study several times before they graduate. Some students experience great pressure from the outside to opt for a career track early; some feel little or no pressure except from themselves. Academic majors and minors are important aspects of the "what am I?" question. Identifying closely with a field of study like environmental science or business, or for that matter with a major like religious studies, art, or music, is one of the primary ways for quarterlifers to answer the "what am I?" question. Obviously, some majors have more career cachet today than others, and this cachet, or lack of it, carries with it ample amounts of pride or shame; success or failure.

Finally, the "what am I?" question is linked to the various socio-biological identities that quarterlifers are dealing with. For example, we often hear them express serious concerns about being summarily boxed by others regarding whether or not they belong to the "privileged" or "non-privileged" classes. Another related identity question has to do with whether or not it is possible to be someone beyond a particular social or racial identity. In this sense, the "what am I?" question is really about whether or not quarterlifers are able to be "more than" the socio-cultural categories and situations they were born into.

The "what am I?" question is also another way to ask: "how can I transcend, or at the very least incorporate, all of my various identities, into a more integrative, original identity?" As one student said to us:

> I want to find a way to exist as a unique person, as a valuable individual, with a variety of *overlapping* identities. As my life now stands, there are just too many people dissecting me in order to reduce to me to my most basic, common denominator. For this reason, I'm not a fan of my multicultural/diversity classes, because the "activists" in it are always categorizing me and, therefore, limiting my possibilities. One of our authors, A. C. Grayling, is right—"the politics of singular identity reduces [me] to an empty symbol and stuffs [me] into a pigeonhole."

Where am I?

Our international students often ask this basic identity question: How does my international citizenship affect my sense of self in the United States? Jennifer sometimes has to remind herself that "where am I?" means literally "where am I

right now?" And, more figuratively—"right here, right now, is where I belong."
For too long, Jennifer has had no "where" she can identify with. She has come to
think of herself as a "cosmopolite"—a citizen of the universe. She has moved around
so much globally during her teen and quarterlife years that the "where am I?"
question is a haunting one for her. She asks: "Where am I from and where do I
belong?"

Another aspect of the "where am I?" question is the one that asks—"am I where
I should be at this particular time in my life?" A student once came to us and said:

> I don't think this university is the best place for me right now. I have very few
> choices in what I want to study. There is no flexibility in the majors. The
> university is just too big. I have not made a single friend among faculty
> members, because they are rarely in their offices. So many of my fellow
> students seem driven. All the teaching is passive rather than active, and the
> classes are huge. The only place that I receive what I need are in the student
> activities offices where I can sometimes find the services that make me feel
> better about being here at this time rather than somewhere else. But, for me,
> time is running out here, because there is just too much of a disconnect between
> the "where I am" and "where I want and need to be" at this important time in
> my life.

How am I?

This is actually an identity question that few college students are encouraged to
ask anywhere on campus, expect maybe in the counseling center. This is as much
an emotional well-being question as it is an objective self-inquiry. We hear several
versions of this type of identity question: "How am I doing?" "How am I feeling
about what I am learning?" "How am I managing my emotions? Do I even
understand what my feelings are, what they might mean, and how they might help
to define me as a unique human being?" "How am I achieving the autonomy that
is so important to me at this time in my life when I feel so dependent on my family?"
"How far along the way am I in creating a sustainable meaning and purpose in my
quarterlife, and what does the buzz-word 'sustainable' mean anyway?" "How am
I doing with making friends—genuine, faithful friends—who will stay the course
with me through the months and years I will be at this university . . . and,
hopefully, long afterwards."

Why am I?

Why ask why? At times, our students are curious as to why we ask so many "why"
questions. In order to get them to think about this rather abstract question, we

give them this "why am I?" prompt—reworded as "why are you?"—and then ask them to free-write some very brief, personal responses. Asking this question pushes our students to explore a basic existential question in a very personal way. For the majority of our students, they have never been asked to do this in a formal educational setting. Here are a few representative examples of what students say.

- "I have no idea why I am. Is this question even answerable? It's a trick question, right?"
- "Why am I? requires the same response as all the questions you have been asking during the semester. Give me a lifetime to think about it, and I'll get back to you."
- "This sounds like a covert religio-spiritual question. Am I supposed to say that 'I am I' because God, or the universe, or some demon made me?"
- "It seems to me that this is the most important identity question of all, because if I can figure out why the hell I am me, with all my contradictions, strengths, and weaknesses, then maybe, just maybe, I can find my true calling in life."
- "Why I am is because of 'shit luck.' There is no larger meaning or purpose for why I exist other than this. I was born, I live, and I will die, like the 100 billion people who have come before me since the beginning of human time. It was all a weird cosmic accident, a product of freak chance, a hapless roll of the dice. And it is up to me, and me alone, to give meaning to another 'why' question: 'why shit luck'?"
- "Why am I? This is easy. I am I because there is nobody else exactly like me. This is the way that God made me. Why I am unique is also easy. I am a special creature of God's love. Why am 'I' the 'I' who is unique, and created by God to do His will, and to love others? Only God knows, and only I know what I can do to make my God proud of me."
- "You know, I really like this question. 'Why am I?' gets to the heart and soul of this unsolvable mystery that I stuggle to live every single day of my life. Why here? Why now? Why then? Why when? Here's my shorthand response: 'Why, oh why?' is the question that I ask myself too much, and, whenever I do, I lose the spontaneous joy of living my life right here, right now. I waste too much time sweating the endless and unanswerable whys. From now on, I'm dropping 'why' from my vocabulary and substituting 'wow.' I want my primary identity from this moment forward to be the 'wow! guy,' not the 'why? guy.' This is really ironic, as you both know, because I am a philosophy major. I hope this doesn't cost me an A this semester, and please don't tell my academic advisor."

"THE DANGER OF DIFFERENCE IS VERY REAL, BUT FEAR IS A CHOICE": ONE STUDENT'S PERSONAL REFLECTION ON BEING GAY—LANCE MATTHEW JOHNSON

For some students, even when they have all their "whys" in order; and even when they are aware of the various identity vectors that they have to deal with throughout their quarterlife cycle; and even when they fully understand the overlapping complexity of their multiple identities—still the "danger of difference" is very real. What follows is a courageous, self-disclosing reflection of a student in one of our recent meaning-making seminars that has universal implications for all students who are facing discrimination because they are "different" in some way. At some level, our student's reflection on being gay is a way of understanding Edward Hall's insight that a "culture hides much more than it reveals, and strangely what it hides, it hides most effectively from its own participants." Our student is in the process of uncovering hidden dimensions of his own fear about coming out—both to the larger culture, and, also, to the "anti-hetero-normative" sub-culture that exists within some sectors of the gay community.

The following reflection resulted from an assignment we often give to our classes when we teach our unit on overlapping identities. The author, Lance Matthew Johnson (name used with permission), is currently an Interdisciplinary Graduate Student in Educational Studies. Lance has taken courses on meaning-making with us. We ask all our students to write an in-class, very honest, 500-word, personally reflective essay. The objective is for them to reflect on a "plaguing self-doubt and very real fear" they might have about *who* they are, *what* they are, and *how* they are at the present time. Here is Lance's wonderfully honest, personal reflection.

I think it is time that I admit I have a problem; or rather, not exactly a problem, but a plaguing self-doubt. I have come a long way in terms of my own comfort with my sexual identity, but there are still some ghosts that linger over my head, and I am not entirely sure how to cope with them. I am becoming hyper-aware of all my own identities and the identities of those I am interacting with. However, it has taken a long time for me to be able to openly express my identity as a gay male, and I believe that stems from a fear of being called out or identified as different. In the movie *After Earth*, Will Smith defines fear as being ". . . not real. The only place that fear can exist is in our thoughts of the future. It is a product of our imagination, causing us to fear things that do not, at present, and may not ever, exist. That is near insanity. Do not misunderstand me; danger is very real but fear is a choice."

While there are certainly instances where presenting a non-dominant identity is truly dangerous, the majority of my experiences lead me to believe

93

that the fear of being identified as "different" is something that I play out in my own head, snowballing until it becomes not only a mental barrier, but a physical one. I am starting to catch on that it is as much a concern over my own opinion of myself as it is of others' opinions of me. Am I accepting myself? Am I comfortable with myself? I feel as if, at least, I am on the right path. In class the other day, I struggled to verbally identify myself as a gay man. Rather than simply state it as a fact, I circumvented the truth by stalling and using unidentifiable pronouns. I was fully aware that the company I was in would be accepting of my whole self, but still something held me back. Later, I found myself quite aggravated at my inability to be able to say "I am a gay male."

I sometimes feel challenged within the gay community about my own identity. There is a large contradiction within my community around hetero-normativity and masculinity. Masculinity is praised within the community, where femininity is often frowned on and discouraged. Yet hetero-normative actions are also frowned upon, and often those who identify as hetero-normative are pushed aside. There are certainly distinctions between the two, but I find that there are far more overlaps between hetero-normativity and what would typically be defined as masculine. I am masculine, and by nature, very hetero-normative. There's nothing wrong with either of those, nor should there be. So in a community that cries out for acceptance of all its different forms and is quick to snap at others, we are sometimes more damaging to ourselves than to others. How ironic!

There are many stages to the coming out process: First to self, then to family, then to friends, then to co-workers and, finally, to the world. In each of these stages, we can either be supportive or destructive. For me, being supportive of others means being authentic about my own identity. If I am able to genuinely represent myself, and hold true to my own identity, my hope is that others will be encouraged to do the same. So I challenge myself to model the kind of authenticity that creates space for others, not only for those who hold minority sexual identities, but for everyone who holds a marginalized identity of any kind.

STRATEGIC TIPS TO HELP QUARTERLIFERS TALK ABOUT IDENTITY ISSUES

When discussing identity issues with our students, we are careful not to minimize the gravity of our students' struggles. When looking at students' challenges and stumbling blocks, it is easy for us, standing on the outside of their unique situations, to make well-intentioned "why don't you . . ." helping statements. Sadly, though, we have found that the overall impact of "why don't you . . ." statements serves further to disempower our students because our advice is often unsolicited. Students want to be heard more than to be told. Moreover, by offering advice from the outside looking in, we unintentionally minimize the personal intensity of their challenges.

What follows are a series of strategic tips that have worked for us in helping quarterlife, meaning-making students to talk about even the most difficult, and sensitive, identity issues. Our overall aim in working with students is to encourage them to be autonomous life-changing activists on their own behalf. Each one of our students has the potential to be an active agent in designing a life plan and in implementing it in a variety of creative ways. Our students are the ones who create their identities; we don't. We are the onlookers who, at best, can offer clarity, understanding, empathy, and personal insights from our own stories whenever relevant and when directly solicited.

In what follows, we include a guiding maxim at the beginning of each tip, because we find that in the meaning-making work we do (especially when the subject matter is as controversial as identity differences), pithy, wise comments about life's complexities are often a good place to start the dialogue with our students. When using maxims, we don't mean to oversimplify; but neither do we want to overcomplicate. Also, we offer the following tips in a spirit of humility. What works for us in our teaching, advising, and consulting may not work for others. In no way do we mean to be dogmatic in sharing our series of strategic tips. Think of these strategies, then, as *describing* our ways of thinking rather than *prescribing* dogmas, because they refer to our own experience as meaning-making educators (see Nash, Johnson, and Murray, 2012).

1. Reflect: "We don't see things as they are; we see them as we are" (Anaïs Nin). As philosophers, we understand the significance of deep reflection. We believe that the cliché "it is what it is" is false. Instead, we hold, with Anaïs Nin, that "the 'it' in the cliche is, in large part, a function of 'who we are' and 'what we, as unique persons, perceive.'" We ask our students to take time to sift through their multiple identities, starting with the who, what, how, where, and why questions we asked earlier in this chapter. Additionally, we sometimes ask: What do *you* bring to the world? How do *you* experience the world? How do *your* identities play a role in your interaction with others? What are *your* perceptions and biases? How many identities define *you*? Do *you* have some hidden identities that you have uncovered recently? How and why have *you* taken the time to uncover them?

2. Self-love: "You yourself, as much as anybody in the entire universe, deserve your love and affection" (Buddha). We sometimes urge our students to take care of their basic need to love themselves first, so that they can be fully present with each other in order to engage in meaningful and purposeful, honest and authentic, dialogue. How, after all, can any of us love others unless we first love ourselves? For the Buddha, the way to others

is first through the self; for Christians, the way to the self is first through others. In our own experience, we find that a salient balance between self and others is the ideal.

3. Inquire and listen: "Courage is what it takes to stand up and speak; courage is also what it takes to sit down and listen" (Winston Churchill). In class, and in one-on-one conversation, we ask it only when we mean it, and we mean it only when we ask it. We listen attentively, and we try to demonstrate to our students that we are listening with care and understanding. We ask empathic, non-judgmental questions. We occasionally ask them to tell a personal story about the point they are trying to make. Every once in a while we might share briefly a time when we, too, might have had a similar experience—not to overshadow the stories of our students but to let them know that at least some of their experiences overlap with others' experiences. We know that when our students can spend non-judgmental time in the classroom with one another, and with us, in order to tell their stories, then they are really learning how to name their experiences and bond with each other. They are also learning that it is the commonalities in their different stories that bind all of us together in some way.

4. Share: "And as we let our own light shine, we unconsciously give other people permission to do the same" (Nelson Mandela). We know well that sharing our life stories can make us feel vulnerable, but that is exactly what ties us together and builds trust. This is why Robert created the genre of Scholarly Personal Narrative (SPN) writing. When we allow our own light to shine, we often encourage others to shine their lights as well. In the midst of talking about our successes, and what gives our own lives meaning and purpose, we are better able to elicit similar disclosures from others . . . and vice versa. There is no better way to connect with others than to show them that we are human . . . fully human in every way. Our humble caveat, however, is that this means talking about not only what *shines* within us, but also what tends to *tarnish* the shine. After all, we want our students to understand that multicultural identity advocates are not perfect. Sometimes they succeed, and sometimes they fail. So, too, do we, and so, too, do our students.

5. Acknowledge: "Most of the shadows in this life are caused by us standing in our own sunshine" (Emerson). We follow a simple rule: we try to think outside the box particularly when that box might sometimes feel like a prison. We allow space for individuals to acknowledge all of their salient identities, whether or not they might be socially constructed, nonconformist, or politically incorrect. We are always available to help our students to understand that they are multiply constructed human beings who have the power, and wisdom, to reconstruct themselves. Both of us, as teachers, have tried to get out from under our own "shadows," and even

though this is an extremely difficult task, change begins with the acknowledgment that sometimes we are too content to stand in our own shadow rather than in our own sunshine.

6. Own It: "When you are right you cannot be too radical; when you are wrong, you cannot be too conservative" (Martin Luther King, Jr). Recognize that as social justice advocates we have been both successful *and* unsuccessful in our work. Therefore, when we see others making mistakes, or using the wrong wording, or being overly critical, don't judge them too harshly. Judges can be sure of one thing: sooner or later they, too, will be judged. We might be hard on the issue, word, or action, but we are always soft on the person. Communication, for us, is more of an art than a science; more *intuition* than *exhibition*. We never forget that one person's radicalism is another person's conservativism . . . and vice versa. And, in the end, who in the world is right *all* the time, or even *half* the time?

7. Forgive: "To forgive is to set a prisoner free and discover that the prisoner was you" (Lewis B. Smedes). We know from first-hand experience with the travails of our own lives that those who have been hurt, triggered, or micro-aggressed against need to practice letting go. Holding onto hurt is like grasping a hot coal with the intent of throwing it at someone else; we are the ones who get burned. To be possessed by our anger is to be a slave to our emotions. To set ourselves free from being tenaciously attached to our self-righteous indignations and to our superior intellect is what personal liberty is all about. Forgiveness is also what makes advocates of diverse identities humble and human. Without forgiveness, particularly in the area of social justice advocacy, we risk promoting only a politics of vengeance.

8. Learn: "The energy of the mind is the essence of life" (Aristotle). At all times, we continue seeking, learning, and absorbing. We especially learn a great deal from how, and why, people identify in certain ways. We, ourselves, make it a point to learn about our own dominant and subordinate identities. We strive to take ownership of our own learning during the semester, and we allow our students to teach us as well as to be taught by us. Good teachers, like good students, are open to all learning possibilities. We have a saying we pass on to our students: "Learn and be energized; learn again and be re-energized. Stop learning, and you stop living, because your energy begins to fade. When this happens, *you* will start to fade away."

9. Patience: "However long the night, the dawn will break" (African proverb). Being the "only one" who thinks and acts in a certain way can be tough, especially in conversations around social justice identity work. We intentionally refuse to adopt a single social justice orthodoxy. Social justice heterodoxy is the best way for us to show respect for difference. We try

to stay strong with our convictions, but we always encourage others to ask questions about what we might believe, often during the dialogue. We are first willing to question ourselves at all times. We are patient with the process, "however long the night," because, sooner or later, we hold that the process will result in a product that brings our students together rather than tears them apart. The dialogical "dawn" will break.

10. Inspire: "With the realization of one's own potential and self-confidence in one's ability, one can build a better world" (Dalai Lama). After making social justice dialogue accessible, relatable, and meaningful, it has been most rewarding for us not to think about what we can *teach* the person. Instead, we strive always to empower and inspire others to learn more, think more, do more, and become more . . . on their own. We are becoming much more self-confident in our abilities to make subtle differences in our students' lives. What follows from this is that our students become self-confident as well. We try to remember always that the Latin root of the word "inspire" is to "breathe into." Thus, our social justice goal is to stimulate our students to do something that is both creative and effective on behalf of equity, equality, and personal empowerment. In our work, *breathing into* is as important to us as *breathing out*. We strive to breathe the gift of overlapping, multiple identities into all of our students so they can live the fullest, richest life of meaning-making they are capable of.

A Personal Reflection from a Practitioner on "Overlapping Identities and Self-Definition"

Randall Laurence Phyall, Special Programs Coordinator
The University of Maryland, College Park, Maryland
Former Assistant Director of the Center for Student Diversity
Mt. St. Mary's University, Maryland

The Truth is Outside of all Fixed Patterns

The questions which one asks oneself begin, at least, to illuminate the world, and become one's key to the experience of others.

James Baldwin

The single story creates stereotypes, and the problem with stereotypes is not that they are untrue, but that they are incomplete. They make one story become the only story.

Chimamanda Adichie

I am a man of color, and I have worked most directly as a diversity administrator in a number of higher education institutions with that population of students. I hope to use my story as a means for other higher education professionals to peer into the student identity development experience. I hope to construct not destruct. I believe, along with Maya Angelou, that "We can learn to see each other and see ourselves in each other and recognize that human beings are more alike than we are unalike."

A Great Controversy: Navigating "Identity Limbo"

Today's student lives in a world where feeling scared can be enough justification for injustice. Even within the walls of a prestigious institution of higher education their identities are minimized to an office, student club, and/or extracurricular activity. However, identities are multifaceted as well as "dynamic" in nature. They are fostered through a continuous process of self-reflection and discovery. But many of us prescribe to seemingly ambiguous perceptions of ourselves because we, simply, have not arrived at that season of life yet. In other words, our life experiences have not exposed us to truths that transcend our current circumstance and "community of knowledge."

Therefore, human beings have an inclination toward compartmentalization. Things that don't fit neatly into *our* "box" don't fit into our perceived reality. When faced with having to accept what I would describe as a contingent reality, we cower. We cower, because we come face-to-face with something we can't name, describe, or empathize with. Thus, we deem it controversial, deviant, and threatening. My story is one such story.

For a while, being a Black man was something that I tried to be, rather than embracing my identity as inherently my own. Other than my skin color, which one would think would suffice, there was no glaring evidence that I was who I had claimed to be — Randall Laurence Phyall, of African-American and Jamaican descent. My name was a testament to the world my parents hoped to create for me, a world which was limitless, conquerable, and guided by God. However, I often struggled to portray myself as "authentic" without compromising the values, beliefs, and worldview that they had instilled in me.

Growing up, my sense of identity became deeply rooted in the expectations of others, because I lacked the voice and ability to proclaim my own identity. Being one of two Black males in my high school class at a private, Quaker institution, there was constant pressure placed on me to conform to stereotypical representations of my race. The "thuggish" and "gangsta" personas that permeated hip-hop and pop culture were often the basis on which others would determine my credibility as a Black male. Being a young Black male in the United States made me particularly "at-risk" for conforming to this societal standard.

Despite my most valiant efforts, terms such as "Oreo" and "Theo Huxtable" were the labels most often imposed on me. The very core of who I am was in stark contrast to the stereotypical norm. As a result, the way in which I portrayed myself was criticized, rather than affirmed and validated. It robbed my White counterparts of their ability to compartmentalize me, which in their eyes was more threatening than my being a thoroughbred gangster.

I faced similar pressures among members of my own race and ethnicity. Being of African-American and West Indian descent posed a unique challenge to me. Fearing not being accepted as a "real" Jamaican or what they call "yardy," I often defaulted to being "just Black." I had to suppress part of my own identity in order to gain acceptance in my own community. Nobody understood my faith as a Seventh-Day Adventist. Instead of asking me questions about my religious beliefs, I was criticized for missing parties and labeled "Bible Boy." Many of these challenges continued into my undergraduate experience.

In college, I struggled to develop a sense of belonging to my institution. Despite being an athlete and very much a part of the dominant social narrative on campus, I felt pressured to overcompensate for what I was not. I felt tokenized, compartmentalized, and that I had little to offer my community outside of making tackles on the football field and hosting the best parties. I was officially indoctrinated into the "Man-Box." For some odd reason, as much as I wanted to "live outside of the box," I feared leaving the one that was created for me. Ms Adichie stated it perfectly when she said, "Show a people as one thing, only one thing, over and over again, and that is what they become." The result was a hyper-masculine, luke-warm Christian wanksta.

Be at Home Wherever You Find Yourself

However, there were multiple intervening agents that enabled me to slowly transition from a state of *conformity* and *dissonance* into *introspection*. Were it not for an advisor of mine at the time, I would have been stuck in my seemingly meaningless and purposeless existence. His genuine interest and personal investment not only in my academic well-being, but in my personal and professional well-being as well, was bizarre to me. I couldn't quite comprehend it. I struggled to figure out what I did to deserve such positive treatment. Well my advisor saw my worth, and that was all that mattered. He exposed me to many of the opportunities that my parents had always told me were mine for the taking. These included diversity dialogue sessions, leadership positions, other supportive professionals, and even a Study Abroad program to London! Most importantly, my advisor made me feel safe in pursuing them without ever forgetting where I came from. I had finally begun to appreciate the value in who I was in all of its forms — Black, Christian, African-American, and Jamaican-American.

Then, I hit a brick wall. Perhaps the most challenging experience that I've had in developing my identity occurred in the summer of 2008, right after I had graduated from college. I had moved to Baltimore to live with my brother for the summer while volunteering with AmeriCorps. One evening, I ventured out to a local 7-Eleven with two of my fellow volunteers (who were Black females) to pick up a few items. After entering the store, I walked across the front of the register and into an open hallway where the bathrooms were located. Just before exiting the bathroom, I was startled by a loud banging on the bathroom door. I was then greeted by the White store manager, who was hurling lewd and offensive comments toward me. He accused me of stealing and adamantly ordered me to leave the building. In utter disbelief, I proceeded to ask him clarifying questions, but to no avail. On my way out of the hallway, I was confronted by a German Shepherd, poised to attack on his master's command. The store owner had also locked me inside the store while the two women I had traveled with stared in horror from the other side of the glass. I was ashamed, felt powerless, and silenced. He robbed me of my manhood and more importantly my humanity. He not only "*told* my story," he "made it the *definitive* story."

The experience above is a testament to the nonlinear, heavily contextual change process that pervades one's identity development. Even in the midst of immense growth, students often have experiences that seemingly take them back to "stage 1." Whether it comes in the form of a bias incident on or off campus, or being singled out in the classroom, students have come to accept such events as the norm . . . just as I did. However, through various experiences in my life, I have truly begun to reclaim the voice that had been taken from me throughout my upbringing. Combating stereotypes and contradictions generated by people who think they see through you is an act of courage. I say this because, while in a state of dissonance, it is hard to find truth. You begin to reassess values and break down belief systems. As your self-esteem fades, you realize that you are but a mere shadow of who you thought you were.

Soon, it became less about controlling what happened to me and more about deciding not to let it reduce me. I began to dictate a different story to myself. As Muhammad Ali stated, "It's the repetition of affirmations that leads to belief. And once that belief becomes a deep conviction, things begin to happen." I directly attribute my current state of self-realization to God, my parents, and the various roles I've served in as a higher education professional. Although issues surrounding bias, intolerance, and prejudice still exist on my campus, I have become increasingly confident in the leaders within my community.

When I speak of leaders, I am referring to those individuals who, despite opposition, have the courage to maintain a struggle against overwhelming odds. I am referring to the individuals who seek to give voice to others even before fully developing their own. I am referring to the peers, mentors, teachers, and administrators who are committed to creating a community that fosters self-discovery and self-appreciation. I hope that we all learn to think and live outside of the "box" to really discover the true essence of who we are inside *and* out.

Conclusion

Given the myriad social, cultural, and academic factors that often challenge college students, providing manageable systems to facilitate their social and academic development is paramount. As student development theory suggests, students (particularly underrepresented students) benefit greatly from meaningful relationships with faculty members and staff whenever we make deliberate efforts to involve students in learning. In this regard our roles can be seen as a means to student empowerment and holistic development. Specifically, effective intervention should identify and cultivate the strengths of each student; inspire curiosity, self-exploration, and independence; and afford advisors as well as coordinators the ability to develop and sustain purposeful relationships with each student.

As higher education professionals, we are called to speak "life" into our students and help them to reveal their own potential to be and do anything. Knowing yourself is liberating; according to Lao Tzu, it's "enlightenment." This begins with your very first interaction with students.

A BRIEF SUMMARY OF RECOMMENDATIONS FROM RANDALL LAURENCE PHYALL'S "OVERLAPPING IDENTITIES AND SELF-DEFINITION"

Randall Phyall, a Cultural Diversity Professional, realizes during his years of work with students from multiple racial, social class, ethnic, and a variety of other backgrounds that each of us, as human beings, is "more alike than unalike." As we point out in our chapter, our individual identities emerge from the complex containers of meanings that each of us resides in every day of our lives. These individual identities overlap with one another, just as our common identities as human beings overlap with one another.

Randall understands how important it is to help our students come to terms with their most nagging identity questions—*who, what, where, how, and why am I?* He wants his students to avoid "compartmentalization," the kind of self- and other-boxing that is characteristic of so much social justice identity-work in higher education today. As an African-American, Jamaican, West Indian, Seventh-Day Adventist, Randall himself is a person of multi-dimensional identifications. He is a complex amalgamation of selves—all of them composited into a respected higher education leader at a major Research I University. His mission in the academy is to help students "to think and live outside the 'box' in order to really discover the true essence of who they are inside *and* out." Here are a few of his salient teachings as a diversity leader:

1. Refuse to be "boxed" by anyone. Be all of who and what you are—proudly, insistently, and humanely. Nobody will ever have the definitive story on you, because, in the end, so-called "definitive" stories only end up stereotyping, and harming, the complex persons that we are.

2. Reclaim your unique voice—whenever and wherever you can. Know your truths and speak your truths, especially to those who want to control and/or silence you. Affirm your convictions. Stand tall when "bias,

intolerance and prejudice seem out of control."You will always have allies who will continue to encourage you to "maintain the struggle against overwhelming odds."

3. Make it a point always to "cultivate the strengths" of all students who come within your purview of influence. The most beneficial identity development begins and ends in relationships. The best way to know oneself is through knowing others.

Chapter 8

How Can I Prepare for a Successful Career, a Soul-Satisfying Vocation, and a Meaningful Life?

> Love and work are the cornerstones to our humanness.
>
> Sigmund Freud (1930)

> Without work, all life goes rotten. But when work is soulless, life stifles and dies.
>
> Albert Camus (1991)

> If you see your work as a job, you do it only for the money . . . if you see it as a career, you are driven by goals of advancement, wealth, promotion, and prestige . . . if you see it as a calling, you find your work intrinsically fulfilling, contributing to the greater good . . . and you're more likely to say "Thank God I am able to come back to work on Monday" instead of "Thank God it's Friday."
>
> Jonathan Haidt

We have found that no issue for quarterlife students is more important than the work/life question in this chapter's title. For years, students have come into our meaning-making classes wondering about the challenge of how to to develop, and sustain, a successful career in order to enjoy all the fruits of a soul-satisfying life. In the last decade especially, career issues have become a near-obsession. Our students' heartfelt concerns about balancing work and life are nagging and recurring. Sadly, up to the point when they walk into our classroom, there has been very little opportunity for them to explore the potential intersections of career, vocation, and a meaningful personal life in any of their previous courses. It is mainly in our career services center where students are encouraged to raise questions and evoke helpful responses, but not every student seeks counseling at our center.

Sadly, some students are too proud, or frightened, to do so. Others simply don't know about the services offered at the center. And still others keep putting off a visit there because they are too "busy," and all of sudden, they are ready to graduate . . . or, unfortunately, they flunk out or drop out of school altogether. We have also discovered that only a fraction of our university's faculty and college staff work together, consistently and systematically, with the professionals at the center. This is a missed meaning-making opportunity for all the parties involved, including, and especially for, students and faculty.

From the very first year of high school, right up to and through college, students feel the pressure to become specialists not generalists, trainees not learners, and careerists not vocation-seekers. These binaries seem to be present in everything they do. The phrase "learning for its own sake" is not something that our students hear much nowadays. Sadly, for some parents and employers, the phrase is almost "immoral." The critics want to know exactly how "intrinsic learning" will provide tangible benefits in the career-world. How, for example, will "intrinsic learning" prepare students for employment at Google, or in the financial markets, or in a national/international corporation, or in an engineering firm, or for graduate work at a medical, law, or business school?

HOW WILL THIS HELP ME TO GET A JOB WHEN I GRADUATE?

As college educators who teach liberal arts subjects in a professional school, we are hardly exempt from exerting these same pressures on students. At a time when higher education, here and elsewhere, is facing dwindling enrollments in many of our humanities- and creative arts-based courses, we are being asked increasingly by administrators, parents, and hyper-driven, careerist students to make sure that what we teach is functional. We are under pressure to demonstrate how the content we are teaching is readily transferrable to the workplace later on. The ever-constant question our students hear from their parents, friends, and significant others is a variation of this one: "How, pray tell, will what you are studying help you to get a job when you graduate? Philosophy? Art? Music? Religious Studies? Creative Writing? History? English? Say what?"

If we in the creative arts, humanities, and liberal arts are being honest, we must also acknowledge that we put pressure on ourselves as educators to demonstrate practicality in order to protect our own best interests. It is important for us to report to our constituencies throughout the university, and to the community outside, that what we do in the classroom has extrinsic, career-preparation value as well as intrinsic-learning value. We often use key pragmatic phrases to demonstrate that we know how important it is for students to be able to transfer the learnings of the classroom to the workplace. We talk about helping our students to think critically and logically, solve complex problems, develop leadership skills, and communicate clearly and cogently. We also want our constituencies to know that we teach students to write rigorously, to research extensively, and to argue convincingly. And, whenever we can, we tout the benefits of work-study programs, service-learning, internships, and other types of field experiences.

While the above is undoubtedly true, what we ourselves have actually found through years of working with college students at both the undergraduate and graduate levels is that it is more than possible to build an integrative work-and-life, meaning-making curriculum that does not set up irreconcilable dichotomies. What is required is the professorial will to do so. Specific career skill sets and disciplinary knowledge, as well as workplace success and soulful living, need not always be in opposition. In fact, we believe that a holistic approach to learning encourages students to understand that the workplace and the soul-space can actually be in complementarity with one another. If they are not, then work/life conflict inevitably follows, as we will show in a subsequent section in a very revealing letter that a recent nursing student wrote to Robert.

Encouraging our students to explore the commonalities between living, loving, and working—i.e., the inextricable connections between learning, yearning, and earning—is what we mean by fostering holistic, soulful meaning-making in the classroom. This will necessitate an approach to teaching and learning throughout the campus that is personal, reflective, intentional, and trusting. Once again, this is what we call "deep, soulful, first-person" learning. And we know from decades of research, and personal experience, that this type of learning can be every bit as rigorous, and vigorous, as any other type.

FREQUENT QUARTERLIFE QUESTIONS ABOUT CREATING A MEANINGFUL LIFE BALANCE

What follows are some of the most common deep-meaning questions regarding work and life concerns that we hear each and every day, in one form or another, from our students:

- Why am I always so worried about whether or not I'm majoring in the right field in order to find a job when I graduate?
- Why is it that I am so preoccupied with learning on-the-job-skills in the classroom and in internships when I really want to enjoy my college experience studying exciting new ideas in the arts and humanities, or in the sciences and social sciences, and having fun in my free time? Isn't this what college should be all about?
- If it's true that I'll be changing careers many times before I retire, what's the sense in taking four to six years to prepare for a particular career in the classroom—a career that could very well change drastically, or even completely disappear, in a relatively short time?

107

- Isn't the best way to learn career skills to learn them on the job? If so, why do I even need a college degree anyway?

- Will I always have to choose between earning a living in a high-paying job and doing what I truly love to do—which seems to be the lament of so many of my family and friends?

- Why is it that very few people I know really look forward each and every day going to work? In fact, so many friends in my life hate, even dread, their jobs.

- How do I really know what the right job is for me anyway? Will I actually be able to identify a lifetime career at age 17 or 18 when I have to declare a college major? Ten years from now, do I want to be held responsible for a bad career choice I was forced to make as a teenager by well-meaning adults in my life?

- Will it be as difficult for me, as it seems to be for so many of my friends, to just walk away from a dismal job experience? Or will my reputation be ruined forever in the workplace because I will be seen as a job-hopping loser?

- What if I'm happier at school than in the workplace at this time in my life and want to go right on to graduate school? Does this make me a work-shirker or a reality-avoider?

- What is "balance" anyway, and how do I create balance in my life when all it seems that I do is study, work, eat, and sleep? Oh, and I also worry constantly about college loans, personal finances, and living from hand-to-mouth!

- How can I avoid over-prioritizing a career during my years in school? I don't want to suffer from "career-fixation" the way so many of my friends and family do.

- Why can't I learn how to enjoy every single aspect of my college education rather than being stressed out all the time about the future?

- Will what I want to do for a living ever be connected to something larger that might give my personal life meaning? Or do spirituality and transcendence have nothing to do with the practicalities of making a living, providing for others, and buying enough toys to make me happy?

- Why is it that jobs, finances, and mainstream ideals of success are so important that they seem to override everything else that is worthwhile in my life?

- Why do I get so stressed out having to keep track of my finances?

- Why is it that when I go to my part- or full-time job I find very little, if any, inspiration there?

- Why do I feel that I have to sacrifice my autonomy and self-respect for a paycheck?

- Where are the imagination and creativity in my work that I need in order to flourish?
- Why is it that I find so much more meaning in my life *outside* of work than *on the job*?
- Why is it that I have learned absolutely nothing about my "inner life" during my years in college? Why do my professors put so much emphasis on the "outer life" and completely neglect what, for me, is far more important at this time—knowing who, what, why, and where I am in my "inner life"?

HOW ESPN LETTER WRITING CAN HELP STUDENTS FIND MEANING IN THEIR CAREERS

We hear versions of the following complaint several times a semester from our students:

> Not a single professor has ever asked me to tell a personal story about what gives my life meaning and what doesn't; or how I might want to live my future as well as how I might *not* want to. Don't they care about me as a unique person with ideals, hopes, and dreams who is able to construct a life of meaning for myself? Why do my professors assume that all they have to do is fill me up with particular information, facts, and skill-sets, and then have me deliver these back to them almost word for word and task by task—and, eureka!, only then will I be an "educated person"? Where, in the end, is the "me" in all of this, or does the "me" not really matter as much as the "them" and the "it"?

What follows in this section is a personal letter that Robert received recently. We present it here, because we believe that it summarizes dramatically what is missing in so many students' lives whenever they undertake a frenzied, career-driven college education, totally devoid of any concern with the various meaning-making questions that we examine throughout our book—*but especially the work/life questions that precede this section*. This letter is further proof to us that education needs to have both extrinsic and intrinsic value in order for it to be relevant, holistic, and potentially transformative. We will then conclude this chapter with a series of reflections on the meaning of loving, soulful, satisfying work derived from the epigraphs that lead this chapter. Along the way, we will also make a few teaching-learning suggestions as to how educators might motivate their students to dig more deeply in order to engage first-hand with the meaning-making, work/life questions that come up both in and out of the classroom.

It is also important to note that, as a pedagogical tool, we ask our students to write a series of first-person, reflective letters (what we call ESPN—Epistolary Scholarly Personal Narrative; Nash and Bradley, 2011) throughout the semester, in addition to their more traditional assignments using the framework of expository research. We employ epistolary *me-search* to help students to connect what they have learned in our course to both their professional *and* personal lives. We encourage this technique as a kind of sanctioned "time-out" for students to draw no-holds-barred, personal meaning-making insights from all the information, knowledge, and skills they have been learning throughout the course.

We make it a point each semester to encourage all our students to move back and forth comfortably among first-, second-, and third-person types of writing expression. We find that subjective meaning-making assignments like writing an honest personal letter to us, or to anyone else of interest—one that contains generalizable themes and relevant concepts from the readings—invariably serve to humanize and personalize the more "objective" subject matter. (The letter that follows, however, was not a class assignment. It appeared in a separate e-mail from someone who was not taking a course with us. This letter was a spontaneous "cry from the heart"—*me-search* without the conventional academic research to ground it.)

The letter writer is Sara Burds (actual name used with permission), a 23-year-old recent graduate of nursing school, who is currently interviewing for positions in the health-care field.

Dear Robert,

My dad has a saying, one that I've heard many times over the years, but much more frequently as I, and my siblings, have begun pursuing our careers: "If you like what you do, you never work a day in your life." My dad is one of the most passionate, work-driven people I know. He loves his job, just about everything about it. He finds passion in working, in creating relationships with co-workers and networking across the country, and even internationally. However, as I've grown up and realized there is more to adulthood than working and paying bills, I've wondered what he does for fun. I still haven't found an answer. I asked him not too long ago what his hobbies included. After a long pause, he simply said "work."

It's easy, I think, to dream of a life where everything is perfect; to have a perfect spouse, a perfect job, and the perfect amount of money for both paying bills and the ability to have hobbies (everything these days seems to have some sort of cost associated with it!). But in reality—is that a reality? I don't know; it almost seems like one of the dreams has to give in order for the others to be greater. For example, instead of each of the three dreams being able to stand on their own value, they all need to add up to one overall dream in order for the perfect life to be a reality. It's either all or nothing.

Having recently graduated with a degree in Nursing, I have decided that I can go anywhere and do almost anything in my field (even more so after I get a few years of experience). This is both incredibly exciting, as well as absolutely terrifying. But my decision was made quite easy. There's this man, and he's wonderful, and he knows, as well as I do, that my place and his place will be wherever we happen to be together. I truly believe that if you aren't happy in your personal life, work will never be good. It will become an escape, certainly, but I don't want to have to escape my life. I want to love it. Whether an escape is work, or alcohol, or any other mind-altering substance, I don't want to have to escape any piece of my life. This, I believe, is where passion falls into the picture. I want to take responsibility for every choice I make—both the good and the bad choices.

Finding something you are passionate about, and putting effort, time, and often money into that passion is a gratifying feeling. Doing all of that AND getting paid for it? This sounds like a great position to be in. Find a person you are passionate about, who you care for more than all others, and who you can't wait to come home to seems like a wonderful way to live! Money, while necessary, is only necessary to an extent. Certainly money is nice to have, and no one I know has ever complained about finding a twenty-dollar bill in the parking lot. But, many people here and throughout the world have lived with much less than the average American is living with. Using money turns into a game of priorities. Following Maslow's hierarchy of needs, the first chunk of each pay check goes towards the rent/mortgage, and then toward food and other sustenance. Spending, or having, obscene amounts of money to throw away on expensive shoes, or jewelry, or "organic" vegetables, while sounding great, is totally unnecessary. I've learned, and decided, to stick to paying for what is important, like food, clothing, and shelter. And, of course, paying off those bills for education, that, thank goodness, I will be using to fulfill my dream of helping others. But everything after that is the frosting on the cupcake— totally unnecessary, and yet, absolutely lovely (even delicious) if it can be acquired.

I've learned over the years what makes me happy, and what frankly makes me miserable and depressed. But I've also learned that no one can change my life for me. In order for something to change, I had to change the variables. For example, I spent one long, miserable year at a college, a year that I've decided truly changed my life. At the end of the most dreadful 12 months of my life, I realized I needed to do something to fix my problem. I had become accustomed to drinking more often than not, napping instead of exercising, skipping classes, and "half-assing" assignments. The moment I left the campus I realized how depressed I actually was, and I told myself I couldn't, and wouldn't, ever do it again. So, I decided to swallow my pride and to drop out of college. It took me two full years to get myself where I needed to be, both physically and emotionally, and damn it was exhausting! But the entire experience made me more focused, driven, disciplined, and passionate, both about myself—giving me a great sense of satisfaction and confidence—and in what I've studied since then. It was exploring that passion at a new school a few years later, that I met the most wonderful man, who I am just as passionate about as beginning my new career. Love and work (and eventually marriage) "go together like a horse and carriage," as the old song says.

It's also been an honor to know you, Robert, since I was such a young girl. At 15, I thought I had all the answers. Now, it is eight years later, and I realize I don't even know the questions I don't know the answers to! But it's been thrilling and inspiring to have you in my life and always teaching me, in small segments, what truly makes up a happy, hearty, and passionate life.

With respect and admiration,
Sara

STRATEGIC TIPS FOR GETTING STUDENTS TO THINK ABOUT MEANINGFUL WORK

As we do with each set of meaning-making questions, we make it a point to start off our units with a series of representative maxims. We ask our students to free-write interpretations of these maxims in their own language. Then we ask them to take some personal risks and compose their own maxims, based on their unique experiences, that may or may not be in agreement with the maxims they are interpreting. What we have found in assigning this exercise is that, when encouraged to come up with their own honest understandings, students are able to think more freely, deeply, and creatively about the key ideas of great thinkers. More importantly, however, they are able to examine, and maybe even resolve, their most vexing meaning-making challenges under the guidance of great minds. In this way, everything our students read and write about is personally relevant, and, therefore, useful. Maxims are an essential tool in the meaning-making quest.

Although we did not ask Sara to respond to the same work/life epigraphs that lead off this chapter, she might very well have responded in the following ways, because this is how other students have reacted to these, and similar, epigraphs in past years.

Sigmund Freud

Whenever our students read Freud on love and work as being the "cornerstones" to our basic humanity, they are not always sure how these two phenomena intersect, if they do at all. So many of them have witnessed the termination of close relationships among their friends and families caused by intense love-versus-work conflicts. Professional work requires long hours, and sustained, focused commitment, especially if fortune and fame are the main measures of career success. If these are the ultimate criteria, then it would seem that there is little time remaining for the cultivation of close personal relationships outside the workplace. Many students see love and work in opposition to one another, because each, in its own way, threatens to diminish, or even undermine, the centrality of the other. Each takes an incredible amount of effort to sustain, and this can be physically and emotionally draining.

Then, there are students like Sara, the letter writer, who see the beneficial connections between love and work, if not immediately then after they have taken time to reflect on what might be causing much, if not all, of the misery and dissatisfaction in their lives. Sara chose to fall in love with someone who offered his unconditional support for all her professional nursing dreams. With this kind of love, Sara is more than ready to venture into a health-care vocation that will fulfill her desires to serve others, no matter what the risks might be. Sara is convinced that her loving relationship *outside* the workplace will make her a better, more compassionate health-care professional *inside* it.

For students like Sara, love is more than an intimate, physical relationship with someone, although this is certainly important. In addition, she knows that love is the gateway to the deepest connections with herself and with others—friends, colleagues, workmates, intimates, and family members. Love helps young people to feel that they belong, that they are respected, that they can be deeply touched by, and touch, others. Sara is learning to develop a healthy, intimate relationship that in the future will transcend the lustful satisfactions included in a few hours of hedonic escape from the dreariness of a sterile work-life. She is creating solid cornerstones in her life because she is making the conscious choice to make a life as well as to make money. She knows that without love in her life, especially the love of close friends, a significant other, and family, she is a lost soul. She has no solid ground to stand on.

Love and work, according to Freud (1930), are the basic cornerstones in making meaning, because they connect us to trusted communities of belonging in all areas of our lives. Love helps us to build a secure identity, decide what is important and what isn't, and opens the way to rich self-discovery and feelings of self-worth. For Freud, love and work make us human, particularly when they feed one another in the never-ending quest all of us are on to make meaning. Love is "deep connection," and the best workplace is one where these connections flourish. The most supportive workplace is the one where care, respect, and generosity are always present, even during the tough times. A sense of deep connection in the workplace is more likely to produce excellent results because it is grounded in trust and loyalty. Deep connection helps workers to solve problems more smoothly together, to take risks and strive for innovation more courageously, and to resolve conflicts more compassionately. This is because workers feel supported, respected, and cared for.

113

One last word on our pedagogy—also inspired, in part, by Freud: We strive in our teaching to create deep connections in our classroom for the same reasons that such relationships are so beneficial in the workplace. Results, almost without exception, are excellent. We believe that genuine learning is more likely to occur in a semester-long, meaning-making seminar whenever our students are willing to be vulnerable; and this can only happen when they, and we, are able to trust one another. To paraphrase Freud: The secret to success in teaching is a combination of building good relationships in the classroom and encouraging a commitment on everyone's part to do exceptional work, both together and separately.

Albert Camus

Our students would agree with Camus (1991) that a life without remunerative employment is not a life they would prefer. Yes, they would say that a life without paid work would be "rotten" in the sense that our bodies would decay and our minds would deteriorate. There would be no resources—either material or intellectual—to sustain them. While quarterlife students are unlikely to use Camus's word "rotten" to describe a life devoid of any type of work activity, they would know immediately what he was getting at. They would say that such a life is for "losers," and it "sucks." They understand very well that work gives life a purpose, if for no other reason than to get up every morning and do something that will bring in the money to pay the bills. They have witnessed first-hand the utter boredom, and sense of uselessness, experienced by out-of-work friends and family members who have lost their jobs for one reason or another. Nevertheless, Camus is getting at something much more complex than this quarterlife take on what a "rotten" life might be.

More tragic for Camus is when work becomes "soulless." When this happens, then life "stifles and dies." We use the term "soulful" throughout this chapter to describe what we think might be the type of work that helps each one of us to create meaning and wholeness in our lives. For us, a "soulful" vocation has little or nothing to do with its more conventional religious connotations, although we are not in the least critical of such meanings. Primarily, we think of "soulful" as that which enhances the universal quest for meaning *both* in religio-spiritual *and* in non-religio-spiritual ways. As for the Ancient Greeks, so too for us, the soul is the unique essence of who and what each of us is and strives to be. Thus, in a more secular sense, a soulful life, and a soulful vocation, are what give our lives depth, essence, meaning, rich emotions, force, substance, hope, ideals, morals, love, heart, art, poetry, beauty, and, yes, spiritual substance. Think of the more worldly references to "soul culture," "soulmate," "soul music," "soul food," or "soul-searching." These terms are closer to the ways that we tend to think about "soul."

Rachael Kessler (2000) has done groundbreaking work on what she calls the "soul of education." For her, teaching to the soul is education's inherent essence or aim, and this essence is all about "helping students find connection, compassion, and character." Kessler's approach to soulful education resonates strongly with us. We want our students always to do soulful writing, soulful reading, and soulful communicating with one another and with us as well. This approach to teaching and learning—an approach that embraces both the heart and the head, the emotions and the mind, of the whole human being—is what we think the meaning-making classroom, campus, and internship site/workplace should be all about. We would make the case that workers in all the professions would be more inventive, productive, and committed if the soul of the workplace were to resemble Kessler's "soul of education."

Sara wants her health-care work to be "soulful." She refuses to settle for a "soulless" daily routine of care-giving. She would agree with Camus that she will not allow her creative juices to be "stifled," nor allow her "spirit" to slowly and painfully "die." The challenge for Sara, and for all other quarterlifers, is this: How can they create "connection, compassion, and character" in a job? Sara learned in her first year of taking courses in college that the career she thought she wanted would not be the career that would help her realize her fondest hopes and dreams. Her classes left her feeling depressed. She turned to alcohol for relief. She went through the motions of studying and taking exams. Her first year of college was truly a soulless experience, so much so that she dropped out and decided not to return to another school for two years. She chose instead to rebuild her self-confidence and her enthusiasm for life. She came to the realization that any future work for her would have to be built on compassionate, caring, and loving relationships with others, particularly with a significant other at the center.

We make it a point to ask our students to reflect on this type of question: If Camus is right when he talks about the need for soulful work, then is the responsibility to create a soulful vocation more on the *organization* you work for or on *you* the worker? Here is another question we ask them: How do you revitalize yourself, both in and out of the classroom, so that your life is more emotionally, intellectually, and spiritually enriched? And, here is yet one more question: Do you believe that some jobs are more intrinsically soulful than others? If you do, would you avoid soulless work, even if this meant earning far less money and fewer, if any, benefits?

Jonathan Haidt

We always assign Haidt's book *The Happiness Hypothesis: Finding Modern Truth in Ancient Wisdom* (2006) in our meaning-making course each semester. Haidt is a philosopher-psychologist who is not only good at explaining difficult concepts—he also knows how to take the ideas of great thinkers throughout the course of history and apply them to the challenges of the twenty-first century. One of these challenges is to find the happiness, and meaning, that often lie "in between" all the

115

activities that seem to dominate every hour of our lives. For Haidt, there is no ultimate or final, objective or universal, answer to what he calls "The Holy Question—What Is the Meaning of Life?" Instead, there is a meaning that exists in the interstices, in the spaces between what we do, think, and feel. Meaning, like happiness, is not always something that we can consciously and purposely seek and find; more often than not, meaning and happiness find us—as byproducts of our being open to all the possibilities and opportunities that come our way.

It is true that we can do our best to set the stage for meaning-making, of course, and this is what Haidt's, and our, books are all about. But there are no money-back, meaning-discovery guarantees. It could very well be, Haidt suggests, that meaning lies in accepting the very uncertainty of making meaning, and then everything that ensues is a wonderful surprise. Now we come to realize that making meaning is a never-ending adventure, more of a process than a product experience. Nevertheless, regardless of the uncertainty, according to Haidt, we are more likely to discover and sustain happiness and meaning in our lives when we have the following resources: love, attachments, autonomy, "vital engagement," and a personal sense of "effectance" (influence).

For Haidt, the work we do in the world is one of the most significant ways for us to make meaning and to be happy, but it all depends on the perspective we take toward our work. As he says in the epigraph, if we do our work primarily for the money and material benefits, then our work is only a "job." If we do our work in order to satisfy our needs for advancement, wealth, promotion, and prestige, then our work becomes a "career." And if we do our work because we feel called to help others, and this is intrinsically fulfilling, then our work evolves into a "vocation." We sometimes get immersed in a "flow-state" of joy, satisfaction, and total contentment, because our work is both intrinsically and extrinsically fulfilling. We can't wait to get back to work on Mondays.

We always ask our students to think of people they know who experience their work as jobs, or careers, or vocations. We then ask these types of questions: Can a job ever become a career or a vocation, depending on your perspective? Was the Roman Stoic and Emperor, Marcus Aurelius, right when he said that "work itself is what you deem it to be"? Can manual laborers find meaning in their work, or is meaning only for the privileged classes who enter the prestigious professions? Is it possible to achieve "flow" in all things that you might do, including your education, personal relationships, and even a part-time, low-paying, chain-restaurant job? How can you create a state of "vital engagement" in everything you do, or is vital engagement primarily dependent on the type of work that you do?

Sara knows that it will be up to her to create the quality she needs in her routine health-care work. She will settle for nothing less. She understands well the need she has for vital engagement in her vocation, and this will come about only if she is convinced that she is contributing to the greater good. She wants a work setting where she can make deep connections to her superiors, colleagues, and patients in order to be genuinely happy. Even though she is still sending out applications and undergoing interviews in order to find the right health-care position, she knows what she needs in order to be fully engaged, connected, and committed. She is pursuing a vocation, and she will not stop until she finds what she needs at this time in her life.

A Personal Reflection from a Practitioner on How to Prepare for Soul-Satisfying Work

Pamela K. Gardner, Director, Career Center
The University of Vermont, Burlington, Vermont

"Soul-Satisfying Work"

Discovering what to do, where to do it, with whom, and for what purpose is a process informed by many factors, internal and external. Some of the wisest people I know— young or old—spend their lives in a process of discovery, asking those questions. Many college students and recent graduates express a desire to build a meaningful life, where their personalities, values and interests align in soul-satisfying work. Unfortunately, many feel as if they are swimming against a tide. Pressured by finances, peers, media, family, and others, some new college students commit to high-demand fields before understanding what the work entails. Others refuse to commit at all because they worry about being trapped in soulless work. Happily, making a successful transition from college to work does not have to be either a giant leap of faith or a guaranteed success plan. It does demand active participation, time, and attention, and for most, some mentoring.

Discovering What Matters

Before seeking intrinsically rewarding work, students must have a basic understanding of who they are and what is meaningful to them. They need to have been challenged and to have stretched themselves inside and outside of the classroom. They need to be encouraged to draw meaning from their experiences and studies. Research in the 2014 Gallup–Purdue study of 30,000 college graduates shows that "support and experiences in college had more of a relationship" to personal and career fulfillment than a college major, type of institution, or selectivity. "Support and experiences" included meaningful engagement with faculty, long-term projects, internships, extracurricular activities and organizational leadership. It included having mentors and faculty who challenged them and cared about them as individuals, being able to discuss their hopes and dreams, becoming deeply involved, and making connections. Graduates with these experiences were much happier with work, family, and all aspects of their well-being.

117

It's relatively simple. In higher education we must encourage deep engagement in learning, in and out of class. This idea is not new. In 1938, John Dewey, educator and philosopher, advocated for education which, rather than imparting facts, enlisted the learner in experiences, connecting current moments with past and future experiences, and to the goals and needs of the learner. Engaging students in finding meaning in what they are learning is an essential part of learning and career development.

Student Stories: Alejandro and Joan

"Alejandro" (a pseudonym) declared an engineering major because he felt it would guarantee him a well-paid job. After struggling through introductory courses, he transferred to environmental science. Bright, engaging, and talented, he held leadership roles in a Latino/a student group, a performing arts group, the debate club, a themed residence hall, and was active on issues of social justice.

When Alejandro arrived in my office, I asked about his major, his activities, his experiences and his needs. Alejandro's animated conversation about his major and activities then became relatively flat as he discussed what he wanted: help getting into law school. Despite my probing, Alejandro shared little about why he was interested in law or what he might accomplish with that degree. Eventually, he revealed that engineering, medicine, and law were respected professions in his culture, and only law remained open to him. He was not interested in reconsidering his decision.

As we prepared application essay topics, Alejandro happily shared that he had created an independent study project where he had researched environmental racism and designed a course. He spent a year petitioning the Faculty Senate and receiving permission to offer and teach that course. He added that his advisor believed Alejandro was the first undergraduate at our institution to teach a credited course.

Looking for a connection, I asked how this project related to his career goal. I expected to hear that he wanted to use law to fight placing landfills near communities of color, or to mobilize communities to demand environmental clean-ups. He made no convincing connections between this experience and law school. What's a counselor to do? He'd rebuffed my challenges. We continued to work through identifying schools. In the end, it was a question about finances that brought Alejandro to reconsider. One look at his projected undergraduate loan payments and projected new loans, and Alejandro abandoned the idea of law school.

Now he was ready to talk. I gave him homework: When in your life have you been the most ablaze? What are those moments where you have felt you have done something really great? Reflect on those. What do they tell you about what matters to you? What do they show about your aptitudes, abilities, interests and life's purpose? What do they show about how you want to engage in the world?

Two weeks later, Alejandro presented me with a résumé and cover letter tailored to teaching jobs. The words flowed; his stories were compelling. Before graduation, he accepted a job teaching in an urban, underperforming high school. In addition to providing salary and mentoring, this program funded his advanced coursework in education. Alejandro excelled as a student and as a deeply committed educator. He started his school's first debate club and, though some of the students could barely read, in their first year they won a citywide tournament. When I spoke to Alejandro last, he was pursuing his doctorate and applying for a principal's job. He was blissful about having found his true calling—soul-satisfying work that was deeply aligned with his core.

Unlike Alejandro, "Joan" (a pseudonym) arrived in the career center torn about what she should do with her life. As we talked, she shared that she had several internships and campus involvements, as well as a paid summer job. Most of her activities focused on business strategy and project management. Joan reported that she felt deeply connected to improving workflow and facilitating communication, but she was conflicted. All around her she saw peers who were struggling financially and who desperately needed well-paid jobs to make loan payments. She felt some wanted the same jobs she did, but she believed others deserved it more than she did. Eventually she revealed that she had significant financial privilege. Because of a trust fund, she could live her life comfortably without ever working.

Should she vow to volunteer? Wouldn't that be the responsible decision? We talked about work, and the role of work in the lives of people. Her interest and skill with business processes were unusually well-developed for a college student, and she had believed she was meant to contribute these gifts to the world in this way, until the recession. As we talked she came to realize that by being good at what she did she might actually create jobs. In fact, her eventual desire had been to build her own business. She shared that both her father and older brother had done the same, and had businesses that employed thousands and hundreds, respectively. As she slowly freed herself of the fear of taking someone else's job, she began to consider the type of business environment she wanted and how she might create a purposeful organization that operated in ways that empowered and rewarded employees. Joan eventually went to work for her brother to learn more about managing a successful business until she was ready to start her own. Once she connected her love of business and her desire make the world a better place, she was off and running.

To find soul-fulfilling work, one must both understand what they bring to the world and find a way or place to apply and extend those talents and interests. Both must be done in the context of the world as it is, with an eye to the world as it might be. Understanding without action is empty, as is action without understanding.

A SUMMARY OF CONVERSATIONAL STRATEGIES WRITTEN BY PAMELA GARDNER TO HELP STUDENTS PREPARE FOR MEANINGFUL VOCATIONS

As a career counselor, I use these experiences when helping students explore options. Though the term "vocation" rarely comes up, students talk about finding rewarding and fulfilling work that allows them to align their core values, talents, and skills to contribute to their personal, familial and societal well-being.

What does that exploration entail? Whether discovered through writing or in conversation, there are a number of questions we might explore:

- What career ideas have you considered? What about them is appealing or off-putting?
- What do you hope for from your work life (e.g., happiness, connection, wealth, meaning, etc.)?
- Do you have deeply-held beliefs or principles that guide or affect the kind of work you do, where, or how you do it? How do they affect your choices now and in the future?
- When have you been happily and deeply engaged in a project, task or activity? Name seven to ten times. What were you doing? What skills were you using? What do these stories say about your deepest priorities? What theme(s) emerge?
- What interests you (e.g., what types of articles or books you read, how you spend your free time, what topics you are most likely to debate or argue, etc.)?
- If you had to describe one main result you want your life to accomplish, what would it be?
- Who are the people in your life that support you? What do they offer you? Are there others with whom you can strengthen relationships?
- What gets in the way of your deciding or pursuing meaningful work?
- How do you make your best decisions? If you aren't sure, ask yourself about past decisions. Which ones were made using a helpful process and which ones weren't? What does this tell you about how best to proceed?

Sometimes the first question gets a student rolling; sometimes it takes several. The goal is to help the student to move as far as possible on their journey of finding challenging, rewarding and meaningful work, *however they define it*. For those who aren't yet ready to have the conversation, our focus may become helping them just to find a good starter job. For students who are ready, our focus may be helping them to explore, and discover, a *deeply purposeful and soulful vocation* . . . in the full sense of what Robert and Jennifer have written about in this chapter.

Chapter 9

How Can I Answer the "Call of Service" to Make the World a Better Place?

I do not know what your destiny will be, but one thing I do know; the only ones among you who will be really happy are those who have sought, and found how, to serve others.

Albert Schweitzer

What we think or what we know or what we believe is, in the end, of little consequence. The only consequence is what we do.

John Ruskin

It doesn't interest me to know where you live or how much money you have. I want to know if you can get up after a night of grief and despair, weary and bruised to the bone, and do what needs to be done to feed the children.

Oriah Mountain Dreamer (2003)

Young people ask, often in subtle ways: Do I have a meaningful place in the social and political world? Are there values that I can make a commitment to and people I can stand with? Am I capable of contributing something useful to others that they will welcome and appreciate?

Sheldon Berman

The terms currently in vogue in higher education for the service quest that we will be examining in this chapter are "civic responsibility" and "civic engagement." Being "civic-minded," and "civically engaged," derive from the word, "citizen," referring to someone who is "public-spirited"; someone who tries to be actively and politically involved in the community in some way. Being civically engaged and responsible—being a public-spirited citizen—is a wonderful way for many young people to make meaning on their own campuses, as well as in their back-home communities.

We have had several students who served the university as student government officers, club and association presidents and vice-presidents, and elected leaders in a variety of organizations such as Greek Life, the Student Senate, and campus social justice groups. And some of our student graduates have even gone on to win elective political offices in their home communities, serving as state representatives, statehouse delegates, members of local school boards, and officers in a variety of other political organizations.

However, for us, we prefer another phrase. This phrase certainly includes civic responsibility and engagement, but it also embraces, and represents, something much more—what Robert Coles describes as "the call of service." This call can be as deep and as committed as a *vocation*, in the way we describe the term in Chapter 8. For many quarterlifers, the call of service is the heart and soul of what it means to undertake an education in the most holistic sense. We both have been greatly inspired by Robert Coles who, in 1993 wrote what we believe is still the classic work (*The Call of Service: A Witness to Idealism*) on getting students away from campus, and outside of themselves, to serve their fellow human beings.

Simply stated, for Coles, "service" represents the most "human side of our nature." Service is "altruism and idealism" combined. Service is compassion. For some of our students, the call is so powerful, welling up from the innermost recesses of their souls and core identities, that it almost takes on the power of a religious duty. For others, service is a "comradeship." Coles goes so far as to say this: the call of service is all about "putting oneself in the shoes of others, absorbing their needs, their vulnerability, their weakness, and their suffering, *and then setting to work*." For Coles, service is not only *what* we do, but also *who* we are. Service to others defines us, not just to others but to ourselves as well. The way we will be using the word "service" throughout this chapter is true to its Latin root—*servire*—to serve others in a caring, non-exploitative, non-self-interested way.

When we use the term "service," we make five assumptions that are in keeping with Coles's pioneering, deep-meaning take on the word:

1. Each of us has a sense of responsibility to help others outside ourselves in a way that enriches their lives and, by implication, ours as well.
2. Each of us has the ability to venture out into the world outside our small, provincial bubbles; and, when encouraged, we can even see ourselves as global citizens, or what we call "cosmopolites".
3. Each of us wants to know deep-down that we can contribute actively and effectively to the greater good, especially when obvious wrongs call out to be righted, and unnecessary suffering calls out to be alleviated.

4. Each of us has a basic social need to know that our individual actions will truly make a difference in the lives of our fellow human beings, no matter how small, or "tall," the difference might be.

5. We are hardwired as social creatures with a need to know that at least one other human being, other than ourselves, will benefit from our presence in their lives.

WHY IS THE CALL OF SERVICE IMPORTANT FOR COLLEGE STUDENTS?

We believe that the call of service is a core quest for college students, because they are at a time in their lives when they are deciding what and who they want to be—trying to learn specialized sets of career skills to prepare for their future, and building their interpersonal networks for a lifetime of flourishing. This is a time when they are wondering how they might fit into the larger world. We need to help them connect both locally and globally. We need to help them to get outside of themselves in order to understand on a deeper level what is on their inside— who they are and who they want to be. Sheldon Berman, one of our chapter's opening epigraphists, sharply captures this core quest for quarterlifers: "Am I capable of contributing something useful to others that they will welcome and appreciate?"

Marcel Proust puts it this way: "the real voyage of discovery is not in seeking new places, but in seeing with new eyes." We all have our own particular style of processing external experience. Some of us are thinkers, storytellers, actors, crafters, healers, or musicians. Getting engaged in one's community is among the many avenues to interpret and communicate thoughts, ideas, and emotions. While the types of involvement with others are varied, all types illustrate the need for human connection. We need to learn how to see our world with "new eyes." We need to understand the human need each of us has to give, receive, and connect. The call of service meets the evolutionary drive all of us have for solidarity, inclusion, and validation. This is the way we humans adapt to our environments that are always changing, always evolving. But what never changes is the universal need for communal belonging. Thus, the call to service in all of our communities confers survival benefits on persons and cultures.

John Ruskin, another of our epigraphists in this chapter, reminds us that "what we think or what we know or what we believe is, in the end, of little consequence. The only consequence is what we do." The call to service gets our students actively and humanely doing something in their larger communities. It gets them out of themselves to socialize, to make meaning in the company of others, and to connect with people around common causes and activities. Being actively involved in a number of internal and external communities motivates students to get out and about . . . doing, interacting, engaging, and living life proactively. Living an action-oriented life reinforces our central theme in Chapter 3: we need to discover a variety of ways to realize our hopes and dreams, and one of these ways is through active engagement with a cause or a community. This enhances the probability of our students finding, and doing, what they love! Our students will need to be willing to try, to do, to risk, to fail, to learn, and to try again, if they are to discover their true vocations. We believe that the call to service is how and where our students get to witness the strength of both individual *and* collective human power.

The beauty of the call to service is that there is a universalizable piece that connects to the human core of each and every one of us. Despite our students' individual heritages, current statuses, or lifestyles, there are fundamental drives, values, and emotions that bind all of us together. For example, Jennifer now identifies as a cosmopolite. She has faced a number of seemingly overwhelming challenges in trying to adapt to a different culture. Her experiences, including both her wonderful successes and painful failures, overlap in some way with all the rest of us, even though most of us have not had to learn a new language, and a new culture, on the fly in order to survive.

Other examples: Foster youths may share Jennifer's ongoing sense of insecurity and a lack of belonging. Youth who identify as LGBTQ (lesbian, gay, bi-sexual, trans-sexual, and "queer") may feel like they are "strange" because their sexual orientations are different. Similarly, bi/multi-racial individuals who drift and are never feel able to find that solid cultural identity and foundation might feel, as does Jennifer, that, as we pointed out earlier, they are "neither here nor there." Some of our students, who straddle a number of socio-economic classes, often experience guilt wondering whether they will have to renounce their lower, working-class backgrounds, and the people in them, in order to fulfill their future ambitions to achieve an upper middle-class professional status. So, too, there are transfer students in our university who feel alienated from their non-transfer peers. There are growing groups of immigrants in our classes, from a number of international countries, who feel totally cut off from their families and their cultural heritages. And there are individuals with disabilities, as well as those who come from a variety of underrepresented racial populations within the United States, who are alienated, estranged, and lonely.

To give, to share, to love, and to receive in our core relationships is to foster belonging, as we discussed in Chapter 6. Inhabiting common spaces together by reaching out to others creates bonds that can be lasting. Shared moments of service to one another hold the promise of producing mutual vulnerability and mutual trust. This, in turn, leads to a sense of belonging. Our students need an opportunity to see their role as larger, and more significant, than achieving a "like" status on Facebook. This type of "status" does not change the *status quo*. Getting actively involved in service to local, regional, and global communities does.

ASKING THE KEY "CALL OF SERVICE" MEANING-MAKING QUESTIONS

Here are the questions that come up time and time again during our unit on the reciprocal benefits (and risks) of providing service to others. It is important to note that our students are not naïve, starry-eyed idealists when it comes to engaging in conversation regarding any of our meaning-making units, but they are especially candid, outspoken realists during this particular unit. Service obviously has a huge upside, and our students describe their service inspirations and satisfactions in wonderful superlatives. But service to others also has a downside. Its hazards can be overwhelming, if pushed to an extreme. We have heard many stories of service burnout, weariness and resignation, doubt, cynicism, anger, bitterness, and, for us, the worst—despair. These are all the "hazards" that Robert Coles writes about so empathically and insightfully in his book. He pulls no punches. Neither do most of our students, as some of the following questions will illustrate:

- Why do I feel such an intense inner need to be more involved with helping others at this time in my quarterlife, especially when so many of my friends seem content just to have fun and "chill out"?
- Just what is it that I, a college student, can offer those who need help?
- In what ways will "the call to service" help me to make meaning in my life?
- Why do I feel so spiritually "nourished" whenever I am helping others?
- But why is it that, no matter how gratified I might feel in serving others, I always go through a very exhausting, burnout stage? (How can I avoid this in the future?)
- What is it I can do in order to share my goodwill and practical skills with people not just in my neighborhood, state, or country, but internationally as well?
- Do I have a moral responsibility to help others who may not be as fortunate as I am?
- Why is it that my inner "ego-maniac" disappears when I'm thoroughly immersed in helping disadvantaged others to learn how to take care of themselves and to grow on their own terms?
- Why is it that my "best self" comes out when I'm so deeply involved in all my volunteer work and service . . . *outside* the classroom? (Sadly, why do my more formal academic experiences tend to bring out my "worst self"?)
- Why do I resent being guilted by some colleagues, friends, and community service leaders at my college to be more actively, even mandatorily,

involved in the community beyond my campus? (Is it possible to force altruism on others?)

- If I am a full-time student but, also, someone who must work during my free time in order to pay the bills, how can I realistically find the time to serve others, even when I feel called to do so?
- Why is it I meet so few people who are content to do community service for its own sake but, instead, always seem to have a particular political agenda to push?
- What is it that I can do to help others when I'm having great difficulty helping either myself or my own family?
- How can I avoid résumé-building as my primary motivation to do community service?
- How can I be sure that my motivation for social engagement, volunteer work, community service, and social justice advocacy isn't a self-imposed "penance" that I'm paying for being a member of the "privileged class"?

A STUDENT REFLECTION ON GETTING INVOLVED IN SERVICE TO OTHERS

In this section, we present a reflection by a student of ours who, during her time with us, asked all of the above questions, and then some. During her undergraduate and graduate years, Juliana felt the strong call of service. She wanted to create a life-narrative that exemplified her passion for helping others. She had her personal doubts about being able to effect change in the larger society, but she was willing to work hard to overcome the obstacles that stood in the way of realizing her dreams. She knew that worldly success was far more than mindlessly accumulating "things," and making, and banking, a lot of money. She understood the truth in Oriah Mountain Dreamer's epigraph:. "I want to know if you can get up after a night of grief and despair, weary and bruised to the bone, and do what needs to be done to feed the children." She was able to craft a life of meaning during her college years by "getting up . . . and feeding the children." What follows is a personal reflection by Juliana Marton, a birth doula and certified professional midwife.

At 19, my friends thought I was crazy for loving childbirth and loving women. I was not crazy: for the first time in my life I felt passionate about some-thing. I steep in birth. Birth makes me feel alive and wild. I felt called by my pack, and I began exploring birth with ferocity. After years of intense reflection and months of study, observation, and inquiry, I decided to become a certified birth doula as my point of entry into midwifery. At this time, I had never supported a woman through pregnancy, birth, and the postpartum. My liberal arts degree program did not offer any opportunities to experientially learn from women, birth, and babies, so I had to create my own path.

A birth doula offers unbiased (to the best of one's ability) and nonjudgmental informational, emotional, and physical support to women during pregnancy, birth, and the postpartum. A doula views birth and women's health through the midwifery model of care: women, women's bodies, and birth are normal and healthy physio-spiritual processes that are natural. Doulas, like midwives, preserve the integrity of birth. A doula's scope of practice is much smaller compared to a midwife or obstetrician. Doulas cannot make health care assessments or provide physical examinations. Despite these limitations, evidence-based research shows the immense presence and benefit doulas offer women, particularly hospital bound women. The continuous support of a doula improves all outcomes for mother and baby, significantly by reducing pharmacological and technological interventions.

I intentionally took time to complete my certification. I knew I needed to act from a center of authentic self-confidence and trust from within. It was always there, but I had to continuously live from it. I attended the 20 hour training, read all the required texts and books, and observed several childbirth and breastfeeding education classes. During the month leading up to the training, as well as the month following, I was immobilized by negative streams of consciousness that corroded my confidence, filling the spaces with doubts, fears, and distrust. "Who will trust me to support them through this great transformation, when I am so young, when I have never been pregnant or given birth, when I have only studied for half a year, when I have never been with woman during childbirth . . ."

I began searching for someone in my Burlington community, and it did not take long. Leah, a fourth year undergraduate student, was a doula without the physical experience of childbirth. We had tea several times together, and shared our love of birth. Listening to her experience refilled me with confidence to put my self in the community as a practicing birth doula. Leah also worked at one of our community shelters and knew of a woman desiring doula support for the birth of her third child. I gladly consented for Leah to provide my contact information to this woman, and she became my first client. Through supporting her birth, the universe opened to me. It is vast, mysterious, and wild, yet filling. I knew there was nothing more beautiful that I wanted to do with my life. I finished my doula training in the fall of 2008. The recommended approach to offering services to pregnant women in our community is to volunteer. I would not have felt comfortable exchanging my services for credentialing and educating purposes any other way. Volunteering doula services is a fast and easy way to generate a substantial number of inquiries. When I volunteered, I made intentional effort to offer my services to women with underserved needs. This

127

included young women, incarcerated women, recovering addicts, homeless women, and survivors of sexual/domestic abuse.

As I practiced, I developed a philosophy of care that aligns with the person-centered therapy, created and articulated by psychologist Dr. Carl Rogers (1995). Person-centered therapy is an approach to care that rests upon the art of being with another person in full, authentic presence. This form of communication, egalitarian relationship, and connection, is the core of person-centered therapy. I believe that we all have the vast potential for understanding ourselves and resolving our own problems without direct intervention, and we are capable of self-empowered growth if we are involved in a special kind of supportive relationship. Thus, clients are responsible for their reactions and actions. This relationship exists in the present—the here and now—and the professional/therapist strives to be with the client in their subjective experiences. I have learned that I can be an effective support and care provider through presence, active listening, nondirective communication, mirroring, and empathy.

When I came to the realization that I did not need specialized knowledge to know how to be with another person, I filled with light and confidence. My client encounters became fluid, relaxed, deep, and authentic. This allowed my intuition to hone to the unique needs and particularities of each client, which could not have happened if these relationships were not created in full-bodied presence. Although we will all personalize our approach to care, the conscious practice of being with another, whether it is a client, partner, friend, family member, etc., is a universalizable experience of relationalism—inarguably its foundation.

STRATEGIC TIPS FOR ENCOURAGING STUDENTS TO ANSWER THE CALL OF SERVICE

> The greatest revolution of our generation is the discovery that human beings, by changing the inner attitudes of their minds, can change the outer aspects of their lives.
>
> William James

Here are *five tips* that we offer our students when they are starting to think about responding to their own unique calls of service. These tips are built on countless conversations we have had with quarterlife students through the years. These tips also emerge from many, many inspiring meetings we have had with service providers on campuses and leaders of community service centers throughout the country. Also, we have been inspired by two national reports on the topic of civic responsibility—one published by the Association of American Colleges and Universities (2009), and the other written by Doris R. Brodeur (2012) that is philosophically grounded in Robert's earlier book on meaning-making, *Helping College Students Find Purpose* (Nash and Murray, 2010).

So, as you read the following, please remember that what we are saying directly to students about service in the form of a "catchy"—maybe, you might think, even an overly simplistic—tip evolves from years of dealing with students like Juliana. It also comes from working with students who are not as far along as they are in recognizing the enormous value that serving others has for making meaning throughout a person's lifetime. Regardless, all of our students are appreciative that sometimes we can give them the advice they seek in a streamlined, motivational way. Here is what we say to them:

1. Start With *You*!

It might sound ironic to start with yourself in thinking about changing the world. But you are the most important asset you'll ever own. As William James said in the above quotation: changing your thoughts and attitude can have a tremendous impact on your life, and consequently, other people's lives. If shame and guilt are your reaction when you think about getting involved in your community, then face your shame and confront your guilt. Why be ashamed of your lack of experience and your youth? Why feel guilt that you haven't experienced the call of service yet? Pull your ostrich head out of the sand. Come out of avoidance and denial. Wayne Dyer says: "Change the way you see the world, and the world you see will change." You will discover that it is not that hard after all. You change the world by seizing opportunities in front of you.

Think of the number of opportunities you have to live up to your full service potential. Take advantage of all aspects of the education available to you to fulfill your purpose to help others, hone your talents and strengths, and give back to the world. If you need more in your education than sitting in a classroom listening to lectures, or hanging out in a residence hall eating and sleeping, or spending hours every day in a library or in a coffee shop writing papers, then ask for what you need, seek it out, and find it.

Supplement your usual campus activities with opportunities to grow in a number of alternative ways. A college campus offers multiple opportunities to provide service to others. Get to know the student affairs staff. Get off campus, and do some volunteer service. Engage in conversations with staff and faculty whom you admire for the work they do in their communities that go above and beyond their paychecks and official titles. Choose elective courses that build in service-learning opportunities. Look for community-based work projects that offer either paid or unpaid employment. Remember, it is *you* who must take the initiative in your own learning. Juliana is someone who took full initiative in her own service-learning from her earliest years in college continuing right through graduate school.

2. Learn About How the *Real World* Works!

Think of the real world as if it were like that first living space you inhabited when you went to college. When you shared a living space for the first time with one or more roommates, it might have turned out to be a disaster, because no one took responsibility for any public areas—the kitchen, the living room, the dining room, the floors, or the bathroom. Dishes piled up, dirty laundry littered the floor, toilets backed up, and after-party messes lasted for days. This is also the way the real world works. We share it with one another, and we're all responsible for doing our part to make it livable. If we go our own way, ignoring the needs of others, then everyone loses. Our mess becomes their mess and *vice versa*. We need each another's help every single day in order to thrive and prosper.

How can you learn more about the difficult life-issues that others are dealing with in both your micro- and macro-communities? How can you help others to address some of these issues now? How can you work on cleaning up your own "mess"? What is it you can do to learn more about what is going on in the various communities of need that surround you and constitute your world? How can you become more globally minded without losing your focus on your most immediate communities. Take advantage of Google, Hulu, online documentaries, Netflix, network news feeds, etc., . . . to become world-wise. Identify those local, national, and international issues and problems that capture your immediate attention. Learn more about them. What are some ways that you might get involved in serving the underserved, in advancing human rights, in mentoring those people who might benefit from your wisdom and expertise (you have both, you know)? Check out resources such as *Break Away—the Alternative Break Connection,* for information on how to bring about real-world change during your mid-year and summer breaks.

3. *Just Start* Somewhere, Somehow. Begin it Now!

> Everyone who got to where they are
> had to begin where they were.
>
> Richard Paul Evans

Once you have educated yourself about the real world and the problems and suffering around you, choose a cause and begin! Juliana found her cause—helping others in the primordial act of giving birth—and, as a result, she found a vocation she can give her life to. It may seem overwhelming to narrow the field and focus on just one injustice or one group's survival need, but just get started on doing something. Delay and denial exacerbate problems, and keep us from activating our better selves. Don't feel like you have to come up with miraculous solutions to the world's problems! Edward Hale reminds us that each of us is only one human being, but we can still do something, even if we can't do everything. The goal, according to Hale, is "not to refuse to do the something that you can do." Begin somewhere from a strength that you have. Get connected with a group of service allies.

Start acting on behalf of something you are drawn to already. Are you a pet lover? Start researching topics regarding your pet. Do you enjoy running outside on the trails? Start thinking about greenery, ecosystems, sustainability, protecting the environment . . . etc. Have you wanted to go to SeaWorld? Then start by looking into how they clear lands, acquire their cetaceans, and how they train their whales and dolphins. Volunteer your services. Maybe you've heard that 20 million people worldwide are being trafficked, and you feel disgusted? What can you do for a start to change things, instead of just giving up in disgust and resignation, and retreating into your own little ego-dominated world.

Whether you donate money, time, or just help by spreading awareness, do something, and do it now. Remember what the world-famous anthropologist, Margaret Mead, once said: "Never doubt that a small group of thoughtful, committed citizens can change the world. Indeed, it is the only thing that ever has." But every small group begins with a single individual to inspire and organize it. Don't begin by asserting that you have a responsibility to change the whole world. This is a sure recipe for never getting started. Instead, say that you are going to change one aspect of your life that will free up time to offer your services to someone, or some group, in need. Lao Tzu said: "A journey of a thousand miles starts with one single step." He thought that if each of us would choose to do just one thing on behalf of our neighbor, then thousands of our small actions would add up to make a major difference. This is the ripple effect that describes one theory of change. No cause is too small. Every step you take will get the rest of us closer to arriving at a more compassionate humanity.

4. Share and Care. *Don't* Glare and Dare!

We know one thing for sure about service: you cannot guilt others to do good. Glaring at, and daring, students to act on what we might think is their moral obligation to leave their comfortable nests of privilege to volunteer their services to the "downtrodden" will always backfire. One of the hazards of doing social justice work that Robert (Nash and Bradley, 2011) has written a great deal about is that so many well-meaning advocates turn into "madvocates" and "radvocates." They become self-righteous, arrogant, and True Believers of the most dogmatic kind. Some of this reversion to our own worst natures is understandable, of course, because we can grow angry at the injustice in the world. We can become bitter, because there appears to be so little improvement on a grand scale in the lives of the poor, the impoverished, and the exploited. We can become angry over what might seem to be the epitome of selfishness and hedonism on the part of so many quarterlifers, politicians, and business executives who seemingly care little about the situation of others much less privileged than they.

Once we faculty and staff get into a cause, it often preoccupies our minds. We have this understandable urge to share our passion to do good with everybody within our circle of influence, including, most of all, our students. There is great injustice and suffering in the world, and we want people to know it! But some students may not be ready to hear our "service-to-others gospel" at this time in their lives. Many are dealing with their own personal crises and issues. We have found that meeting students on a more personal level by sharing our stories of service success *and* failure with them is a good place to start. Personal stories humanize us, especially if we acknowledge our own guilt, shame, and motivations for wanting to do more for people who have less. In so many ways, our students are reliving our own doubts and fears about what we might have had to offer others that would make a real difference.

Robert remembers a student complaining in class that he was no longer involved in voluntary community service one day a week because his supervisor made him feel that he could do "nothing right" in working with ghetto children to help them become better readers. She once screamed at him: "You need to spend more time with these kids, because it's people like you with your upper-middle-class entitlements who have kept them down!" In our opinion, instead of shaming others, we need to show that we care by sharing our own human vulnerability. A genuine call of service is not acting out of guilt, shame, or obligation; instead, for service to work well, we must recognize it as a natural human urge to care for others when they most need us.

5. *Glow* in Your Own Light!

We sometimes say to our students: Let your passion and conviction shine through your joy and demeanor. Juliana is a role-model for midwifery in every way, but especially in her ability to "show her glow" throughout the total cycle of the birthing process—from start to finish. We, too, as instructors and advisors try to "show our own glow" through our gratitude at being able to help others in some way, by including all those students who appear before us everyday in our classes, offices, and in other campus locations. We never miss the opportunity both before and after a class to thank our students for showing up, taking an active part in discussions and assignments, and then leaving us, and themselves, richer for the experience each and every time that we are together. So many students have told us that few if any professors and administrators have ever thanked them for anything. In fact, as one student said, some professors "can't wait to beat us out the door" when class ends. Obviously, this is not the best way to "glow" while serving our students.

While we get paid well to provide service to our students in our official capacities as college faculty and administrators, we always let them know that it can be pure pleasure (not pure torture) working with them. On some days, Robert has even said that he would do what he does for free (please don't tell this to his faculty union). When our teaching goes well (and we have our challenges like everyone else), we are able to find that unbeatable mix of friendship, instruction, guidance, mentoring, inspiration, and assorted other mutual benefits in our relationships with students. We let them know that they, too, will have those miraculous moments (not always, of course) when they achieve this "unbeatable mix" in their service to others.

We make it a point at the end of the semester to read the following words of Dorothy Day (1952), founder of the Catholic Worker in the 1930s. Few, if any, students, have ever heard her name before we introduce it. Day considered the call of service:

> a call toward others—heart, mind, and soul—but also a call inward, a call to oneself, a call that is a reminder: Watchmen, what of the night? The darkness that defines the moment of light in us, the darkness that challenges us to shine for one another before, soon enough, we join it.

A Personal Reflection from a Practitioner on Answering the "Call of Service"

Kyle Dodson, Director of Community Service and Civic Engagement
Champlain College, Burlington, Vermont

Am I My Brother's Keeper?

Several years ago I attended the Saint Michael's College (SMC) Commencement exercises where the keynote speaker was Arne Duncan, U.S. Secretary of Education. Arne and I attended the same college, Harvard University, and we played on the same basketball team. He was two years ahead of me and once he graduated we did not stay in contact. Arne was swarmed that day at SMC by all sorts of folks who wanted to meet him and pick his brain. It didn't help that Senator Patrick Leahy (an SMC alumnus) was also at the commencement and his whole entourage was also there. I ended up following Arne into the men's room so that I could have a moment to reconnect with him. He was incredibly gracious and was still the down-to-earth guy I remembered from our college basketball days.

For several years prior to crossing paths with Arne, I was a Principal of a quasi-charter elementary public school in one of Boston's most challenged neighborhoods. We had an incredibly ambitious agenda for how we were going to provide a radically different education for the children at our school. I was keenly interested in various educational reform issues playing out across the nation, and I was a voracious consumer of articles, essays, white papers, anything I could get my hands on that dealt with urban education. One day in one or another of the dozens of media outlets that cover education, I came across an announcement that the Chicago public schools had created a new leadership role named the President of Schools (as opposed to the more common Superintendent) and that the person was none other than Arne Duncan. I was excited and awed. Here was this guy who I knew only in the context of jumpshots and help-side defense and he was just appointed to the highest leadership position in urban public education in the nation.

As I dug into my memory to make sense of how a guy who in college had seemed so unassuming and unspectacular rose to such a position, some relevant pieces of his story that helped to connect things came back to me. I knew that Arne was from Chicago and from the way he played basketball and spoke, it was clear that he had spent some significant time around Black folks like me. I remembered that his dad was a college professor in Chicago, and Arne's sister Sara came to Harvard as well. I learned from his SMC commencement address that his mother ran a tutoring program in one of Chicago's notorious housing projects and Arne came of age in those classrooms. All of a sudden things made a little more sense to me. Arne's father was a respected professor at University of Chicago and a connected social activist. His mother was also an educational activist. Arne and his whole family were very familiar with what was happening in the schools and households of Chicago's most challenged neighborhoods. In some ways he was perfectly suited to the job.

As I listened to Arne's commencement address I reflected on my own time as a school leader in a challenged urban community and thought about my decision to leave that work. I have a great deal of ambivalence about resigning as a Principal and moving out of Boston and back to Vermont. Although my five years as Principal presented me with some of the most difficult experiences of my life both personally and professionally, it also was the most exciting and rewarding time of my life. Public education, particularly in urban communities, is one of the most pressing issues of our time. My time as a Principal helped me to develop a personal mission that is about "mobilizing communities of caring people into changing their behavior so that we can have a different world" (Parks, 1997).

I am personally torn between my desire to be on the front lines of national education reform, working in a leadership role in an urban school or district versus my desire to be a present and involved husband and father. The challenges that most urban schools face require an amount of effort and time that is incompatible with the time that I want to be able to dedicate to being with my family. Yet, when I look at Arne Duncan and the work he is doing I wonder if I am "copping out" by living a comfortable, "artificial bubble" existence up here in Vermont?

I didn't want to spend too much time in this essay detailing my own individual journey, but it struck me that the personal aspect of this reflection piece would benefit greatly from an exploration of the things that influence my sense of civic responsibility that I try to share with my students.

The Crucible Within Which I was Formed

The earliest influences on my sense of civic duty and the call to service were my parents. Joyce and Charles Dodson were not activists. They didn't take us to volunteer at the soup kitchen every week. And they weren't Peace Corps Alums. In fact, Joyce and Charles weren't college graduates, and they grew up in circumstances that landed them more squarely in a demographic group that is more likely to be the recipients of humanitarian service, rather than the providers. But my parents were decent people with strong convictions, among which is the idea that human existence is inherently reciprocal. Basically, they believed you give when you have and you get when you need.

Beyond my parents, the most powerful influence on my sense of personal civic responsibility was a high school mentor named Artie Williams. Artie was about 30 years old and a Vietnam Vet who had a very bad military experience. I am not sure of the specifics, but part of the outcome of his time in the Army was an injury that left him disabled and receiving government payments. Since Artie had a small income and injuries that made it difficult for him to work, he had lots of time on his hands. What he did with that time was hang around with my group of high school guys who loved basketball. During after-school hours and in the summer we went to the local playground almost every day and usually Artie was there as well. He would rebound for us so we could shoot hundreds of jump shots, occasionally he would serve as the extra man if we were short a guy, and always he would lend a sympathetic ear and offer little nuggets of wisdom about life.

Artie's greatest gift to me (figuratively and literally), and one that I didn't fully appreciate until much later in life, was the book *Brothers and Keepers* (Wideman, 2005). This book was written by a Black man who grew up on the tough side of Pittsburgh and went on to a successful basketball career at the University of Pennsylvania. He later became a Rhodes Scholar. He also had a brother who was serving a life sentence for murder. The book is his questioning of how he and his brother's paths diverged so dramatically, what he owes his brother, and the broader question of what we owe to each other to help us get through life. It is this last question that still sticks with me today. I was too young (and a bit too self-absorbed) to fully appreciate the thoughtfulness and appropriateness of Artie's gift at the time (I, too, am an African-American male who was headed off to play basketball at an Ivy League Institution, and I was about to embark on a journey that would substantially widen the gulf between me and many of my Black brothers).

I and Thou

In college, I took a course with Robert Coles, and recently I was reminded of that course when reading Coles (1993) book, *The Call of Service*. One of Coles's heroes is the poet/physician William Carlos Williams, and in the book Williams says the following about serving others:

> We're completely lost in our own world—egoists! Or maybe we're locked into ourselves, and even though we want to break out, we can't seem to do it. It takes someone else to help us, a person who breaks in or has a way of letting us out.
>
> (Coles, 1993, p. 24)

I think that service can provide us with this "way out."

I continue to struggle with this question of how much does each of us "owe," and what is the best way to fulfill that duty. This reflection doesn't lead me to guilt, but rather keeps me motivated and inspired to strike the right balance in my life. Reciprocal human giving strikes me as a dynamic, rather than static, proposition. There are multiple variables that influence how service plays out in one's life depending on what else you have going on. One thing I know for sure is that I am called to service, and it is up to me to create the balance in my life that serves my own needs, the needs of clients, students, and colleagues, and, most of all, the people I love—my family, friends, and others. I am also called to the service of my African-American community whenever and wherever I am needed.

INSIGHTS FROM KYLE DODSON'S PERSONAL REFLECTIONS ON A LIFETIME OF SERVICE

Kyle Dodson has been responding to the call of service for the better part of two decades. When Robert first met him in his graduate class, Kyle was the Director of the Multicultural Affairs Office at neighboring St Michael's College. Even then, early in his career, his commitment to community service was exemplary and inspiring. When he moved on to become an elementary school principal at a charter public school in Boston, Kyle did this because he felt the call of service to work with inner-city children, parents, and teachers. As an African-American man, he felt that working, and living, in a multi-racial neighborhood in the inner city would be the best way for him to provide service.

Even though Kyle had the privilege of being an Ivy League student in both undergraduate and graduate school, he made it his mission to help others outside of his own elite educational spaces. Because of the personal influence of such service luminaries as Arne Duncan and Robert Coles, Kyle looked for tangible ways to put into realistic action his strong sense of altruism and beneficence. At the present time, Kyle is an upper-level college administrator in the area of civic engagement. He spends his days attempting to bridge the ever-distant space between a private college in Burlington, Vermont and all the working-class neighborhoods that surround it. Champlain College (where he currently works),

136

along with the University of Vermont, are often referred to as the "elite colleges on the hill."

Here are some motivational tips that Kyle is excited to offer those of us who try to provide service to communities that might need it the most:

1. We are our "brother's keeper," always and everywhere—no matter how far removed we might think we are from where people actually live out their lives. As members of the human community, we "owe" one another whatever we might be able to share that will help us to live productively and harmoniously together. This call to service to our "brothers" comes, not from guilt, shame, pity, or out of the embarrassment of being privileged, but from a sense of genuine, civic duty to our fellow human beings. We are an interdependent species, and we need each other for our mutual survival far more than we might realize.

2. One of the best ways to provide service to others is to "mobilize communities of caring people into changing their more egoistic behaviors." Unfortunately, egoism is frequently the law of the university jungle, both among students and faculty; but the university also has the potential to inspire, and exemplify, altruism. To do this, we will need "to break out of our own little worlds," at least for a while, and risk sharing our special talents with others. We, the service providers, will be as much the beneficiaries as those who will be receiving our services. How so?— because the principle of reciprocity is activated whenever people help one another without the intention to profit from that service.

3. The call of service to others must begin with "balance": how can we balance our own needs, along with the needs of loved ones, and all those who are in our inner circles of belonging, with the needs of those (many of whom are strangers) in the outer communities we seek to serve? This is an ongoing challenge, and learning how to balance a variety of competing interests in our lives needs to begin on the college campus in a variety of venues. There needs to be more emphasis in the classroom, residence hall, and student affairs offices on cooperation . . . not competition.

Chapter 10

How Can I Cultivate the Art of Self-Care and Balance in My Life?

Be yourself. Everyone else is already taken.

Oscar Wilde

Don't ask me to list my mistakes. Ask me instead what I have learned from my mistakes. Only then will you truly know me.

John Gardner

Being authentic, resilient, transparent, and centered are my personal strategies for achieving self-care and balance.

Jennifer J. J. Jang

Because of the insatiable demands on their lives to be, to do, and to achieve, so many of our quarterlife students are thinking about self-care and life-balance. Actually, the need to cultivate both of these qualities is an "equal opportunity employer," in the sense that we hear the same question in our chapter title frequently, even desperately at times, from staff, faculty, and administrators at our university and throughout the country. We think of *self-care* as an *art* to be cultivated, because it takes creativity and imagination to take good care of ourselves amid the turbulence of our daily lives. Self-care is all about knowing how to understand, maintain, and rejuvenate ourselves. This is especially necessary for all of us in higher education (and this includes our students as well) who work every day in the service of others. Because of our never-ending "to-do lists," there seems to be precious little time left to practice self-care.

For us, as for the Ancient Stoics, *balance* is about finding an equilibrium between who we are and who we want to be; between what we want and what others want from us. Balance is living life consistent with one's values. Balance is aligning our core selves with the work we do, the subject matter we study, the activities we enjoy, the people we like and love, and the hopes and dreams that ignite our passions and push us forward. Balance is seeking to fulfill our potential,

139

no matter how great or small the obstacles might be that threaten to diminish us. Balance is not static; it is dynamic, fluid, and action-oriented. Balance is living our lives consistent with what we believe, cherish, and enjoy. For Stoner and Robin (2006), balance is knowing your limits while realizing that growth is only possible when we are willing to push those limits. This means accepting that we have "gifts" (core understandings, skills, and talents) we can tap whenever we choose to do so. The choice, in the end, is ours . . . and ours alone.

POSITIVE PSYCHOLOGY AND SELF-CARE

Positive ("happiness," "flourishing") psychologists have inspired us greatly in thinking about self-care. In some important ways, they have taken the work of Abraham Maslow's (1962) self-actualization theory, and his groundbreaking "psychology of being," to the next level. Their findings, along with Maslow's, underlie most of what we will be saying in this chapter. Briefly, for happiness gurus, and scholars, like Martin C. P. Seligman, self-care and balance require attention to *five elements* of self-actualization (2011). When these elements are front and center in a person's life, then, according to Seligman and other researchers (e.g., Gilbert, 2005; Lyubomirsky, 2007) who have studied the conditions necessary for "authentic happiness" for several decades, we are able to live our lives in a "flow" state (Csikszentmihalyi, 1990). Being in "flow" is the best way to find balance and to flourish, even when we are at our busiest.

Here, in brief, are the five *sine qua non* "elements" of human flourishing and self-care:

1. *Positive emotion.* This is all about knowing how to maximize feelings of satisfaction, happiness, and contentment in one's life, even when it might seem that everything is falling apart.

2. *Engagement.* To be engaged is to be totally absorbed in what we are doing, even when this might not be something we look forward to. Engagement is all about "flowing." Engagement, or flow, often happens *after the fact*, in retrospect, when we go back and relive the time that we have been helping others in some way. We might say something like "where did the time go?" or "I completely lost myself in the process." To be fully engaged is to get outside of ourselves in order to get fully inside the work at hand. Robert often says that when he is absorbed completely in a three-hour seminar discussion, "there is no Robert there." Instead, there are the topics being discussed, the seminar room, the 20 or so students, and his co-teacher. All of his attention is focused—without his usual, irritating ego distractions—on those he is conversing with—listening to, sharing with, clarifying, and responding with non-ego-driven empathy and understanding.

3. *Meaning.* We have written this entire book on the element of meaning. Suffice it to say that, for positive psychologists, meaning is both a subjective and objective state of mind. It can exist both inside and outside of us. The sum total of all the quests that we cover in this book add up to both subjective *and* objective ways to evaluate what gives our quarterlifers, midlifers, and later-lifers a sense that their lives have meaning, both for themselves and for others. Meaning, for positive psychologists, can be validated by three criteria: it enhances well-being; it can be pursued for its own sake as well as for the sake of others; and it produces an overall sense that what we do in our lives is valuable and worthwhile. The ultimate validation of whether we have created lives of meaning is whether or not we have moved beyond a belief that life is empty and pointless to a belief that our lives are full and purposeful. There is no better way to take care of the self than to live a life of meaning—every day in every way.

4. *Accomplishment.* When achievements are pursued for their own sake, more than for the sake of the achiever, then well-being is more likely to result. It is mainly when achievers become preoccupied with success, and unable to learn from their failures to achieve it, that accomplishment can become a terrible, self-destructive addiction. There is nothing better during moments of stress and struggle than for each of us to know, and genuinely believe, that we are winners even when we might be tempted to think of ourselves as losers; that no matter how unachieving we can be at times, accomplishment is right around the corner. Moreover, accomplishment is more likely to happen when we pursue it for its own sake, without coercion, and when we are able to enjoy it fully in the moment . . . before we let it go and move on.

5. *Positive relationships.* We have already written much about the healing power of wonderful, loving relationships in our lives. Self-care begins with others in the sense that Seligman points out: "When you are feeling down, why don't you go out and help someone?" Seligman (2011) goes on to state that "according to the most rigorous measures, helping someone (kindness and generosity) produces the single most reliable increase in well-being of any element that scientists have tested" (p. 20). Just to know that you care deeply for people, and they care deeply for you, is one of the best ways to do self-care, find balance, and be happy.

INSPIRING STUDENTS TO BE AUTHENTIC, RESILIENT, TRANSPARENT, AND CENTERED

We have decided to change the format of the final chapter in this Quest section, by incorporating self-care advice that Jennifer wrote to her "self" in her graduate thesis three years ago. She has added some updates when relevant. She will clarify some operative concepts that she draws on for being true to, and taking care of, herself. Since writing her thesis, Jennifer has found it necessary to be concerned about her, and others', self-care, if she is to continue to flourish amidst the frenetic, current, day-to-day activities of being a high-level administrator and educator committed to diversity work. In her letter to herself, Jennifer will also draw out some of her self-care techniques in her extremely busy worklife with quarterlife students—as an advisor, mentor, and teacher. In her own way, Jennifer exemplifies the five elements (positive emotion, engagement, relationships, meaning, and achievement) of well-being (flourishing/positive psychology) we introduced in the previous section by the way she takes care of herself, and tries to create balance, all while providing deeply committed service to others.

Dear Self,

"Burnout," "exhaustion," "compassion fatigue," "deprivation," "running on empty," "self-care compromise," etc. These and other words and phrases are the ones I hear so frequently both from my colleagues and my students. Upon deep reflection, searching inwards, and very careful consideration, I realize that the Art of Self-Care is a recurring theme in my own journey through adversity. Being authentic, resilient, transparent, and centered are my personal strategies for achieving self-care and balance. In what follows, I will try to shed light on what has helped me endure times of hardship, sustained my sense of balance and wellness, and maintained my distance away from unnecessary, negative, and preventable stresses in my life.

Being Authentic

I have always been inspired by Oscar Wilde's maxim: "Be yourself; everyone else is already taken." The United States often values individuals being down to earth, genuine, and authentic. But what does that mean? The Latin authenticus means "original, genuine, principal." Derived from the Greek noun authentes, the word was formed from autos, "self" and hentes, "worker, doer." To be authentic is to be original; to be a doer; to be a creator. Being authentic, for me, means to live my life according to my own standards and values, to be fully myself, and to have authorship over my life and intentions.

In the work I do as a student affairs administrator and teacher, I often find myself stretched to assist, give, provide, facilitate, connect, and help others. This dynamic works well in the reciprocal collectivist Taiwanese culture I was raised in where people are socialized to look out for the needs of others. In an individualistic society like the United States, however, life balance is not as easy to achieve in the service-related professions. When my own strong compassion tendency is to give, give, and give, most of the times others in this new culture of mine are socialized to just take, take, and take. I sometimes feel in my professional space that the people I serve have taken it all, and I have nothing more left to give. In an individualistic society where most people are watching out for themselves, the only person I can rely on to take care of my well-being is me. No one else is going to take care of me for me. I all too often tend to leave myself with no energy to return to myself with love.

Everything I experience today is the result of choices I have made in the past. As the author of my life, I have control over the thoughts I think, the words that I speak, the images I visualize, the emotions I feel, and the actions I take. If I do not like what I am experiencing or producing, I can change my responses. I can change how I proceed with my thoughts, change what I speak about, change who I surround myself with, change the knowledge sources I tune into, change how I allow myself to be impacted and influenced by events and others. I can decide to take breaks from being in front of the computer, stay hydrated, eat natural and wholesome, stretch, laugh every day, exercise regularly, sleep more, get up earlier, trust my intuition, believe in myself, call upon my courage and be vulnerable, stay in touch with friends, go the extra mile, and take care of myself. I can also decide to live by my own high standards, take on only those projects that align with my life goals, ask for help without shame, stop beginning my sentences with "sorry," practice reflective listening and nonviolent communication, seek belonging in a group instead of merely fitting in, call my sister more often to connect, and be a class act.

Living a life of authenticity means actually living my life in line with how I want it to be. This is logical, but difficult to do. Living out my life authentically involves risk. Living out my lifestyle choices of no drinking, drugging, gossiping, and sniping, I risk being out-casted by my peers. By taking time to rejuvenate my selectively-social introverted-self, I risk losing the opportunity to connect with a potential friend. Practicing the art of asking for help brings up concerns of appearing incompetent and needy. Choosing to follow my intuition involves fear of it not being reliable or correct. Allowing my natural feeler side to surface calls forth a deep insecurity of being too emotional, less stable, or unprofessional. Taking a chance to branch out into new, perhaps controversial, areas of administering, teaching, and learning, I risk the possibilty of failing, and succumbing to those miserable feelings of defeat, disappointment, alienation, and marginalization.

From this "risk-obsessing" mindset, I need to remind myself that the only way I will never make a mistake is if I never take any risks, and if I avoid authentic risk-taking, then I remain stationary in my life. I know that I cannot keep on repeating what I have always done and expect to produce a different, more innovative result. I am the author of my life. I design, create, and script it, while reserving the right to make edits, changes, and revisions. I want to be authentic, and, therefore, I will fully accept the benefits and risks in taking responsibility for shaping my own life.

143

Authenticity has been one of the best ways to care for myself. In being authentic, I am able to find the living in life compared to only existing. I am able to discover the fine line between doing what I'm good at and what I enjoy. I am able to differentiate the non-imposing advice I cherish from the well-meaning advice that limits my potential. Most of all, though, when I am authentic I am acting on my own power rather than being powered by others. This is a sure-fire recipe for taking care of myself in a balanced way. This is not to say that I am always able to find the agency within myself to stay authentic, even when I know that is what I want. We all have baggage and influence from family, society, media. It is a constant revolving cycle of un-learning, learning, and re-learning who I want to be before the world told me what I am supposed to be. Remember, Jennifer, that you have gained so much from being true to yourself. Don't let go of your authentic self. Stay.

Being Persistently Resilient

Life can be like ocean waves, full of natural rhymes of ups and downs, crescendo and diminuendo, gradualness and abruptness. Life can be vibrant, pulsating, and vivacious; yet, beautifully painful, and painfully beautiful at the same time. There will always be the inevitable hardships, struggles, and, often, conflicting pressures from societal norms, cultural values, family standards, social dynamics, and personal beliefs. In the face of obstacles, challenges, and what may feel like overwhelming odds, I know I need to be persistently resilient. The Latin root of the word resilience is resilire, *meaning "to bounce back." I do not wish for everything to be smooth sailing in life, but I do wish for the courage and perseverance to carry on.*

It is not about me sticking to an optimistic, happy-face outlook on life, which was the only face I allowed myself to have for years, regardless of what's happening, or always managing to be at a good place emotionally—but being able to encounter those equally valid emotions of sadness, disappointment, and anger, and still bounce back with vitality. It is about having the tolerance level to bear the blow, having the strength to climb back up from the abyss, and having the ability to accumulate experience-capital to emerge nothing less than totally transformed and strengthened. This is what makes me the person I am today.

Even though the classroom of my real-life experiences has tested me with pop quizzes even before I received the lessons, I knew deep down that I would come out better on the other side. You see—it is all about resilience. It was all about taking care of myself when I first came to this country when nobody else was able, or willing, to take care of me. My past has taught me that I need balance in my life because of all the risks that I must take each and every day in facing up to my challenges. On a day-to-day level, it means that I have to be committed to the particular goal I am pursuing—obtaining my doctorate, cultivating my AcroYoga© practice, enhancing my college teaching, strengthening my friendship network, enriching my professional practice, and infusing a sense of wonder, joy, and play into my life. All of this requires resilience and steadfastness, often at the same time.

Resilience is vital for all of us to stand strong in times of hardship. David Campbell says:"Discipline is remembering what you want."It is not about avoiding challenges or denying difficulties, but how I choose to react to these trials when they confront me.Whether it is by words, actions, or sheer personal energy, I decide what to accept and how it impacts me. Sometimes I succeed; sometimes I do not. The rollercoaster ride of my life will inevitably present low points where I feel defeated. However, I have not really been lost if I learn from my challenges. Just as the American inventor, Thomas Edison, claimed never to have failed 200 times at inventing the light bulb, because along the way he discovered all the ways how not to make one. I got to keep the eyes on the prize, focus on my goals, and remember what I want.

From math, the universal language, being the only subject in which I ever earned an A in Saipan due to a language barrier, to being on the President's List for the rest of my high school, college, and graduate education (once I learned the English language), I found ways to survive and thrive. I overcame, because I refused to become discouraged by my defeats. I chose to have my resilience be my badge of courage and honor. I realized early on that resilience was a precondition for my self-care. I could only find a balance in my life and take the best care of myself when I was intent on bouncing back from my everyday failures.A source of inspiration for me has always been John Gardner's resilience-maxim:"Don't ask me to list my mistakes; ask me, instead, what I have learned from my mistakes. Only then will you truly know me." I stand by that if we learned from our mistakes then it is not really a mistake. It is like when we ask to be granted more patience, we are given a line at the bank . . . It is simply a lesson generously provided to grant me the opportunity to learn first-handed.

Every single setback, challenge, and struggle in my life has its significance and meaning. I choose to use my sense of rootlessness, my nightmarish journey to learn a new language in order to survive in a culture not my own, my being bullied by my grade-school classmates because I wasn't "like them,"my distorted perception of healthy body image and desperate eating disorder, my inexperience in handling emotions and only knowing the need to suppress them, my decade-long absence from my consanguinal family, and my heavy financial responsibilities—all these challenges, while difficult, have been my restorative vitamins.The journey has required me to keep going and not to give up, while, along the way, I learned new lessons, made difficult, and always life-changing, decisions, developed new and necessary perspectives, practiced these newly acquired skills, and discovered more about myself. My learnings?—Don't give up. Stay in the game. It is still not easy, I know, but it can be worth it. Stay persistently resilient.

Being Transparent

Growing up in a collectivist Asian culture where people naturally tuned into each other's needs, direct verbal communication about these needs was virtually non-existent. As a person who places high value on relationship-building, this lack of open communication about feelings frequently left me frustrated, disappointed, and, even, very lonely. As a result, then, and even now, I avoided those much-needed conflict conversations in order to arrive at what my Chinese ancestors considered to be the ideal interpersonal "harmony"—most of which existed on the surface, rather than in the depths, of human communication.

Since my time in the United States, I am learning that being transparent, and speaking with integrity and intentionality, is to speak a language of life. This language of life is closer to my truth, and it is just what I need in order to take care of my authentic self. Speaking my truth in an honest and caring way allows me to communicate my observations, thoughts, needs, and requests openly without blame, criticism, accusation and attack, that too often dominates majority dialogue. It is extermely rewarding, but this is not to be confused with it being simple or easy to carry out.

Transparent nonviolent communication takes a tremendous amount of strength and trust in the other person. Letting that person into my brain and my heart is scary, because now I am clear and see-through. Ill-intended people can sometimes exploit, and harm, those of us who are transparent. But, I try to be clear with what the other person needs as well as with what I need. Naming where I am in any given situation allows the other person to do the same. Voicing and updating my status to the other person takes a lot of courage, trust, strength, and clarity, because essentially I am living up to the anonymous quotation "sing as if no one is listening, dance as if no one is watching, and love like you've never been hurt."

But, even if my transparency makes me feel vulnerable, I need to remember that a healthy amount of vulnerability shown to a carefully selected group of core people in my life is completely acceptable. The whole point of transparency in living a self-caring life is for me to open up and be vulnerable, to ask for help when I need it, and to open up the opportunity for the other person to do the same with me. At some point, we end up caring for one another in a genuine spirit of reciprocity.

Among all my recent awakening moments, being transparent has been by far one of the most gratifying, and liberating, self-care learning experiences for me. I no longer hide from conflicts, shove things under the rug, or avoid awkward conversations like the plague. Transparent nonviolent communication allows me to honor myself as a human being along with my basic, natural, and valid needs that I used to minimize. Now I cultivate the agency within myself to believe I am worth advocating for, and I trust others to be kind and to listen and value my communication when I speak it. Honoring my thoughts and feelings, while communicating with utmost care, trust, sensitivity, integrity, and intentionality, has been the way I cultivate self-care.

Being Centered

In order to find my center, it is important to know the difference between what it means being alone versus being lonely. How can you be centered if you constantly lean on others for a sense of worth, comfort, and ease? If my situation of solitude is inevitable, why can't I become comfortable with the one, single person I am going to spend the most time with in my life—myself? Most of us have been socialized by being plugged into technology and the internet, which often means instant communication with others around the globe. This makes it very difficult, at first, to transition into situations where one has to be by oneself.

However, getting over that initial discomfort of being alone is crucial. There is a big difference between being alone, and feeling lonely. I can be alone by myself, and feel completely comfortable, at peace, relaxed, and reflective—journaling, experiencing a kind of Stoic serenity, and feeling completely at ease. And I can be surrounded by a group of people and feel the most lonely. Being alone, I can find "home" within myself. It is in my "home" within where I am best able to do the self-care and to find the balance that enables me to revitalize and renew myself before I return to my busy professional life each and every day. You can be alone and not feel lonely.

In order be centered and balanced, I must also get in touch with myself. I may have great breadth and depth of knowledge, but being out of sync with myself makes me feel like what Robert calls an un-alphabetized encyclopedia with all my thoughts jumbled together, unorganized, and frenzied. My own life story is like knotted thread, a ball of entangled yarn that I cannot find the ends to, and an un-chronologized autobiography. In order to get to know myself better, I need to make close contact with my inner self, so that I can have a rich, coherent autobiography that is both alphabetized and chronologized. How can I ever truly actualize self-care, if the coherent self that I don't know is dispersed into a thousand incoherent selves, each wanting, indeed craving, something different?

What exactly is my coherent self? This is a question I frequently ask. Growing up in a family filled with classical music, rehearsals, performances, and recitals, expressing and feeling my self through music pieces has allowed me to be in a zone where I am relaxed and centered. Music enables me to find peace, serenity,

147

and tranquility inside myself, to see the image of the island, Saipan, I lived on, to feel the tropical breeze, and move at a calmer pace. It is what I need and desire at this precious moment of me-time. On the same note, these music pieces also embody for me the emotions of tension, sadness, tears, struggles, issues, stress, challenges, and hardship. Music has its beautiful side, but also its painful moments, because it brings back memories that are not always pleasant. My musical memories can sometimes be difficult, because they remind me of a home I can never really return to. There are many times in the present, as well as in the past, when I play the piano by myself—with my family nowhere present, except in my distant memories.

One of the first things that I do when I am feeling frazzled, distressed, impacted, influenced, or just not where I would like to be emotionally, physically, or psychologically, is to breathe mindfully. I take a deep breath in, and then a deep breath out. The inhale is just as important as the exhale, and vice versa. I make it a point to be mindful of my breathing at all times. Taking a deep breath helps me to focus, concentrate, and be here in the now. It gets me ready to listen, problem solve, and be present. I am able to ask how I can be supportive, name where I am in the process, and successfully manage my, and others' expectations. Intentional, deep inhales and exhales allow me to think with more clarity, feel with more calmness, communicate more effectively, and make observations more strategically.

The Latin root of "breath" is spiritus, which means "breath, the soul, vigor, that which animates life." Perhaps breathing is a major part of my spirituality. To be spiritual for me is to live a life of breath. Breathing allows me to feel grounded and aligned with my inner self. I access and maintain my spirituality through the breath. The result of having oxygen in my mind and body gives me the literal strength to take ownership of my life, the endurance to face seemingly overwhelming obstacles, and the courage to face what is not working and then embrace the change that is to come. Everything feels possible through the breaths.

And, so, dear self, please remember to revisit these tips often. "Please keep your seatbelt fastened until the captain has turned off the fasten seatbelt sign." In addition to your seatbelt, you need to put on your oxygen mask before helping others to put on theirs. You need to be well holistically for your compassion and assistance to be sustainable. Continue to strive for excellence . . . not for perfection. In the end, you are all you really need in order to take care of yourself.

You are enough, and you are worth it,

Jennifer

TEN STRATEGIES FOR ACHIEVING SELF-CARE AND BALANCE

We offer the following sets of simple and practical strategies that have helped so many of our students through the years at least to get a start on restoring self-care and balance to their busy lives. Each and every one of these strategies are grounded in the principles of positive/flourishing psychology that we described at the beginning of this chapter.

Breathe

Always remember to take a deep breath. The exhale breath is just as important as the inhale breath. Enough oxygen does everyone good. It will grant you happier cells, a calmer mood, better circulation, and far greater concentration and clarity.

Constant Reflection

Ask yourself the *Six E* questions below. They are split into two parts. The first three questions require contemplation. The second three questions require more action in your daily life.

Exploration: Who am I?
Expression: Why am I?
Expansion: Where do I want to go?
Enrichment: What *is working* for me (provides the *flow* experience that I need to be happy) that I should do more of?
Enhancement: What is *not working* for me (tasks that take me *out of my flow* and cause anxiety and boredom) that I need to do less of?
Enlargement: What is something new that I could try, for it may produce the desirable outcome?

Be Patient with Yourself

Aim for *good enough* rather than *best enough*. Persistence is key. It is a never-ending cycle of constant and continuous improvement. What you are doing is an art form requiring patience and mindfulness. When you have mastered your goal, what you aim for will be a natural integration of your life. But remember, according to Malcolm Gladwell, 10,000 hours of subsequent mastery will not come in a few minutes!

Listen to Your Body

The human body is a magnificent and intricate system of brilliance. It is wise beyond our understanding. When it signals you pertinent information about your health, do not mute your body with drugs or indulge in self-destructive, escapist hedonism. It is worthwhile for you to listen attentively to your body, and appreciate the wisdom of the messages it is sending to you.

Cultivate a Rejuvenating Hobby

What fuels your energy at the core? Where do you feel tremendous love by being yourself? That's belonging in the truest sense. Find that. Stick to that. Feed your soul. *AcroYoga*© (blends mindfulness and breath of yoga with playfulness and strength of acrobatics), Jennifer's advocation, helps her to lean into discomfort, cultivate trust, enrich connections, and practice the art of letting go. What's your hobby?

Be Gentle and Kind to Others

It is scary to be vulnerable, but putting others down does not bring you up any higher than where you are now. Do not let your own insecurities get in the way of treating yourself and others with respect and dignity as it will inevitably come back to you in some way.

Live by Your Own Highest Standards

You may be conditioned and socialized to see life as a 100-meter dash, but in the long run, it is not a competition with others. It is more like an ultra-ultra-marathon where pacing is the key. Be a class act: live by your own highest standards and empower others to do the same.

Up Your Average

Carefully select the individuals you surround yourself with, as you become them over time. Up your average, by choosing to have a vacancy in your core group, rather than to lower your standards. Interview candidates wisely, and be selective.

Solicit Feedback

Ask for feedback in all settings, from trusted individuals around you, and incorporate it into your constant and continuous improvement. The value of feedback is incalculable. Do not be afraid to ask for ways you can become better.

Trust Your Intuition

You usually know the answers to your own questions. All the resources you need you already possess in your inner genius. Now you just have to cultivate and trust in your gut feeling, your sixth sense. You are the expert on your life. You know yourself better than you think.

A Personal Reflection from a Practitioner on Self-actualization, Self-care, and Balance

Leslie Averill, Vice President of Student Life,
Champlain College, Burlington, Vermont

"When You Say 'Self-care and Balance'—I Think Self-actualization"

As the Vice President of Student Life at a small private institution in the northeast, I often encounter students and staff who suffer from burnout, who feel out of balance, and are making decisions that are less than healthy. These young adults come to me with low motivation and feeling lost and overwhelmed. When they sit in my office and begin to share their stories, my heart bleeds with them. I can feel their pain, and I can hear their cry out for help, wishing for a magic answer to life's most challenging questions. Unfortunately, I have not found an easy answer or magic solution to help. Our journeys toward finding inner peace, living well and creating balance are unique and demand our daily attention.

These encounters make me feel alive. When I recognize something or someone who awakens my spirit, I try really hard to have more of it in my life. Given this, I prefer not to use the word "balance" in my own vocabulary. Instead I use the term self-actualization, as is identified in Maslow's (1962) "Hierarchy of Needs." Thinking of how one achieves balance drains my energy, makes me feel tired, and many times hopeless. On the other hand, the idea of self-actualization peaks my interest, makes me pay attention, and awakens my spirit. For me, finding balance or equilibrium, as defined in popular American culture, can be a tantalizing idea, but it is an idea that seems impossible and, therefore, remains just an idea, and not one I support.

What Grounds You?

Existentialism, Appreciative Inquiry, and Positive Psychology are grounding concepts in which I shape my life, my management practice, and my leadership practice. These concepts shape how I think and how I act as I navigate my day-to-day life and long-term journey toward self-actualization.

Because I consider myself an existentialist, I believe my life is in my hands and is mine to create. "Existentialism" (a word first coined by Victor Frankl), asserts that

"There is no metaphysical essence; there is only being or existence, and it is up to us to create our own values and meanings in a world where all the old certainties have disappeared." To me this means I cannot rely on anything supernatural or metaphysical to show me the way to a meaningful life. It means I am on my own; I am the sole *bricoleur*, or builder of my life. With this at the front of my mind I am free to build my own understanding of balance and empowered to practice my personal definition of the concept.

Positive psychology is defined as "the study of optimal functioning." It is the science of everyday human strengths and qualities. Originally conceived in 1998 by Martin Seligman, former president of the American Psychological Association, positive psychology expands the traditional practice of working to cure the ill to also identify what is healthy in individuals and builds off of what is working for them in their lives. A primary aim of positive psychology is to focus on "positive subjective experiences, positive individual traits, and positive intuitions." Given the influence of positive psychology, when working to achieve balance/self-actualization, I prefer to reflect on positive experiences I've had in my life, identify what positive traits I bring to the challenge such as energy and determination, and what my gut tells me.

In addition, Dr. David Cooperrider (2005) has conceived of a new organizational change management methodology called Appreciative Inquiry (AI). AI is an inquiry-focused practice and methodology aimed at empowering, encouraging, and energizing an individual, organization or system. It requires attention be paid to "root causes of success" rather than "root cause analysis of failure." It is an alternative to the traditional organizational change practices that are grounded in identifying problems and designing problem-solving solutions. AI presumes that questions encourage individual thinking, creativity, and empowerment and that supports the idea that "the questions we ask set the stage for what we find, and what we find is what becomes the knowledge out of which the future is constructed." This suggests that individuals have the power to influence and construct their ideal future. If the questions we ask set the stage for what we find, then rather than asking the questions "How can I balance my day? Or, how can I find balance in my life?," I ask,

- How will I create joy in my life today?
- What can I do today to stimulate my mind or get my blood flowing?
- What will make me feel invigorated and energized?

These questions are life-giving and generate energy in me rather than lead me on a quest for achieving balance.

Conversing with a Student

When I am sitting in my office with a student who is burned out, feeling out of balance, overwhelmed, and down I have a few hopes and intentions of the meeting. They are:

1. to hear the student or staff (let them know I am listening, that I care, and that they are important),
2. to be sure they realize there isn't a magic answer and that they have the power to create their own definition of balance and their own lives but that it takes daily attention and work,
3. that they can take one step toward making that particular day better and another step the next day,
4. and, of course, that they leave my office feeling, if nothing else, that they can make a difference in their own life.

As an example of how I approach the conversation I've written a brief narrative of what I might say:

Final Thoughts

As I mentioned throughout this short, reflective essay, there is no magic answer to this particular type of life ailment. However, as professionals in higher education, we can provide time and coaching to those who are showing us they are struggling. And it is my belief that an hour of our time and coaching could be one of the most important hours of one undergraduate's experience; most of the time we don't know if we have helped, but I believe every conversation does make a difference and is worthwhile. I hope you do, too.

For Your Next Meeting with a Quarterlife Student or Millennial Staff

Here is my advice for the next time you find yourself working with students or young professionals who are burned out and looking for some balance in their lives:

- Inspire them to listen to their inner voice. If they can't hear it, tell them to listen harder and longer.
- Encourage them to take note every day (at home and at work) of moments that bring them joy, inspire them, or get their hearts beating faster.
- Remind them to be intentional and create more time in their week to do more of the things that bring them joy.
- Empower them to feel that they own their reality. Encourage them to be unabashedly aggressive. Reiterate that there can be no excuses and remind them that this is their life and now is the best time to act.
- Introduce and reiterate the importance of following positive energy. Emphasize that importance of identifying what it is that energizes life and breathes life into them.

153

- And with compassion and clarity remind them that like the journey of meaning-making, the journey of self-actualization is a lifetime of work.

A SUMMARY OF PRACTICAL TIPS FOR ENCOURAGING STUDENTS TO SELF-ACTUALIZE AS A WAY TO ACHIEVE SELF-CARE

Leslie Averill studied with Robert during both her master's and doctoral programs. From her beginning as a graduate student, Leslie has been concerned with getting college faculty and staff to commit to the goal of helping others to cultivate what she calls "self-actualization." She prefers this term rather than "balance," and even "self-care," because, for her, self-actualization is a lifelong process of "awakening the spirit." This means that, while we will always experience the highs and lows in living our lives, self-actualization requires that we accept the challenges and move full speed ahead to the highs. Sometimes this requires balance and equilibrium; sometimes this requires risk, boldness, and dynamic energy. Leslie cautions us against the downside of putting balance and self-care first because, as we say in this chapter, authenticity, resilience, transparency, and centeredness are the preconditions for constructing a life narrative.

Leslie knows well from all the ups and downs in her own life (which she wrote about in her SPN dissertation) that there is no "magic formula" for happiness or success. For her, life is an evolving, unfinished act of self-creation, and it is in nobody's hands but our own. Like the positive psychologists, existential philosophers and therapists, and the Appreciative Inquiry management leaders who have been such an inspiration to her, Leslie chooses to focus on the adventures in life, and to inspire others to reach beyond themselves. Leslie is a strong believer in the five core elements of self-care and human flourishing—positive emotion, engagement, meaning-making, accomplishment, and positive relationships that we talk about throughout our chapter. As we can see in Jennifer's letter to her "dear self" earlier in the chapter, these qualities can be both self-actualizing and self-balancing. In sum, they enable us to live full, rich lives without suffering the ravages of burnout, compassion fatigue, or self-compromise. In actuality, Jennifer and Leslie are closer than might first appear in how they approach self-care and self-actualization in their work with students and faculty.

In closing, here are some practical "final thoughts" in an *ex post facto* personal reflection written by Leslie:

I believe that we all get to write our life story. I get to write mine and you get to write yours. This means you get to define the idea of balance (insert the your own topic here). Personally, I don't believe in the idea of a universal balance. Finding your own personal balance is unique to you. No one can find it for you or tell you what balance in your life should look like or feel like. My sense of balance is different from yours and yours is different from mine. This is good because we are unique and motivated by different things in life.

For me, the popular idea of balance in America is limiting and unrealistic. Given that I don't believe in the popular understanding of balance it doesn't make sense for me to work toward finding it, but to instead redefine balance in a way that excites, engages, and empowers me to live the life I want to live. For me this means identifying the origins of my life story and continually rewriting my life story.

Questions of Origin

So let me ask:

- What do you believe balance is?
- Why do you believe this?
- What are some alternative stories in your history that could lead you to a different understanding of balance?

Energy-generating questions:

- What can you do today that will create moments of joy in your life?
- What can you do today to stimulate your mind or get your blood flowing?
- When is the last time you felt invigorated?
- What was going on? What were you doing? Who were you with?

These are questions that generate energy for me, and I expect they will for you, too. So let's move to action.

- What can you do today to create a moment of joy in your life before you go home and go to bed? It can be small but you need to do something that will make you feel good even if for just a minute. And then you need to give yourself some credit for taking the action.
- What can you do right now to begin working toward your ideal tomorrow?

I believe it's important to identify where, who, when and what conditions exists when you feel alive, excited and inspired, and then try and create those conditions as often as possible. This is your life and you have the capacity to make it great. Are you ready to take the next step?

The Next Steps

We will include in Part III two chapters of personal-insight reflections illustrating how to be an effective meaning-making leader; why interdisciplinarity in meaning-making education is crucial; and what an effective interdisciplinary capstone experience looks like. All of the personal reflections in these last chapters were written by past and present students who have studied meaning-making. These reflective insights represent the distinct voices of a high-level, college administrator, an instructor, a recent quarterlife college graduate and English teacher, and a non-traditional, mid-life student. We will conclude each of these chapters with a brief series of practical take-aways for teachers, leaders, and students on the topics of meaning-making leadership, interdisciplinarity, and capstone seminars.

Chapter 11

Meaning-Making Leadership and Interdisciplinarity

Hell is a place where nothing connects.

T. S. Eliot

Today, the word "interdisciplinary" is bandied about at every academic conference and praised in every dean's report, but in fact most of our academic institutions are much less interdisciplinary than were their counterparts in the past.

Andrew Delbanco

We have spent several chapters describing, exemplifying, and elaborating upon the content and pedagogy of meaning-making on college campuses. We have identified, and unpacked, the core quarterlife meaning-quests. We have tried to create a convincing, meaning-centered vision for helping students to prepare not just for their quarterlife years but also for their mid-life and later-life years beyond college. We hope that what we have said will serve as the impetus (and inspiration) for faculty and staff to go one step further in educating college students at all levels. We realize that advocating for meaning-making is a gigantic step to take for many educators and administrators in academia because, not only is it controversial, it is also intellectually unprecedented in so many of the disciplines and professional schools.

We are grateful to each of our respondents in these final two chapters for their willingness to offer their insights on meaning-making, leadership, and interdisciplinarity in both a personal and professional way. Each of them is unafraid of being vulnerable. Each of them is determined, at this stage of their careers, not to come across as "detached," impersonal teachers and leaders. Each of them identifies as a "passionate" meaning-centered educator *and* a determined change-agent. Each of them, therefore, models in their writing what they believe an authentic, meaning-centered education should be.

LEADERSHIP INSIGHTS OF AN ACADEMIC DEAN

Jonathan Haidt (2012) makes a crucial distinction between what he calls "transactional" versus "transformative" leadership. *Transactional* leaders are adept at motivating individuals to become team players—able to contribute to the growth and power of their organizations— and, in so doing, end up better enhancing their own power. A transactional leader emphasizes, first and foremost, *what's in a person's self-interest.* Thus, if individuals can produce benefits for others, they are better able to produce benefits for themselves. In corporate businesses, especially those with a strong capitalist bent, transactional leaders are preferred.

A *transformative leader*, however, is someone who is able to "activate pride, loyalty, enthusiasm, and togetherness" in individuals, who then go on to become true team players committed to a unifying cause. The unifying cause is, first and foremost, doing *what is best for the group.* According to Haidt's research, these individuals are "happier, more productive, and connected" to one another than those whose leaders tend to be transactional. They see themselves as "we," not "I." Therefore, and Haidt is adamant on this point, transformative leaders are the most effective in educational settings, and, by extension, in facilitating meaning-centered experiences.

In Mika Nash-Gibney's insight-reflection that follows, she spells out the type of transformational leader she tries to be in her role as an academic dean. For her, the major task of an educational leader is to develop "deep connections" between and among all the persons in her division, including students. In her own words: "Our success is made real every time we put our students at the center of a strategic initiative, and success looks very much like connection." In the college classroom, as well as in the administrative office, "deep connections" are most likely to produce the "deep learning" that a meaning-centered education requires if it is to be successful.

CONNECTIONS . . . ALL THE WAY DOWN

Mika Nash-Gibney, Academic Dean and Associate Professor
Division of Continuing Professional Studies
Champlain College
Burlington, Vermont
Contributing Monthly Education Columnist for *The Huffington Post*

I never expected to end up in education, but the first time I stood in front of a high school classroom as an English teacher, my heart swelled to fill my chest, and I knew I had found home. While sullenness was the initial response of the 15-year-old skills level students to my teaching of a short story, they became animated as I encouraged them to connect their own stories to that of the main character.

The more time I spent with these kinds of students—the ones who approach education warily, guardedly—the more I was convinced that these were the people to whom I would commit my professional life. And so I have, from high school to community colleges to higher education administration, where each day I play a central role in ensuring we touch as many students as possible in the most meaningful and effective ways.

Today, I am well into a career in higher education administration, and my aim has remained high-quality connections. As the academic dean of a centralized continuing education unit that delivers online education to adult students, I must regularly answer questions about the rapidly changing landscape of higher education and the legitimacy of our modality. My response is always the same: regardless of how much higher education changes or what technologies are used, for those institutions offering students the most profound experiences, the objective endures—an environment where students can partner with others in making sense of their academic journey.

"Hell is a Place Where Nothing Connects"—T.S. Eliot

Recently I was asked to speak to a group of graduate students about the "controversy" inherent in online education. I redirected the audience to share their worries about education in the twenty-first century. They expressed apprehensions about feeling alone, being unable to connect with a professor, feeling cut off from others. As we parsed these concerns, it was clear that each of these students was describing real life experiences. They talked about the prospect of not knowing how they were doing in their classes because teachers didn't get assignments back to them and not feeling as though it would be appropriate to speak their truths. In short, the problems they had isolated as being specific to the classrooms of the future were, in fact, those that characterized their current experiences.

The take-away is that education done well—regardless of how it is delivered—must first and foremost provide a forum for connection. There are a thousand innovations that will change the way we receive education, but in the end, a high quality academic experience is one that enables students to find their voices and connect with one another. Our responsibility, as administrators who are seeking to use new technologies to reach students and support them to completion, is to hold as our touchstone the enduring goal of education: connection—to self, to others, to content, to ideas, to the future, to the past, to meaning.

Enduring Principles of Leadership to Inform Leaders and Students

Ultimately, regardless of the modality through which we offer education to students or the changes that are under way as we think about the future of higher education, there are some enduring principles for how to do it well, all of which are informed by a *philosophy of connection*.

1. *Cultivate space for meaningful relationships*. Students, regardless of how they are taking courses (either online or on campus), want someone to know their stories. This can be easily accomplished by increasing outreach and providing a network. At graduation, students consistently tell us that this deep, powerful connection made it possible for them to persist through the distractions and crises that are part and parcel of an educational journey.

The most effective institutions are providing these networks for their young, face-to-face students as a way of recreating the support systems they had growing up with eagerly involved parents, coaches, and teachers. As we develop new ways of working with students at a distance, we must remember the importance of meaningful relationships for everyone, and find ways to place them at the center of a student's experience.

2. *Demand evidence-based pedagogy*. We come to our methodology from a particular pedagogical perspective, in which we meet our students where they are and support them toward achieving their goals. Everything we do, both inside and outside the classroom, is grounded in working with the quarterlife, and older, student; we provide meaningful social connection, real world application of theory, and fluid interplay between didactic and hands-on academic experiences. This grounds our methodology in best practice, lending credibility to the work we do.

Pedagogy aside, the classrooms of the future demand evidence-based practice as a way to provide students with the best, most innovative methodology for getting them to completion. As we consider responses to those anxious about how quickly things are changing in higher education, it is much easier to imagine changing people's minds about new teaching interfaces if we can base our usage in research and best practice. Meaning-making education is a multi-modal pedagogy, effective anywhere, as long as it is grounded in the basic principle of what I am calling making "connections all the way down, across, up, and over."

3. *Think facilitated learning*. It is time to move away from the tired concept of the "sage on the stage" and toward the idea of faculty as "guides on the side." It's unclear whether students ever enthusiastically embraced sitting silently for hours as a weathered professor stood at a lectern reading yellowed lecture notes. There is no evidence that students can absorb more than ten minutes of monologue at a stretch. Studies from as far back as the mid-1970s have shown that students need interaction and connection to the material and the concepts under study to be invested in their learning.

Done right, for example online learning as well as on-campus learning, make this varied methodology easy to accomplish. Students immediately engage with the content and make sense of it in a variety of ways—thus, producing an engaged, interactive seminar, as opposed to a disengaged, teacher-centered lecture hall. There is no sitting silently in the back of the room when facilitated learning takes place; everyone must explicitly engage with the material however and wherever. As we consider how we educate students, we must ask ourselves whether our methodology encourages engagement or stifles it, whether it's central to the experience or peripheral, so that we can confidently speak to the inclusivity of the learning environment. It is in this type of space where everyone has a voice, and there are safety, encouragement, and affirmation built into the practice.

4. *Keep it small*. While it is efficient to fill cavernous auditoriums with hundreds of students and a professor (all too often a graduate assistant, instructor, or an adjunct faculty member), this is no way to engender connection between students and the material they are studying or among one another. The ideal size in most courses is much smaller. All the research about persistence and retention supports smaller educational groups, and the value of meaningful relationships and connections for students. These are tough to create or sustain in an echoing amphitheater. We can tell ourselves that the Teaching Assistant (TA) will do this face-to-face work, but the hierarchical message we send to students with this dynamic is not only troubling to ponder, but may, and often does, undermine the efficacy of the learning.

We encourage keeping all courses smaller, particularly online, so that discussions don't get unwieldy and so that students can get to know one another as kindred fellow travelers in the learning process. Again, as administrators make these kinds of student-based decisions, we further legitimize the work we are doing both online and on-campus.

5. *Get out of the echo chamber*. If you are in higher education administration and you are not squirming right now, then you are not paying attention. There is no eco-dorm, or climbing wall, or green space, or library turned into an internet hangout café, that is going to fix what's broken in higher education. Astronomical tuition costs are forcing students and families to reconsider whether college is a viable option, and for those who decide to enroll, the staggering debt they take on is often not offset by high-paying jobs. College as we know it is becoming a thing of the past.

Those administrators who are willing to change the way they do business are the change-agents who will create environments where students thrive and, as a result, so will their institutions. The key for any of us in positions to effect change is to stay abreast of the shifting landscape, and maintain a commitment to the teaching-learning mission of connection and engagement. This will make it possible to respond to student needs in new ways and to consider tweaks to existing systems without grasping at a past that no longer is relevant.

I started my professional life in a classroom, where I matched students' gazes with my own. I read body language, coaxing out their stories when I saw students wanted to speak but couldn't find the words. I came to a high-level administrative position in a continuing education division whose emphasis was online learning with an open, but dubious, mind. What I've found, which is not surprising, is that when the student is at the center of decisions made about programming, pedagogy, faculty training, and support, the quality of the product is often not only equivalent to what is taught in the classroom, but sometimes better; and research bears this out. The key to ensuring that a campus is both prepared and eager for change is clarity about the mission and alignment of decisions with those guiding principles. It is, then, our job to communicate our mission in everything we do. Our success is made real every time we put our students at the center of a strategic initiative, and success looks very much like connection. To paraphrase T. S. Eliot: "Hell is an education where nothing or nobody connects."

INTERDISCIPLINARY INSIGHTS OF A UNIVERSITY FACULTY MEMBER

Unfortunately, "interdisciplinarity" is fast becoming an all-too-common "buzzword" in higher education, even though it contains eight syllables and is hard to say quickly. Thousands of references have appeared on Google during the last decade promoting the benefits of interdisciplinary studies. Often, authors use synonyms such as "multi-disciplinary," "trans-disciplinary," and, lately, "post-disciplinary," in order to tweak the concept of interdisciplinarity. We are not necessarily being critical of the term, but we do want to be clear about how we are using the word in connection with meaning-making. Once more, we are not discipline-phobic. We love the disciplines (therefore, we are discipline-philes), and we are proud to have specialized degrees in several of them. In fact, we appreciate the disciplines so much that we cannot get enough of them. We want to introduce them to one another, so that they can be close friends, and so they can interact with, and enrich, one another.

We want to connect and integrate as many of the disciplines as possible so that our students become "multi-perspectival" (a concept invented by Friedrich Nietzsche) when it comes to critical thinking, problem-solving, and creativity (Strober, 2011). In fact, how is it possible to understand the complexities of meaning-making without being aware of a number of disciplinary perspectives? For us, interdisciplinarity is a word that applies to the fullest understanding of the real world that we, and our students, live, work, learn, and love in.

Think of the various subject matters that quarterlifers will have to understand, and integrate, if they are to make sense of the "eight meaning-making quests" that we discuss in Part II of this book. Each of the quests requires, at the very least, a rudimentary literacy in a number of disciplines in the social sciences, humanities, arts, and sciences. Even more, if the meaning-making quest is to be part of a "holistic" education, our students will need to understand the interconnections, and integration, of as many of the discrete disciplines as possible. Why? Because this is the reality of the complex meaning-making world that we live in today—there are no simple, mono-disciplined answers to the complex questions of meaning. For example, in this book alone, we have generated hundreds of questions about ethics and morality, hopes and dreams, religion and spirituality, love and friendship, overlapping identities, work and vocation, service, and self-care. How, pray tell, can a single discipline provide answers to even one set of these inquiries?

Andrew Delbanco (2012) echoes our take on the need for interdisciplinarity. In today's world, few problems of any significance are either confined or narrow. Rather, they aggressively cross boundaries that render the perspectives and methods of single disciplines "incomplete and inefficacious." In effect, then, we are teaching undergraduates to think in ways that may prepare them less than adequately for the problems they will face once they leave the college environment and face the outside world.

Debora Teixeira, a former dentist and now a college instructor in Romance Languages, understands well what all of this has to do with teaching and learning in the real world. For her, there is no dramatic disconnect between dentistry, teaching a language, and meaning-making. Her interdisciplinary insights follow.

HOW INTERDISCIPLINARITY FUNCTIONS IN THE REAL WORLD: FROM DENTISTRY TO FOREIGN LANGUAGE TEACHING

Debora Teixeira
Instructor of Portugese
Doctor of Dentistry
College of Arts and Sciences
The University of Vermont

I consider myself a living example of how interdisciplinarity functions in the real world. After being formally trained as a dentist in Brazil, my country of origin, I became increasingly interested in education. My first experience as a professor was in the field of Dentistry, where I trained dental students how to conduct initial patient examinations. Later in life, circumstances changed, and I became interested in the opportunity to pursue training in TESOL—Teaching English as a Second or Other Language. It was surprising to me, at first, to observe the multiple connections that existed between two very distinct and apparently unrelated careers. It became gradually very clear to me that both fields required that I dealt with people who felt vulnerable and, at times, severely stressed.

As I look back and think about how I feel while performing in each of these professions, I am convinced that I can be equally happy fulfilling either role. Each offers me the opportunity to help human beings feel better and to empower these individuals, by allowing them to preserve, or to improve, their self-esteem. In order to successfully accomplish the goals of either function, though, I have to determine how I can connect with these individuals and inspire trust. Only then, after my patients or students feel that I can be trusted, can I proceed forward and attempt to achieve my objectives.

What is interdisciplinarity? What is my personal view on its impact in one's life?

According to the *American Heritage® Dictionary of the English Language*, *interdisciplinary* is defined as something "of, or relating to, two or more academic disciplines that are usually considered distinct." I now am aware that inter-disciplinarity has been a constant throughout my life: I was not a child who showed definite interest towards anything specific. I remember at a young age, when I started taking piano lessons, noticing the connections between mathematics and music. I had to count, add, and divide the sounds and the pauses when reading music and playing the notes.

Throughout childhood, I was more like a "hopper," shifting my attention from place to place, up to the point where my parents were led to worry that I was unable to focus. I just was, and am, still interested in too many things, and I tend to feel it is a waste not to take advantage of the opportunities presented to our senses and to wonder about all the amazing things that surround us. Maybe humans are by default interdisciplinary beings, who are steered away from this natural tendency when they are "taught to focus."

As a matter of fact, I see the entire world as interdisciplinary. Nature itself is interdisciplinary! Disciplines are an artificial way of categorizing knowledge into neat little compartments, in order to facilitate the dissemination of bits of information. An interdisciplinary approach is nothing more than the natural way of recognizing how different realities interconnect to form what we define as knowledge. Compartmentalizing knowledge, as is generally the norm in conventional education, adds an unnecessary burden to the process of learning by negating what is natural. Currently, humankind needs much more than individuals with sophisticated technical training, if this expertise cannot be applied to different fields.

Solidarity and the Current Educational Model

In today's reality, excessive specialization has led to undesirable consequences: if individuals are trained to focus on a single aspect or facet of a given issue, the end result may lose its status as the main goal to be achieved. Instead, each professional will concentrate solely on his or her own field of expertise, and the responsibility for the outcome will be somewhat diluted. Let us imagine, for example, a group of health professionals belonging to different specialties, who happen to be treating the same patient. Oftentimes, each of these professionals will place their efforts on the one "part" of the patient they specialize on, forgetting that the ultimate goal is helping the patient, as a whole, to feel better. This example can easily be extrapolated to other circumstances, such as construction, or how any company functions. The only effective way, I believe, of refocusing the group's attention, and working as a team in order to reach the desired outcome, is through solidarity.

To most people, the word "solidarity" initially evokes ideas that relate more to social relations than to a health-care context—referring back to the example above. However, "solidarity" derives from the Latin word *solidus*, which means solid or whole. In other words, for a group to work in solidarity, it has to function as a whole. It is essential for each individual to perceive that the group shares a common goal, and that selfishness, or the desire to "shine" individually, has to be put aside. This is not to say that individuals should not strive to excel in their own capacities, but rather that it is important to keep in mind that the shared outcome as a whole is more important than the success of each "player" in isolation.

The issue at hand is that the conventional educational model tends to emphasize fragmented specialized tasks, instead of collective efforts towards a common goal. The prevalent models of education have isolated concepts into specific contexts in their respective subjects, without necessarily highlighting the interconnections between the different fields of knowledge. To make matters even worse, savage competition for resources in academia is increasingly widespread, with some of the STEM disciplines being given more importance or prestige than others, at various times. Maybe it is time for the system to re-think itself, and start infusing more solidarity into education. A good start would be accepting and accentuating the connections between different fields of knowledge, as opposed to having them compete against each other. We are back to interdisciplinarity.

Interdisciplinary Strategies for Faculty and Students

1. *Learn how to work toward common goals.* We are living in a world where uncertainties are much more abundant than certainties. If we want to succeed as a whole in this large group that we all belong to, namely the human race, we need to re-learn how to work towards common goals, in solidarity. For a group to function in solidarity, there has to be true dialogue. Moreover, for true dialogue to occur, there has to be respect. We can only respect someone if we recognize their value. Thus, individual expertise in any field—and, here, I mean expertise in the broadest sense of the word, which surpasses mere technical knowledge—is deserving of respect, due to its intrinsic value. Each and every person is able to contribute if they feel valued by the other elements in the group.

167

2. *Broaden perspectives.* Ever since I started working in the field of education, I viewed my career shift from dentist to educator as something that broadened my perspectives in life and provided me with great flexibility to adapt to different work environments. However, I sensed that changing careers was interpreted by some as a negative aspect of my résumé, as a weakness instead of a strength in my professional profile. People sometimes viewed my switch as an indication that I could not focus in a certain field, much like when my parents worried that I had a limited attention span. Unfortunately, this is an issue that I still face, to some degree, depending on the situation I am in. It appears to me that the traditional model usually values vertical progression within a certain field, with not enough value being placed on the ability to connect knowledge and interact in different settings.

3. *Connect with students.* There are several ways to make that connection. The *sine qua non* condition for such a connection to take place is for the instructor to recognize students as human beings who have feelings and dreams; as people who are striving to make meaning of their lives. This, in turn, can only be accomplished if the instructor demonstrates genuine interest in who these students are and who, and what, they want to be (also a sign of respect, in my view). This allows students to open up and let go of any barriers that may prevent them from effectively engaging with the subject being taught. It also helps students to start seeing that a particular skill is something that truly carries some sort of value to them.

   In other words, the course objectives have to be unanimously recognized as meaningful. Only then will the course objectives be perceived as a truly shared common goal. In my experience, when this happens, a magical sense of community develops among the students, and achieving this state is one of the most rewarding aspects of my work as an educator. Once again, the benefits of an interdisciplinary model of education are validated: an interdisciplinary instructor will be more capable of recognizing potential connections between what sparks the interest of the students and the topics being covered in class. Hopefully, we will soon be shifting towards an educational model that values interdisciplinarity as much as vertical specialization.

Chapter 12

The Capstone Meaning-Making Seminar: Personal Experiences and Recommendations

"Capstone": the highest point of achievement in a person's life.

Webster's New World Dictionary

Of course, research and writing have their own rewards, but nothing like having a student come to you and say, "I feel I'm starting to figure out what to do with my life, and your class made a difference."

Andrew Delbanco

In Robert's graduate program—Interdisciplinary Studies in Education—all students elect to take a capstone meaning-making seminar. For many of these students, this is the first class they take in their course of studies. For some who are finishing their degree, it is the last. And for others still, mostly undergraduate students looking for an unconventional elective where they can do some self-exploration, the meaning-making capstone is an energy-restoring pause along the way; and the seminar can come at any time during their education. The first definition of a *capstone* experience in *Webster's New World Dictionary* is the "highest point of achievement" in a person's life. Thus, it is not necessarily the final step in an academic program. Our capstone meaning-making seminar, taught jointly by Robert and Jennifer, meets once a week for three hours at a time. Often, our seminar goes way over the three-hour period each week, because students—both graduate and undergraduate—are so thoroughly engaged in an academic experience, many for the first time, that they just don't want the class time to end. For them, it is the "highest point of achievement" in their education so far. It is also the highlight of their week.

We believe that the content we cover in the course, and the questions we ask throughout, rivet our students' attention because they have never been asked to deal with such real-life material before. We also believe that for educators to be oblivious to the power of the meaning questions we ask is to unconsciously reinforce for students that the only life worth living is one lived in the present, hedonistic moment, or, worse, one lived in the "not yet" of a future only dimly and, depressingly, perceived. Sadly, the consequences of living this way, both for educators and students, can be disastrous. We are convinced that an inability, or refusal, to rise above the humdrum routines of our everyday personal and professional lives, and beyond the lures of an unknown, frenetic future, means that our fundamental need for love and creativity, hope and joy, goes unfulfilled. Whenever this happens, we burn out, or we dry up. Worse, some of us become aggressive, hostile, and alienated. We get paranoid, or we grow numb.

We want all of our capstone students, whether they are undergraduates, graduate students, teachers, or practicing professionals, to experience a deeper and richer meaning in the day-to-day lives they lead. We tell our students at the outset that we want our capstone seminar to reach the minds and hearts of all of those who might be restless, unsatisfied, even bored; or who aren't sure what they are going to do, not only during the rest of their formal education, but perhaps even with the rest of their lives.

What follows are two reflective student-essays, written by two very different people—one a quarterlifer, and one a mid-lifer—describing how a capstone meaning-making seminar can change lives. Both of these student writers, and so many like them through the years, continually remind us of Andrew Delbanco's (2012) wonderful observation about how much we, ourselves, benefit from teaching our capstone, meaning-making seminar:

> For one thing, this kind of teaching has benefits for faculty too, since it can save them from creeping anxiety about the value of writing books that other faculty will have to read in order to write their own books. Of course, research and writing have their own rewards, but nothing like having a student come to you and say, "I feel I'm starting to figure out what to do with my life, and your class made a difference."

WHY ARE YOU HERE?

Anna Stern
Graduate Student in Interdisciplinary Educational Studies
High School English Teacher

It was August 26, 2013, my first day ever of graduate school, and I was sure that I was in the wrong room. Even though I had checked the room number twice, read the "Meaning-Making Seminar" course description over and over, used the closest zoom function on Google maps to locate the building on the UVM campus, and done some quasi-creepy stalking of both my professors' backgrounds, it still felt entirely feasible that not only was I in the wrong classroom, but possibly in the wrong building, at the wrong time, on the wrong day.

This assumption felt reasonable because I was not only walking into my first course at UVM, but I was also new to Burlington and to graduate school. The night before class, I couldn't sleep because it dawned on me that in my two-year lapse between undergrad and graduate school, I had forgotten everything I knew about being a student. Had I gotten the right editions of the assigned textbooks? What if we were expected to have read something I didn't know about? What if everyone in graduate school was noticeably, irrefutably smarter than I?

When the four o'clock class finally rolled around the following day, I had worked myself into an anxiety-fueled mess. I spent the morning double- and triple-checking that I was, in fact, an accepted student to the UVM graduate school who was walking into the correct classroom, and when I finally took a deep breath, squared my shoulders, and pushed opened the door, I saw a dimly lit room with no desks. Rather, all the desks were pushed into a crowded heap in the back of the room. There was not a podium, a PowerPoint screen, nor a clear front of the room. A few people were mumbling while they focused on organizing the twenty or so, non-desk chairs into a circle, and a massive bag of M&Ms was lifted off of a mini-singing bowl to be passed around. Just as I was about to turn to double-check the room number, Professor Nash (who preferred that we call him Robert) smiled broadly at me and boomed, "Welcome!"

I had imagined graduate school as a mysterious and intimidating world of strict, industrious, and competitive adults, compulsively collecting data to write brilliant reports, but this classroom had M&Ms, and a singing bowl to call our attention to the start of class, for crying out loud. As I sat down in the circle with a small pile of chocolate on my notebook, I wondered if the class was going to be one of those "touchy-feely" courses that I had heard about where no one works hard, and everyone gets an A+ and a smiley sticker on their report cards. The mindfulness activity that got us started for that first class (and all the classes after that) reinforced my fear that we were all going to become Buddhist disciples chanting "Om" mantras. However, the very first question Robert asked the class ("Be perfectly honest: why did you choose to be here in this elective course at this time?") was one that got me thinking more deeply than I had in a very, very long time.

Graduate school was the next step for me; embarrassingly enough, that was my first thought. In order to teach high school English, I had to build a résumé that pushed my name to the forefront of principal's minds, and graduate school was a major part of that. I had known that teaching English was my dream ever since I was 16, and I had spent all my time since then methodically going after that goal. Full of drive, I sought out educational experiences everywhere I went. I studied English and Education at college, did my educational observations, spent

171

a semester student teaching, completed an intensive TESOL certification program, worked for an alternative educational program in Oregon, taught Humanities at the "wrong" school, worked as a para-educator at the "right" school, and tutored on the side all the while. I had been moving forward for almost a decade, step after step, my eyes set forward at all times.

But there I was, suddenly halted by Robert's question. Why *was* I there? I noticed my seat was only a few yards from the door, and perhaps I didn't have to be there after all. But I had worked hard to get to the seat I was sweating in, and I was not going to give it up. As my classmates went around the circle, honestly and bravely answering the question with vulnerability, my mind raced. Why was I getting my master's degree now? Why did I choose UVM? Why had I chosen this elective course on the long list of offerings? I had endless logistical, financial and personal validations for my choice, but they all seemed too complicated and convoluted for such a straightforward question. When the student next to me finished speaking, and my turn had arrived, all of my reasons (a sense of duty, my own curiosity, respect for the subject matter, relevance in the classroom) boiled down to one simple truth: "I want to be here. Period." The moment this statement left my lips, I knew it was true, and I knew I was in a class that would change my perspective indefinitely.

That semester, Robert and Jennifer led us each and every week to think deeply about how we derive meaning from our lives, which for me meant that I thought a lot about education. I learned things about myself I thought I already knew, but it turned out that I had only seen the outline of many of my beliefs without ever digging deeply into their cores.

When I was little, my parents did me the great service of reading me bedtime stories. My mother's ideal daily schedule would be a 5am sharp arousal followed by a consistent 8pm bedtime, but she dutifully marched upstairs around 9 to read to me anyway. I used to prop myself up on her shoulder and follow her voice through my favorite book, *The Story of Ferdinand*. Every night around page three, my mother's valiant battle with sleep was lost, and I would have to jab her very hard in the ribs to get her to continue. She jerked up, widened her eyes, and began anew at the top of page three, until the words . . . the words . . . the words . . . were lost to sleep once again. We must have read pages one through three a dozen times, before I learned to follow the shapes of the words to her flickering voice, and when her eyes popped open in response to my prods, my finger would be pointing to the word she nodded off on. Before long, we finished the entire book, and not long after that I could read independently; once I could read on my own, I never stopped.

Reading enraptured me, thrilled me, brought me all over the world and taught me about people who were different from the ones I knew. Roald Dahl let me sit in the pocket of a gentle giant, Ann Patchett let me sprint around the Harvard track with effortless grace, and Ernest Hemingway showed me what it truly feels like to be lost. Reading was (and is) an integral part of my life, and without my love of reading, I am sure I would be a drastically different person. Books have taught me most of what I know, and I have always been comforted by their presence. You might be wondering, *what does this lauding of all things literary have to do with meaning making?* Robert and Jennifer asked me the same question for our first paper, and I didn't know why reading meant so much to me until I wrote it. What I learned from doing this paper was incalculable in helping me to understand what gave, and gives, my life the most ongoing meaning.

Of course, I knew I loved books, but it wasn't just that. After hours of unsuccessful brainstorming, writing explanations that didn't quite feel right, and flipping through passages from some of my favorite books, I decided to take a break. I had just finished re-reading *Catcher in the Rye* by J. D. Salinger, and I wanted to talk about how much Holden had changed in the five years since I'd last wandered around New York City with him. As I picked up the phone to call my father (a great fan of American literature), I suddenly understood: it was sharing my love of books and the ideas they inspire that gave my life meaning. Khaled Hosseini, the author of literary masterpieces such as *The Kite Runner* and *A Thousand Splendid Suns*, said "Writing fiction is the act of weaving a series of lies to arrive at a greater truth." Literature, and readers of literature, are both seeking to make meaning of life. Books use fictional characters and conflicts to shed light on the people and struggles in our own lives. The late and great Maya Angelou once said, "Words mean more than what is set down on paper. It takes the human voice to infuse them with shades of deeper meaning." The raised hand that asks what happens to Boo Radley, the voice that thinks Piggy is a whiner, and my phone call to my father pitying Holden's heartache—we all seek to find truth in literature; we are a meaning-making community.

Needless to say, my first capstone paper poured out of me, and by the time I saved and printed my work, my understanding of who I was as an aspiring English teacher had deepened. It was as if now there was a solid foundation built beneath my values that had always been strong, but invisible to me. I spent the entire semester in the capstone exploring that foundation, and marveling at how firmly the pieces of my communities, my family, my experiences, and my core identity as an individual built who I am today.

Without our capstone meaning-making class, I might not have understood the answers to the "why?" questions Robert and Jennifer were constantly pushing us to explore. I now understand why I love reading, why I love writing, why I love exploring ideas, why I am who I am: a daughter, a friend, a learner, and a teacher. Without Robert and Jennifer, I might not someday turn to my own class, look my students in the eyes and ask them, "Why are you here?" "Why are you here?"

"WHEN ANGEL DIES"

Ida M. Russin
Non-Traditional Master's Student in Interdisciplinary Studies

The Sounds of Silence

In his book *The Power of Kindness* (2007), Piero Ferrucci says: "In our society, the silent treatment is never deliberately practiced by an entire community on one individual. But even a tiny dose on an individual level can have disastrous effects— destruction of self-esteem, insecurity, depression." You don't have to be a quarterlifer for meaning-making to be an important part of your life experience. Even when you're older and you *think* you know everything, meaning-making can happen. "Bullying" was the word I had used to describe what was happening to me in my office; being in episodic post-traumatic stress disorder was really what was happening. And though I was in my early fifties, I communicated in the language of a 12-year-old girl with the term "bullying." That's what it felt like to me. I felt that everyone in the office was against me; everyone had stopped talking to each other. It's no wonder I found myself on the cold institutional bathroom floor one day, sobbing uncontrollably.

I had the good fortune of serving graduate students as a Student Services Specialist for more than eight years. It was a wonderful and rewarding job, and it was the highlight of my career in education. I had been trained by someone who equally loved supporting students. A woman named Mike, another Student Services Specialist, had been my main co-worker and trainer. She had natural, bright, curly red hair, a boisterous laugh, and made everyone feel welcomed into the office. She had worked all of her life in education, following her children in their schools with jobs as a playground assistant, then as a bus driver. Then when they were nearing college age, she moved to a job at the university, so her two children could get their bachelor's degrees.

Learning the Job

One of the technical parts of our positions at the university was to perform a "format check" for graduate students in programs that included presenting a final thesis or dissertation. The best way for me to learn seemed to be simply to sit in on Mike's format check appointments for some time. So I sat quietly beside Mike and the student, just listening and paying careful attention to her kind instruction. I focused intently as Mike checked each nervous student's pages, learning which common errors might occur. Were the margins 1.5 inches on the left? Did the lowercase Roman numerals appear properly in the introductory pages? Did it have a proper *Table of Contents* and a *Comprehensive Bibliography*? While we certainly did not need to read or comprehend their papers, we needed to make sure that their work was technically perfect for the day of their defense and presentation to their committee. But the thing I most enjoyed while listening to Mike do a format check was when she was almost finished. As she neared the end of each format check, Mike would lean in with a warm smile and ask the student ". . . So where are you from?"

You see Mike had traveled to almost all of the 48 states in the US. It was rare that someone mentioned an area that she hadn't already visited, toured, or ridden through on the back of a motorcycle. Her family had also taken many vacations when she was young in the old "station weapon," as she called it. Finding out where a student was from made an instant meaning-making connection. Putting the students at ease, in order to allow them to accept our help and not simply "point out errors" was her goal. I'm not even sure Mike did this consciously. But she has a wonderful soul, and it had a way of shining through in everything she did at work.

After Mike made this very natural connection, the student stopped worrying about the technical part of their defense, and they started talking. They spoke of where they came from, and where they hoped to live after graduation. They spoke of their loved ones back home, their favorite regional foods, or the favorite memories of places in their pasts. They were meaning-making, even while fulfilling their academic requirement for a format check. By the time they left their meeting, Mike had achieved several goals: 1. The student had all of the information they needed for a successful defense presentation. 2. The student felt a sense of pride in their accomplishments at the university. 3. The student felt as though someone cared about them and their success. These were the final conversations we held with graduate students, and so we listened carefully as they opened up about their challenges and inspirations of their graduate coursework.

Taking Good Advice

The best advice I received from the many inspirational faculty members at the university was to work towards my own graduate degree because simply, "You don't know . . . what you don't know!" I took that good advice, and both my children and husband looked puzzled when I announced to them that the "Capstone Meaning-Making Seminar," taught by Robert and Jennifer, would be my first graduate course after having been accepted to the Master's program. Their questions came in rapidly: What is meaning-making? What would it have to do with my degree? What would it teach me? My two "twenty-something" children were intrigued with the course choice of their "fifty-something" mother. It had been a difficult year, as I moved unconsciously, quietly, and meekly from abled to disabled with post-traumatic stress disorder. If there was ever a time in my life that I needed to stop and get a new foothold on meaning, it was now. Mike had retired; the office had fallen into a negative and hostile environment. All of this was having "disastrous effects" on my emotional health. Being in a course that spoke of challenges we all shared led me back closer to "abled," while many of my co-workers simply ignored my suffering.

I don't know if Mike ever read Victor Frankl's *Man's Search for Meaning* (1959), but I know she would understand his thoughts on how we all share suffering in this world, as we all face loss. Frankl writes: ". . . suffering completely fills the human soul and conscious mind, no matter whether the suffering is great or little. Therefore the 'size' of human suffering is absolutely relative." Mike knew that students could be very stressed at this time, and she taught me to respect their vulnerability. We were not the students' advisors. We were not even their peers who could share the language of their discipline. But we offered support and encouragement, along with the acknowledgment that they had met all of the requirements for their specific degree.

When I started performing the format checks alone, I wondered how I might also connect with and calm these nervous students. I had lived in Boston for a time, but hadn't traveled anywhere else. I certainly couldn't ask them where they were from, and hope, like Mike, to pull out a funny and warm story about the area. But naturally and organically, my approach to reach students on a personal level appeared. For me, the question near the end of the format check became "Who will be attending your defense besides your committee?" As soon as I asked this question, I learned so much about the student. Would it be parents, a spouse, friends and/or cohorts? Did they have people that loved and supported them either near or far? Their responses poured out as they left their theses and dissertation worries behind, and looked forward to life after their degree.

Shared Sufferings

It was clear in our meaning-making class that the stories we shared pulled us together and connected us on a deep level. We felt confident in how the instructors and classmates viewed confidentiality, and so each student was able to speak to their own, very personal, risks, benefits, challenges, gains, and losses. Aristotle wrote "Moral excellence comes about as a result of habit. We become just by doing just acts, temperate by doing temperate acts, brave by doing brave acts." If the lessons we learn in college apply only to our academics, then we will miss significant lessons that will help us in life. I believe we find meaning in our lives by sharing our own stories of how we have faced, and overcome, life's inevitable challenges. What are the "habits" that we have created, even amidst the terrible stresses and strains in our lives, that have helped us to become responsible, moral beings?

I believe that academic *rigor* will help this next generation of college students to find solutions to the world's complex problems through interdisciplinary research. I believe even more strongly that meaning-making *vigor* will help this same generation to be caring and ethical researchers who know how to face controversy and hardships, and who will be prepared to do so. Students empowered with both *rigorous* and *vigorous* interdisciplinary, meaning-making experiences are more likely to have rich and fulfilling lives. Moreover, they will have the resources to draw upon for strength and encouragement while they navigate their unavoidable challenges. This is what meaning-making, interdisciplinary education is doing for me . . . even at my late age and stage of life.

Music to Our Ears

My husband of 26 years, Dean, and I curled up on the couch together on a recent rainy day to watch the musical *Rent*. We sang along loudly and off-tune with the familiar music. We had seen the Broadway tour of the play several years ago, we had watched the movie many times, and we had memorized the lyrics from blasting the soundtrack in the car. It had been some time since we dusted off the DVD player yet, just as I expected, during the part that Angel dies, my husband looked at me with sadness and surprise and said, "I didn't remember that Angel dies!" He says that same thing each time we watch the movie. I'm not quite sure why Dean can remember so many of the lyrics to the songs, and forget that in this movie, Angel dies. Every single time.

Meaning-making has also helped me to deal with my own personal challenges. You see, Dean has end-stage liver disease, and as a result of his failing liver he has hepatic encephalopathy. It took me weeks to say those difficult words, the second one, mostly, because it's a tongue twister. The "hepatic" part of this diagnosis simply means that it pertains to the liver. But the "encephalopathy" part of it means that there are periods of time when my husband has general confusion and short-term memory loss. It can be something as small as saying the word "sandwich" as "sangwidge," while indignantly insisting that this is how he's said that word all of his life.

I look back now and see how the capstone seminar has helped me through my own post-traumatic stress challenges, leading me back to a life on steadier ground. We will all face loss and challenges. We will all need to make meaning of what happens to us and to those we love. We need to be prepared for a variety of situations, good and bad. We need to prepare for times like when your husband forgets things he used to know—things that I'm surprised he's forgotten—like when Angel dies.

RECOMMENDATIONS FOR TEACHING A CAPSTONE MEANING-MAKING SEMINAR

What follows are a series of brief recommendations for teaching a capstone meaning-making seminar. Obviously, there will be no all-purpose, cookie-cutter, pedagogical model that will apply to every seminar situation. The various academic disciplines, as well as individual teaching and learning styles, are much too diverse for this. Therefore, we make these recommendations knowing that what has worked for us may not work in the same ways for others unless tweaked or drastically revised. We leave it up to our readers to adjust the following recommendations to suit their particular disciplinary and pedagogical needs.

What we offer below regarding the process and content of a capstone meaning-making seminar has been inspired by countless students through the years, like Anna and Ida. As different as they were in ages, interests, and backgrounds, both Anna and Ida responded incredibly well to an entire semester of meaning-making activities—sharing personal reflections on the readings, actively participating in both small- and large-group conversations, and being enthusiastically involved in student-generated presentations. Anna became much more comfortable with our seminar-teaching style. She managed to discover the ever-silent extrovert residing within her introverted self. And Ida used the seminar as a start to put together the fragmented pieces of both her professional and personal lives. Both of them are now pursuing Interdisciplinary Graduate Degrees in Educational Studies.

1. Make sure that one seminar theme is always front and center.

How will a college education prepare students to grow as whole human beings throughout their lives, both professionally and personally? Tell students that for the first time in their education they will be spending an entire semester in a classroom exploring, in a very personal way, eight meaning-making themes that they have to deal with sooner or later during the course of their lives. These themes include hopes and dreams; ethics and morality; religion and spirituality; loving core relationships; overlapping identities; vocation, career, and finances; the call of service to others; and self-care and balance. It is important that we let students know that it is impossible to live a coherent, holistic, hopeful life without a heightened sense of expectation, a sustaining reason for being alive, and an opportunity to fulfill their hopes and dreams.

2. Let students know from the outset what they can expect.

They will do lots of personal narrative writing. They will read books that are written in down-to-earth, life-relevant language. They will be involved in an authentic seminar atmosphere with lots of large- and small-group conversation. They will use the internet and social media on certain occasions. They will be expected to treat each and every person (including their instructor) in the seminar as valuable, unique individuals whose voices are worthy of the greatest respect. And, by the end of the course, if all goes well, they will be able to put together a tentative life plan for now, and in the future, based on all the rich, probing, honest, and instructive meaning-making conversations that will be a feature of the capstone seminar.

3. Explain the academic differences (and commonalities) between rigor and vigor in the pursuit of truth and meaning.

Rigor sets high disciplinary and interdisciplinary standards. *Vigor* calls for vital, creative responses. Required readings in a meaning-making seminar—books, articles, and websites—will be plentiful, but they will also be as jargon-free and spirited as possible. All the readings will be both disciplined-based and applied; intellectually challenging and down-to-earth. All the writing will be personal as well as conceptual, particular as well as generalizable. Remind students that they can have some fun in their learning. They can actually "play" with ideas. Their reading and writing can be both creative and accessible while still being scholarly. Meaning-making is both rigorous *and* vigorous. It requires a seriousness of purpose, and a lively sense of adventure.

Finally, meaning-making is an interdisciplinary, not a mono-disciplinary, activity. Let students know at the very beginning of the seminar that they will be dipping into a number of disciplines in the professions, humanities, arts, and in the pure and applied sciences, in order to understand the multi-dimensionality and rich complexity of meaning-making content. Therefore, they will need to be serious about learning new concepts, languages, and disciplinary ways of thinking. They will need to be both rigorous *and* vigorous adventurers.

4. Be clear about the meaning of meaning.

Meaning is what sustains us during those hard, perplexing times when everything seems to be up in the air, and there are no certain answers anywhere to the most confounding questions that plague all of us . . . throughout our lives. Emphasize that meaning is different from purpose in some respects. The words are not synonymous, although, at times, there might be some overlap. Meaning is what we create, and it is inside of us and ever-evolving. Purpose is what is created for us, and it is outside of us and rarely evolving. Meaning is existential; purpose is metaphysical. Meaning is a process; purpose is a product.

5. Stress the style of seminar conversation that works best in meaning-making.

Because meaning-making requires an educational dynamic that is organic, interactive, and often spontaneous, students need to understand what Michael Oakeshott (1950) means when he says that we must "taste the mystery without the necessity of at once seeking a solution." Spirited and candid inquiry about the

179

multiple mysteries of meaning-making, therefore, is more likely to occur when conversationalists feel safe and supported to speak their truths to others. Remind students that everyone in the seminar is a genuine seeker of meaning, and meaning is always growing and changing. Generally, the more heated someone's comments, the more intense someone's search. Few of us have made up our minds once and for all on controversial matters, especially what gives our lives a satisfying meaning to live for. Thus, it is essential that we need to treat each other with exquisite respect and sensitivity.

Critique and feedback, when appropriate, ought always to come out of a framework of generosity and empathy, and with an intention to make the other person look good. An effective meaning-making capstone seminar ends up generating more questions than answers. Participants learn to talk with one another by ending their sentences in question marks or ellipsis points, or even, on occasion, with open-ended *vice versas*. Delightfully absent are the definitive, conversation-stopping periods and exclamation points that are a feature of so much seminar discussion in the more traditional mono-disciplines . . .

Bibliography

Allison, D. (1994). *Skin: Talking about sex, class, and literature.* Ann Arbor, MI: Firebrand Books.

American College Health Association. (2012). Undergraduate Students: Reference Group Executive Summary, Spring 2012. www.acha-ncha.org/docs/ACHA-NCHA-II UNDERGRAD ReferenceGroup ExecutiveSummary Spring2012.pdf. Accessed May 2014.

Anton, C. (2001). *Selfhood and authenticity.* Albany, NY: State University of New York Press.

Association of American Colleges and Universities (2009). *New data on how campuses educate students for civic engagement.* Retrieved from www.aacu.org/press_room/press_releases/2009/civicresponsibility.cfm. Accessed June 2014.

Baggini, J. (2004). *What's it all about? Philosophy and the meaning of life.* New York: Oxford University Press.

Baumeister, R. F. (1991). *Meanings of life.* New York: The Guilford Press.

Bennett, W. (2008). *The moral compass: Stories for a life's journey.* New York: Simon & Schuster.

Brodeur, D. R. (2012). *The ethics of globalization.* Retrieved from www.cdio.org/files/document/file/the ethics_of_globalization.pdf. Accessed May 2014.

Browne, K. (2010). *An introduction to sociology.* Cambridge, MA: Polity Press.

Camus, A. (1991). *The myth of Sisyphus.* New York: Knopf Doubleday (reissued).

Canfield, J. (2005). *The success principles: How to get from where you are to where you want to be.* New York: HarperCollins.

Carver, G. W. Retrieved from www.ideafinder.com/history/inventors/carver.htm. Accessed May 2014.

Chickering, A. W. (1993). *Education and identity.* San Francisco, CA: Jossey-Bass.

Coelho, P. (1987). Retrieved from www.brainyquote.com/quotes/authors/p/paulo_coelho.html. Accessed May 2014.

Coles, R. (1989). *The call of stories: Teaching and the moral imagination.* New York: Houghton Mifflin.

Coles, R. (1993). *The call of service: A witness to idealism.* New York: Houghton Mifflin.

Cooperrider, D. L. (2005). *Appreciative inquiry: A positive revolution in change*. San Francisco, CA: Berrett-Koehler Publishers.

Crouse, J. S. (2014). Sad truths about teen suicide. *American Thinker,* January 9. Retrieved from www.americanthinker.com/2014/01/sad_truths_about_teen_suicide.html. Accessed May 2014.

Csikszentmihalyi, M. (1990). *Flow: The psychology of optimal experience*. New York: Harper and Row.

Day, D. (1952). *The long loneliness: The autobiography of the legendary Catholic social activist*. New York: HarperCollins.

de la Chaumiere, R. (2004). *What's it all about? A guide to life's basic questions and answers*. Sonoma, CA: Wisdom House Press.

Delbanco, A. (2012). *College: What it was, is, and should be*. Princeton, NJ: Princeton University Press.

Dewey, J. (1938). *Experience and education*. New York: Macmillan.

Eagleton, T. (2007). *The meaning of life*. New York: Oxford University Press.

Erikson, E. (1994). *Identity and the life cycle*. New York: W. W. Norton & Company.

Ferrucci, P. (2007). *The power of kindness: The unexpected benefits of leading a compassionate life*. New York: Penguin.

Fish, S. (1982). *Is there a text in this class? The authority of interpretive communities*. Cambridge, MA: Harvard University Press.

Flanagan, O. (2007). *The really hard problem: Meaning in a material world*. Cambridge, MA: The MIT Press.

Ford, D. (2007). *The search for meaning: A short history*. Berkeley, CA: University of California Press.

Forleo, M. [marieforleo]. (2012, September 10). *How do I figure out what I want*. Retrieved from www.youtube.com/watch?v=mIztYzUgIOE. Accessed May 2014.

Frankl, V. ([1959] 2006). *Man's search for meaning*. Boston, MA: Beacon Press.

Freud, S. (1930). *Civilization and its discontents*. New York: W. W. Norton & Company.

Gallup–Purdue Study on College Graduates (May 6, 2014). J. Ray and S. Kafka. Retrieved from www.gallup.com/poll/168848/life-college-matters-life-college.aspx. Accessed May 2014.

Gardner, H. (2006a). *Multiple intelligences: New horizons*. New York: Basic Books. (First published in 1993.)

Gardner, H. (2006b). *Five minds for the future*. Cambridge, MA: Harvard Business School Press.

Geary, J. (2005). *The world in a phrase: A brief history of the aphorism*. New York: Bloomsbury.

Gilbert, E. (2005). *Eat, pray, love: One woman's search for everything across Italy, India, and Indonesia*. New York: Penguin.

Gladwell, M. (2011). *Outliers: The story of success*. New York: Back Bay Books.

Goethe, J. W. (1820). Retrieved from www.goodreads.com/quotes/929-whatever-you-can-do-or-dream-you-can-begin-it. Accessed May 2014.

Goodman, E. (2007). *Paper trail: Common sense in uncommon times.* New York: Simon & Schuster.

Grayling, A. C. (2010). *Ideas that matter: The concepts that shape the 21st century.* New York: Basic Books.

Haidt, J. (2006). *The happiness hypothesis: Finding modern truth in ancient wisdom.* New York: Basic Books.

Haidt, J. (2012). *The righteous mind: Why good people are divided by politics and religion.* New York: Vintage.

Havighurst, R. J. ([1972] 2005). *Developmental tasks and education.* (Third edn.) Harlow: Longman Group.

Kessler, R. (2000). *The soul of education: Helping students find connection, compassion, and character at school.* Alexandria, VA: Association for Supervision and Curriculum Development.

Kettering, C. Retrieved from www.todayinsci.com/K/Kettering_Charles/Kettering Charles-Quotations.htm. Accessed May 2014.

Kronman, A. T. (2007). *Education's end: Why our colleges and universities have given up on the meaning of life.* New Haven, CT: Yale University Press.

Lama, D. (2011). *Beyond religion: Ethics for a whole world.* New York: Mariner Books.

Lamott, A. (1994). *Bird by bird: Some instructions on writing and life.* New York: Anchor.

Layard, R. (2005). *Happiness: Lessons from a new science.* New York: Penguin.

Lyubomirsky, S. (2007). *The how of happiness: A new approach to getting the life you want.* New York: Penguin.

Marinoff, L. (2000). *Plato, not Prozac!: Applying eternal wisdom to everyday problems.* New York: Quill.

Marinoff, L. (2003). *The big questions: How philosophy can change your life.* New York: Bloomsbury.

Maslow, A. (1962). *Toward a psychology of being.* Eastford, CT: Martino Books.

Mountain Dreamer, O. (2003). *The call.* San Francisco, CA: HarperOne.

Narvaez, D. (2013). The future of research in moral development and education, *Journal of Moral Education,* DOI:10.1080/03057240.2012.757102

Nash, R. J. (1997). *Answering the "virtuecrats": A moral conversation on character education.* New York: Columbia University Teachers College Press.

Nash, R. J. (2002). *"Real world" ethics: Frameworks for Educators and human service professionals.* New York: Columbia University Teachers College Press.

Nash, R. J. (2004). *Liberating scholarly writing: The power of personal narrative.* New York: Columbia University Teachers College Press.

Nash, R. J. (2009). Crossover pedagogy: The collaborative search for meaning. *About Campus*, March-April, pp 2–9.

Nash, R. J. (2015). Teaching about religion outside of religious studies. *The Oxford handbook of religion and American education*. Eds. M. D. Waggoner and N. C. Walker. New York: Oxford University Press.

Nash, R. J. and Murray, M. C. (2010). *Helping college students find purpose: The campus guide to meaning-making*. San Francisco, CA: Jossey-Bass.

Nash, R. J. and Bradley, D. L. (2011). *Me-search and re-search: A guide for writing scholarly personal narrative manuscripts*. Charlotte, NC: Information Age Publishing.

Nash, R. J. and Viray, S. (2013). *Our stories matter: Liberating the voices of marginalized students through scholarly personal narrative writing*. New York: Peter Lang.

Nash, R. J. and Jang, J. J. (2013). The time has come to create meaning-making centers on college campuses. *About Campus*. September-October, 2013, pp 2–9.

Nash, R. J. and Viray, S. (2014). *How stories heal: Writing our way to meaning and purpose in the academy*. New York: Peter Lang.

Nash, R. J. and Jang, J.J. (2014). *Education for making meaning. In search of self: Exploring undergraduate identity development*. Ed. C. Hanson. New Directions for Higher Education Series. San Francisco, CA: Jossey-Bass.

Nash, R. J., Bradley, D. L., and Chickering, A. (2008). *How to talk about hot topics on campus: From polarization to moral conversation*. San Francisco, CA: Jossey-Bass.

Nash, R. J., Johnson, R. G. and Murray, M. (2012). *Teaching college students communication strategies for effective social justice advocacy*. New York: Peter Lang.

Oakeshott, M. (1950). The idea of a university. *Listener*, 43, p. 424.

Obama, B. (March 7, 2004). Obama's religious beliefs: An interview with Barack Obama on his religious beliefs. Cathleen Falsani. *Chicago Sun-Times*.

Palmer, P. (2000). *Let your life speak: Listening for the voice of vocation*. San Francisco, CA: Jossey-Bass.

Parks, S. D. (1997). *Common fire: Leading lives of commitment in a complex world*. Boston, MA: Beacon Press.

Pollock, D. C. and Reken, R. E. V. (2001). *Third culture kids: The experience of growing up among worlds*. Boston, MA: Nicholas Brealey Publishing.

Robbins, A. (2004). *Conquering your quarterlife crisis: Advice from twentysomethings who have been there and survived*. New York: Perigee.

Rogers, C. (1995). *On becoming a person: A therapist's view of psychotherapy*. New York: Mariner Books.

Rohn, R. (2012). *My philosophy for successful living*. Melrose, FL: No Dream Too Big Publishing.

Rorty, R. (2000). *Philosophy and social hope*. New York: Penguin.

Rosenthal, N. E. (2013). *The gift of adversity: The unexpected benefits of life's difficulties, setbacks, and imperfections*. New York: Tarcher.

Schwehn, M. R. (2005). *Exiles from Eden: Religion and the academic vocation in America*. New York: Oxford University Press.

Seligman, M. (2002). *Authentic happiness: Using the new positive psychology to realize your potential for lasting fulfillment*. New York: Free Press.

Seligman, M. (2011). *Flourish: A visionary new understanding of happiness and well-being*. New York: Free Press.

Sinek, S. (2011). *Start with why: How great leaders inspire everyone to take action*. New York: Portfolio.

Snyder, C. R. (2003). *Psychology of hope: You can get here from there*. New York: Free Press.

Stangroom, J. (2010). *Would you eat your cat?: Key ethical conundrums and what they tell you about yourself*. New York: W. W. Norton & Company.

Stoner, C. and Robin, J. (2006). *A life in balance: Finding meaning in a chaotic world*. Washington, DC: University Press of America.

Strober, M. (2011). *Interdisciplinary conversations: Challenging habits of thought*. Palo Alto, CA: Stanford University Press.

Tivnan, E. (1996). *Moral imagination: Confronting the ethical issues of our day*. New York: Touchstone.

United Nations (2013). *World Happiness Report*. Eds. J. Helliwell, R. Layard, and J. Sachs. Retrieved from http://unsdsn.org/wp-content/uploads/2014/02/World HappinessReport2013_online.pdf. Accessed May 2014.

Watts, A. (Sept. 22, 2009). *On the meaning of life*. Retrieved from www.goodreads.com/work/quotes/58911-the-culture-of-counter-culture-edited-transcripts-love-of-wisdom. Accessed May 2014.

Wideman, J. E. (2005). *Brothers and keepers: A memoir*. New York: Mariner Books.

Wiesel, E. and Friedman, T. L. (2010). *An ethical compass: Coming of age in the 21st century*. New Haven, CT: Yale University Press.

World Psychiatric Association (2014). *A newly identified group of adolescents at "invisible" risk for psychopathology and suicidal behavior*. Retrieved from www.ncbi.nlm.nih.gov/pmc/articles/PMC3918027/. Accessed May 2014.

Wyland, R. (2010). Interview. Retrieved from www.youtube.com/watch?v=IxPLVM pkHSs. Accessed May 2014.

Young, K. (2010). *Internet addiction: A handbook and guide to evaluation and treatment*. San Francisco, CA: Wiley.

Index